TREATMENT OF BORDERLINE PERSONALITY DISORDER

Treatment of
BORDERLINE
PERSONALITY
DISORDER

A Guide to Evidence-Based Practice

JOEL PARIS

THE GUILFORD PRESS
New York   London

© 2008 The Guilford Press
A Division of Guilford Publications, Inc.
72 Spring Street, New York, NY 10012
www.guilford.com

Printed in the United States of America

This book is printed on acid-free paper.

Last digit is print number: 9   8   7   6   5   4   3   2   1

The author has checked with sources believed to be reliable in his efforts to provide
information that is complete and generally in accord with the standards of practice
that are accepted at the time of publication. However, in view of the possibility of
human error or changes in medical sciences, neither the author, nor the editors and
publisher, nor any other party who has been involved in the preparation or publication of this work warrants that the information contained herein is in every respect
accurate or complete, and they are not responsible for any errors or omissions or
the results obtained from the use of such information. Readers are encouraged to
confirm the information contained in this book with other sources.

Library of Congress Cataloging-in-Publication Data available from the Publisher.

ISBN 978-1-59385-834-6 (cloth : alk. Paper)

To my colleagues
in the personality disorders research community

About the Author

Joel Paris, MD, is a Research Associate at the Sir Mortimer B. Davis–Jewish General Hospital in Montreal. Since 1994, he has been a Full Professor at McGill University and served as Chair of its Department of Psychiatry from 1997 to 2007. He has supervised psychiatric evaluation with residents for over 30 years and has won many awards for his teaching. Dr. Paris is a past president of the Association for Research on Personality Disorders. Over the last 20 years, he has conducted research on the biological and psychosocial causes and the long-term outcome of borderline personality disorder. Dr. Paris is the author of 135 peer-reviewed articles, 11 books, and 25 book chapters. He is also Editor in Chief of the *Canadian Journal of Psychiatry.*

Preface

*P*atients with borderline personality disorder (BPD) are famous for being difficult. Their problems can challenge even the most experienced therapists.

The most frightening symptoms of BPD are chronic suicidal ideation, repeated suicide attempts, and self-mutilation. These are the patients we worry about—and are afraid of losing. After a difficult session, therapists may not be sure if they will ever see the patient again or whether someone will telephone to report a suicide.

Even in patients not threatening suicide, therapists face serious difficulties. BPD is associated with many symptoms, and each one presents problems. Mood instability is difficult to manage and shows only a weak response to medication. Impulsive behaviors, both in and out of therapy, are highly disruptive. Intimate relationships are often chaotic, and this pattern can repeat itself in treatment, disrupting the therapeutic alliance. Cognitive symptoms (paranoid ideas, depersonalization, and auditory hallucinations) also present problems for management.

Given this clinical picture, there can be no doubt that BPD is a serious mental illness. While BPD is classified as a personality disorder, it differs from most of the other categories listed on Axis II of DSM-IV-TR. Many people with personality disorders see themselves as normal. This is not true of patients with BPD, who suffer greatly and seek treatment.

Patients with BPD make therapists sweat. These are the cases on which we are most likely to obtain consultations from colleagues. BPD is often the focus of case conferences and invited talks and workshops by experts in the field.

Even so, BPD can be ignored. All too frequently, it is diagnosed as a variant of major depression or bipolar disorder. Moreover, patients with BPD are often mistreated. They receive prescriptions for multiple drugs that provide only marginal benefit. They do not always get the evidence-based psychotherapy they need.

THE PURPOSE OF THIS BOOK

Because BPD is a troubling clinical problem, it has been the subject of an enormous scientific literature: Medline and PsycInfo list over 3,500 articles, with at least 200 new papers published every year. Only a few diagnoses have such a strong research base.

This book aims to aid clinicians in understanding this literature and in showing how empirical data can inform clinical management. Although much about BPD remains unknown, science is beginning to unlock its secrets. This book will show how research can come to the aid of the harried clinician. Even though we are only beginning to understand the causes of the disorder, the outlook for patients is much better than previously thought, with several methods of psychotherapy proven effective. Although therapy can be difficult, we know much more than we did in the past about what works (and what doesn't).

Thus, this book differs from many others in its emphasis on *evidence-based practice.* I am profoundly committed to this approach. Much of what has been written on BPD in the past has been based on clinical opinion. But no matter how long you have practiced, the generalizability of your experience is limited by the patients you see and by your own preconceptions. These biases are precisely what research corrects for.

In principle, everyone agrees that treatment for mental disorders should be based on empirical findings. But the problem is that, all too often, there are not enough data to go on. We are forced to make decisions based on what we have done before or on our "gut feelings." Yet there are now enough rigorous investigations that one can ground the principles of management in empirical data.

I present clinical vignettes of patients with BPD to illustrate these principles. I also describe my approach to therapy. But it is not possible to write a book on the treatment of BPD with an evidence base for every intervention. Inevitably, some of what I have to say must be based on my own experience. On the other hand, everything I recommend will be at least *consistent* with current empirical evidence.

I reference many previous books on the treatment of BPD. I have learned a great deal from each of them. However, research findings and clinical trials have often been used to support a single method of therapy. In contrast, this book teases out the essential elements of *all* successful therapies.

Thus I avoid identifying myself with any "school of thought." I have always thought that excessive allegiance to any single perspective, whether cognitive or psychodynamic, is an obstacle to understanding patients. Instead, I draw on whatever ideas have the most science behind them and make the most clinical sense.

To show how research can be translated into practice, each chapter ends with a bulleted section reviewing the implications of empirical findings for therapy. Although I cannot make the treatment of BPD easy, I will show how it can be rational.

HOW THIS BOOK IS ORGANIZED

The book is divided into three parts. Part I focuses on the problems in defining BPD and in describing patients. Chapter 1 reviews problems in the DSM definition: Making the diagnosis more specific could make treatment more specific. Chapter 2 examines the boundaries of BPD to determine whether it is "really" a form of some other condition such as depression, schizophrenia, or posttraumatic stress disorder. It presents a detailed critique of the currently influential view that BPD falls within the bipolar spectrum. Chapter 3 reviews the development of BPD in childhood and adolescence and describes research directions that identify traits that are precursors of disorder.

Part II reviews research on the etiology of BPD. Chapter 4 reviews biological, psychological, and social risk factors associated with the disorder. Chapter 5 presents a model combining all these factors into an integrative model.

Part III reviews research on treatment and makes recommendations for management. Chapter 6 reviews data on the long-term outcome of patients with BPD and describes their implications for therapy. There are new (and encouraging) findings from large-scale prospective studies showing that most patients with BPD recover—a frame around which we can build treatment. Chapter 7 critically reviews data on pharmacological treatment for BPD. It suggests that current expectations for drugs are not supported by clinical trials and that most patients are being overmedicated. Chapter 8 examines evidence for the efficacy of psychotherapy. Talking therapies are the mainstay of treatment; a large body of data support that conclusion. But just as there is no single cause for BPD, there is no one way of conducting therapy. Research now supports several methods specifically designed for these patients. Chapter 9 makes recommendations for overall management consistent with this evidence. Chapter 10 discusses which therapeutic interventions are most helpful for patients. Chapter 11 suggests ways of handling the special problems that emerge in therapy for BPD. Chapter 12 addresses some thorny clinical issues related to managing suicidality and considers whether to hospitalize patients. Finally, Chapter 13 examines what we know and what we don't know about BPD and suggests what future research is needed and how such knowledge could further illuminate treatment.

ACKNOWLEDGMENTS

Roz Paris and Hallie Zweig-Frank read earlier versions of this book and made many suggestions for improvement. Marina Petel helped with references and tables. Members of my clinical team provided me with useful clinical illustrations. Jim Nageotte was a thoughtful editor.

I have dedicated this book to my colleagues in the personality disorders research community. This book could not have been written without them. Over the years, I have greatly benefited from my interactions with researchers, both at McGill and at universities around the world, who are as interested as I am in understanding BPD. Our research community consists of a few hundred people worldwide, but our numbers are growing.

JOEL PARIS, MD

Contents

PART I

Definitions

CHAPTER 1

Making the Diagnosis

*T*o treat borderline personality disorder (BPD) you first have to recognize it.

There is a common belief that you cannot diagnose a personality disorder in an hour. That is not true. You have to ask the right questions and make sure you have taken a detailed life history. If you do not get enough information, you may need to see the patient again or interview a family member or key informant. Most of the time, however, it is not that difficult to determine whether a personality disorder is present and whether the patient's pathology falls within one of the Axis II categories.

The real problem with the diagnosis of BPD comes from the way the construct has been defined. It needs to be made much more precise.

The term *borderline* is a misnomer. No one believes any more that patients lie on a border with psychosis. Moreover, "borderline" fails to describe the most salient features of the syndrome: unstable mood, impulsivity, and unstable relationships. This vagueness has contributed to the tendency for BPD either to be seen as something else or to be ignored entirely.

The problem is that we do not yet have a better term to describe this form of pathology. Most proposals focus on one aspect of the disorder (emotional dysregulation or impulsivity) but do not do jus-

3

tice to the complexity of the syndrome. But if we do not understand the mechanisms behind the disorder, renaming it would be premature. Until we know more, we might as well as well continue to use the diagnosis of BPD.

A BRIEF HISTORY OF THE BPD DIAGNOSIS

A historical perspective helps in understanding the problems of diagnosing BPD. Adolf Stern (1938), the psychoanalyst who first described borderline personality, observed that these patients became worse, not better, in therapy. He suggested this group was unsuitable for analytic treatment because their pathology lay on a "borderline" between neurosis and psychosis. Stern documented their clinical features ("psychic bleeding," inordinate hypersensitivity, difficulties in both reality testing and relationships), and his description is as relevant today as it was 70 years ago.

However, following Stern's article, there was only sporadic interest in borderline pathology over the next 30 years. Robert Knight (1953) published a study that added little to what Stern had said and had little impact beyond the psychoanalytic community.

Three psychiatrists were responsible for reviving and popularizing the concept of BPD. The first was Otto Kernberg (1970), a psychoanalyst who first worked at the Menninger Clinic and then at Cornell University. Kernberg proposed that character pathology (or what we now call personality disorder) has three levels: one milder (close to "neurosis"), one moderate, and one severe (i.e., borderline). However, there were two problems with his concept of "borderline personality organization" (BPO). First, it was entirely psychoanalytical in that it was defined on the basis of theories about mental mechanisms rather than on observable behaviors. Second, BPO defined a very broad group of patients with personality disorder as "borderline."

The second pioneer was Roy Grinker (Grinker, Werble, & Dyre, 1968), working at Michael Reese Hospital in Chicago. Grinker published the first empirical study of borderline patients, which gave more weight to clinical observation than to psychodynamic speculation and subgrouped patients based on observable symptoms. Grinker's group also conducted the first systematic follow-up studies of patients with BPD (see Chapter 6).

The third, and most influential, pioneer was John Gunderson of McLean Hospital and Harvard Medical School. Gunderson and

Singer's (1975) article in the *American Journal of Psychiatry* was a turning point for the acceptance of BPD. It showed that this form of pathology could be operationalized with behavioral criteria and that a semistructured interview yielded a reliable diagnosis.

I have vivid memories of reading this report. Up to that point, under the influence of my teachers, I had rejected the validity of BPD. The concept seemed all too vague and wooly, and I actually refused to let residents make the diagnosis. However, Gunderson and Singer convinced me, and many others, that the construct was valid.

The work of these pioneers influenced the definition of BPD adopted by the *Diagnostic and Statistical Manual of Mental Disorders* (third edition [DSM-III]; American Psychiatric Association, 1980) 5 years later. The BPD diagnosis was included in DSM, and personality disorders as a whole were given a separate axis. As a result, research took off. In 1987, the International Society for the Study of Personality Disorders (ISSPD) was founded and has met every 2 years ever since. (ISSPD also publishes the *Journal of Personality Disorders*, now 20 years old.) Because BPD is the most important clinical problem described on Axis II, most personality disorder research has focused on this category.

However, there continues to be controversy about the best way to classify the pathology that BPD describes. I discuss three ways to do so. The first is the DSM system (American Psychiatric Association, 1980, 1987, 1994, 2000), which lists nine criteria, of which five must be present to make a diagnosis. The second is based on four domains of pathology, each of which can be scored on a scale. The third is a dimensional approach, in which BPD (as well as all other personality disorders) are described by scores on measures of their underlying traits.

BPD IN THE DSM SYSTEM

When I went to medical school, I learned DSM-I. I used DSM-II as a resident. Neither of these systems had the influence of DSM-III (American Psychiatric Association, 1980), a manual that revolutionized psychiatry. The use of observable criteria and algorithms for diagnosis in DSM-III was a great advance. The DSM system has made it more likely that clinicians are talking about the same kind of patients when they categorize them. From this point on, psychiatric diagnoses became, at least in principle, reasonably reliable.

The highest levels of diagnostic reliability are found in research studies, where everyone is trained to observe the same phenomena. However, years of teaching psychiatric residents have shown me that one cannot expect everyone to take the time to use DSM criteria in the prescribed manner. It is all too easy to jump to conclusions based on one or two features rather than to open the book and count.

This problem applies to BPD. I have seen many clinicians make this diagnosis when patients present with overdoses or when they show what Kernberg (1976) called "splitting" (the tendency to see people as all good or all bad). BPD is a complex disorder that cannot be defined by any single feature.

Although defining reliable criteria for diagnostic categories is a good thing, reliability does not prove validity. Psychiatry needs to develop diagnoses that are as valid as those used by other medical specialties. However, as long as categories of mental disorder are based on clinical observation (as opposed to biological markers such as blood tests or imaging findings), their validity is bound to remain weak (Paris, 2008).

What are the best criteria for a valid diagnosis of mental disorder? Nearly 40 years ago, two psychiatrists, Eli Robins and Samuel Guze (1970), wrote an influential report on the subject. These authors proposed that diagnoses are valid if based on (1) a clear-cut clinical description; (2) laboratory studies; (3) delimitation from other disorders; (4) follow-up studies documenting a characteristic outcome; and (5) family prevalence studies.

BPD fails on most of these grounds. It greatly overlaps with other mental disorders. It lacks a specific biological profile. It does not have a specific family history. At best, BPD is a coherent clinical entity with a set of typical outcomes.

Yet if we were to apply the Robins and Guze criteria to most of the mental disorders listed in DSM, very few would be valid. Even the most intensively studied categories, such as schizophrenia and bipolar disorder, have serious problems with overlap, lack laboratory tests to confirm their presence, and do not conform to an expected family pattern. All these diagnoses could turn out to be syndromes (i.e., symptoms that occur together as opposed to true diseases with a common pathogenesis).

Although the proposals of Robins and Guze were sensible (and remain so today), diagnoses are not advanced enough to apply such stringent criteria (and will not be for decades). Thus, even if BPD is short on validity, it is no better and no worse in this respect than other widely accepted disorders. In the meantime, there are ways to refine the diagnosis.

The eight diagnostic criteria for BPD introduced in DSM-III have not changed since 1980, but a ninth criterion was added in DSM-IV (American Psychiatric Association, 1994) to describe cognitive symptoms. This change was positive in that it added an important and characteristic set of symptoms, but I am still not satisfied that the current definition is adequate.

Following the rules set out in the DSM definition, clinicians refer to a list of criteria and must identify five of them in a patient to make a diagnosis. This "Chinese menu" approach is typical of the DSM system. However, the manual fails to specify any core features, without which a diagnosis should *not* be made. (This problem is not specific to the BPD diagnosis but applies to almost all disorders.)

The nine criteria in DSM-IV-TR (American Psychiatric Association, 2000, p. 710) fall in several domains. Affective symptoms are described by Criteria 6, 7, and 8. Impulsive behaviors are described by Criteria 4 and 5. Interpersonal problems are described by Criteria 1 and 2. Cognitive symptoms are described in the "extra" Criterion 9. However, this criterion fails to consider one of the most frequent cognitive symptoms in these patients: transient stress-related auditory hallucinations (Zanarini, Gunderson, & Frankenburg, 1989). Criterion 3 (identity) does not quite belong in any of the four domains. Although there has been some research on measures to operationalize the concept of "identity disturbance" (Wilkinson-Ryan & Westen, 2000), the construct has never been precisely defined.

The problem is that any combination of five symptoms gives the diagnosis, even if not all domains are represented. In addition, there are no core symptoms for diagnosis. When a "polythetic" system is used, patients with the same diagnosis can be very different (Clarkin, Widiger, Frances, Hurt, & Gilmore, 1983). There are too many ways to reach the same conclusion, and the problem is even worse with nine criteria than it was with eight. BPD is a complex syndrome that cannot be defined by a limited number of criteria. Any expert in psychometrics will agree that many more than nine items may be needed, either in questionnaire format or as part of a semistructured interview.

In summary, Clarkin et al.'s criticism is as valid today as it was 25 years ago. The DSM criteria were a good start but cast much too wide a net. They need to be revised in DSM-V, but not everyone agrees on how to proceed.

THE DOMAIN APPROACH

Because I am dissatisfied with the DSM criteria for diagnosing BPD, I do not use them, either in research or in clinical practice. (Nonetheless, I teach them to psychiatric residents, who are expected to know DSM thoroughly.)

I suggest, along with Mary Zanarini (2005), that because BPD is a multidimensional disorder and patients have symptoms in multiple spheres (mood instability, impulsivity, unstable relationships, and cognitive impairments), the presence of *all* these features should be required to make a diagnosis. A narrower definition would describe a more homogeneous group of patients.

For this reason, I prefer a system first developed at McLean Hospital by John Gunderson: the Diagnostic Interview for Borderline Patients (DIB), later revised by Mary Zanarini (DIB-R; Zanarini et al., 1989). This semistructured interview assesses patients in the four domains of BPD pathology (affective, cognitive, impulsive, and interpersonal). Each is scored separately (0–2 for affective and cognitive and 0–3 for impulsive and interpersonal). The maximum score is 10, and 8/10 is the cutoff for BPD.

The DIB-R scales parallel DSM but follow a more rigorous algorithim. The Affective subscale taps affective instability and emptiness (DSM Criteria 6 and 7), but to attain a full score of 2 the patients must have serious problems with anger (DSM Criterion 8). The Cognitive scale taps depersonalization, paranoid trends, and pseudohallucinations (a broader range than DSM Criterion 9); if all these features are absent, then the other three domains will have to score fully. The impulsive scale taps suicidality and cutting (DSM Criterion 5) as well as other self-damaging behaviors (DSM Criterion 4). The Interpersonal scale describes problems with abandonment, instability, and identity disturbance (DSM Criteria 1, 2, and 3).

Patients with a score of 8 on the DIB-R always meet DSM criteria. However, quite a few who meet 5/9 DSM criteria will not meet DIB-R criteria. These patients have borderline traits but either lack the impulsive behaviors seen in the full syndrome or do not have conflictual relationships (because they avoid getting involved with other people). This group has what Zanarini et al. (2007) have described as "subsyndromal" pathology: Their symptoms resemble BPD but do not meet full criteria. They might be called "borderline" borderlines.

Zanarini et al. (1989) noted that if one requires six or seven DSM criteria instead of five, the same result could be achieved (i.e., describing a more homogeneous population of patients who could be clearly distinguished from those with other personality disorders). The criteria in DSM-V could, therefore, be narrowed down in the same way as with DIB-R. The patients I treat all meet those criteria. Although they are hardly peas in a pod, they are reasonably similar to each other.

Case 1 (Typical BPD)

Wilma was a 39-year-old illustrator who had been living with the same female partner for 15 years. This relationship had originally been sexual but gradually evolved into a friendship. Wilma had an affair with a man and then became involved with another woman. Telling her girlfriend about this development led to a crisis followed by two suicide attempts (leading to hospitalizations). In the second attempt, Wilma went to a hotel to overdose but called her partner to rescue her. At the time of evaluation, Wilma was still carrying out a secret affair with the lover and was having trouble making a decision. She was sleeping poorly, feeling empty, and experiencing mood swings with angry outbursts. Wilma was thinking of suicide and was cutting herself regularly (something she had been doing for many years) and was binging with alcohol. Other symptoms included depersonalization, paranoid trends, and visual hallucinations. (Wilma would see people in her house but knew they were not real.) Wilma met all nine DSM criteria for borderline personality disorder and scored 9/10 on the DIB-R.

Case 2 (Typical BPD)

Tania was a 23-year-old student about to graduate from college. Tania's problems started in high school with severe bulimia; she still forced herself to vomit several times a day. She also cut herself regularly and thought about suicide. Recently, Tania had been involved with a boyfriend who was a drug dealer and who took cocaine daily. Tania was drinking heavily and using marijuana on a daily basis.

Tania had many difficult and highly conflictual intimate relationships with both men and women. She described feelings of emptiness and hopelessness. She also experienced several cognitive symptoms: depersonalization, paranoid thinking, and occasional auditory pseudo-hallucinations.

Tania met all nine DSM criteria for borderline personality disorder and scored 9/10 on the DIB-R.

Case 3 (Typical BPD)

Sarah was a 26-year-old nurse who, despite having had problems since adolescence, was presenting for treatment for the first time. She had recently been seen in the emergency room at two hospitals for suicide threats. Sarah suffered from diabetes but was noncompliant with treatment. She was a heavy user of alcohol and drugs but had managed to do well in nursing school. Sarah was sexually promiscuous and had many relationships with drug addicts and criminals, whom she tried to save. Sarah never made a suicide attempt but once hit her head with a rock to injure herself.

What had changed was that Sarah's difficulties began to affect her work. Sarah had angry outbursts with colleagues and on several occasions stormed off the ward. Similar problems had long occurred with boyfriends, usually associated with jealousy.

Sarah met all nine DSM criteria and scored 8/10 on the DIB-R.

However some patients who meet DSM criteria do not score in all domains, as required by DIB-R.

Case 4 (BPD by DSM but Not DIB-R Criteria)

Melissa was a 19-year-old woman working part time in a bakery. Since the age of 14, she had had seven hospital admissions for anorexia nervosa (without bulimia). Melissa had attempted suicide 3 years previously after a quarrel with her psychiatrist and still had suicidal thoughts. Melissa also had been cutting herself since early adolescence.

Melissa was diagnosed in the course of an eating disorder program as having BPD based on DSM criteria. She met Criterion 1 (abandonment), Criterion 3 (identity), Criterion 5 (self-mutilation), Criterion 6 (affective instability), and Criterion 7 (emptiness) but not Criterion 2 (unstable relationships), Criterion 4 (impulsivity), Criterion 8 (emptiness), or Criterion 9 (paranoia). On the DIB-R, Melissa scored 1/2 for affective symptoms, 1/2 for cognitive symptoms, 2/3 for impulsivity (based on self-mutilation and aggressive behavior), but only 1/3 for interpersonal relationships (only one friend, and most "borderline" behaviors occurred with professionals), giving her a total score of 5/10.

Some patients who have had BPD in the past will have recovered to the point at which they no longer meet criteria (see Chapter 6).

Case 5 (Lifetime but Not Current BPD)

Nathalie was a 36-year-old woman living alone. Recent symptoms followed a breakup with her boyfriend of 2 years. Nathalie had been treated in a hospital for suicidal threats but did not attempt suicide. From adolescence, Nathalie had been a recurrent self-mutilator and carried out multiple overdoses. However, she stopped these behaviors in her late 20s. Nathalie had been unemployed for 10 years, only had a few friends, and was estranged from her family. She had never had a successful intimate relationship. These problems went back many years. Nathalie had only completed high school and had never developed a career.

Nathalie had a lifetime diagnosis of BPD but not a current one, and scored 6/10 on the DIB-R criteria, mainly because of a reduction in the level of her impulsivity over time as well as the absence of intimate stormy relationships.

Other patients have features of BPD but have never met criteria and require a different diagnosis.

Case 6 (Personality Disorder but Not BPD)

Maureen was a 29-year-old woman who was being mentioned at a community clinic. She was seen after making a serious suicide attempt by ingesting 150 pills of various kinds.

Maureen's problems went back many years. She had graduated from a community college but never held any job for long. She lived with her parents and had no relationships with men, but retained some intense friendships with women. The breakup of a friendship, as a result of Maureen's excessive demands, was the precipitant for this overdose.

Although Maureen was referred with a presumptive diagnosis of BPD, she only met three of nine criteria listed in DSM-IV and scored 4/10 on the DIB-R. Even a lifetime BPD diagnosis would not fit because of a low impulsivity and limited involvement in relationships. Given her long-term problems in work and relationships, Maureen met overall criteria for a personality disorder not otherwise specified (NOS), with traits lying mainly in Cluster C (the anxious group of personality disorders).

Diagnosis is important to the extent that it provides a guide to management. We aspire to treat patients on the basis of a reliable and valid categorization. An overly broad and fuzzy diagnostic construct fails to identify a core group of patients who show all, or most, clinical features associated with the disorder and will include too many people with milder symptoms who need different methods of treatment.

The DSM system tends to overdiagnose BPD. Even so, some clinicians are reluctant to identify patients as having a personality disorder, categorizing them within other diagnoses. We need to improve the diagnosis of BPD and make it more valid to convince clinicians who doubt its validity. The best way to do that is to make criteria more precise and more stringent.

DIMENSIONAL SYSTEMS

I prefer to fix the BPD diagnosis rather than eliminate it. However, some researchers have concluded that problems of definition for personality disorders as a whole are intractable. Criticism has been particularly strong from trait psychologists, who are trained to prefer constructs that describe continuous variations rather than sharp categories. Their approach leads to a solution in which BPD is described through personality trait profiles rather than as a category. That is a *dimensional* model.

A dimensional approach replaces the categories of BPD (and other personality disorders) with a series of scores. This is a radical alternative, intended to solve most problems of heterogeneity and overlap. Dimensions are being seriously considered by the committee preparing DSM-V and might be adopted either as an alternative to or a replacement for the current Axis II system.

One of the leading proponents of this view is John Livesley (2003), editor of the *Journal of Personality Disorders*. Other key supporters are Paul Costa and Tom Widiger (2001), psychologists who performed a large body of research on traits related to Axis II disorders. These authors have made cogent critiques of categorical diagnosis and propose dimensional measures as a replacement.

The most widely used of the measures in trait psychology is the five-factor model of personality (FFM; Costa & Widiger, 2001), which describes personality on five broad dimensions: Neuroticism (the tendency to experience negative affect), Extraversion (the tendency to interact with other people), Openness to Experience (a measure of absorption and creativity), Agreeableness, and Conscientiousness. Patients with BPD (and other personality disorders) tend to be high on Neuroticism, with low scores on Agreeableness and Conscientiousness.

It requires a conceptual leap to link self-reported traits to neural mechanisms. Nonetheless, that trait dimensions factor in a consistent way and are heritable suggest that they reflect something about the way the brain organizes personality (Livesley, Jang, & Vernon, (1998). In this view, personality traits are hierarchically organized: A large number of narrower dimensions are associated with genetic and biological mechanisms, which cluster together into four or five "super-factors."

One of the main arguments in support of a dimensional system is evidence that most personality disorders tend to be continuous with normal personality traits (Livesley et al., 1998). Research in community and clinical populations usually fails to show any sharp separation between pathological and normal personality traits.

The principle of continuity between traits and disorders is applicable to most of the Axis II categories. Narcissistic and obsessive–compulsive personality disorders are obviously exaggerations of normal personality. These traits are very common, and we can readily identify them in our friends and colleagues (even if they do not always cause major dysfunction). On the other hand, trait dimensions do not readily account for the wide range of symptoms seen in BPD.

Another argument in favor of dimensions is that whereas traits are stable over time, personality disorder categories, and the symptoms on which they are based, are unstable (Skodol et al., 2005). As Chapter 6 shows, BPD traits can continue to cause dysfunction, even when the disorder no longer presents enough symptoms to meet criteria.

One of the strongest criticisms of categorical diagnosis in Axis II of DSM-IV-TR is that many of the personality disorders listed have not been researched. We have serious empirical data on only three categories: antisocial personality (6,000 publications since 1950), borderline personality (3,500 publications), and schizotypal personality (1,700 publications). The literature on the other seven categories is very slim. They are there mainly for historical reasons. We would probably not miss any of these diagnoses much if they disappeared.

Retaining so many categories on Axis II was based much more on tradition than on empirical data. British researcher Peter Tyrer (1988) suggested that the problem with Axis II is that it used too many categories; 3 or 4 would work much better than 10.

But there is another problem. Axis II is a mixture of highly symptomatic disorders and "egosyntonic" traits that other people (not necessarily the patient) consider to be problems. We need to separate diagnoses with prominent symptoms (the categories that have elicited the most research) and those primarily reflecting traits (most of the others).

In this way, BPD is not like most personality disorders. It has a wide range of troubling and unusual symptoms that most people *never* experience. Although it can be mapped by scores on trait measures, that does not account for its clinical presentation. Some features of BPD, like affective instability and impulsivity, are indeed traits seen in community populations. However, others are symptoms far out of normal experience. Overdosing and cutting are the most striking examples; it is hard to see how these behaviors can overlap with normality. The more general point is that symptoms differ from traits: They are present in people with diagnosable disorders and absent in those who only have trait vulnerabilities.

A separation between traits and symptoms in BPD has been supported by research. In a large-scale follow-up study of patients with BPD and other personality disorders, Morey and Zanarini (2000) administered a measure of the FFM. They confirmed that BPD patients scored higher on Neuroticism. However, scores on this dimension did not account for scores on Impulsivity items from the DIB-R, and although neuroticism remained stable over time, the diagnosis of BPD did not (symptoms waxed and waned at various points of follow-up).

Saulsman and Page (2004) reported on a meta-analysis of studies that applied the FFM to patients with personality disorders. They found almost *all* personality disorders to be associated with high scores on Neuroticism, and most were also associated with low Agreeableness and low Conscientiousness. (Axis II categories vary most with respect to Extraversion.)

These findings suggest that the FFM offers a very broad picture that lacks necessary clinical details. FFM profiles are better measures of personality than of personality disorders. Instruments developed in community populations to describe normal variations on trait dimensions are not ideal for assessing pathology.

If DSM-V were to adopt a dimensional measure, it would need something better. One possibility is to develop a revised FFM with more psychopathology items. Some instruments have been designed in that way. The Schedule for Non-Adaptive and Adaptive Personality (Clark, 1993) and the Diagnostic Assessment of Personality Pathology (DAPP; Livesley et al., 1998) made a special effort to include pathology-oriented items in their questionnaires. (I have used the DAPP in my own research.) However, although these measures provide different information from categories, the coherence of the BPD construct depends on how traits interact.

How would a dimensional system work? Livesley (2003) has proposed that DSM-V should allow clinicians to make an overall diagnosis of personality disorder without invoking categories. Specific features would then be described using a profile of scores on personality dimensions. Even if some categories were retained (on a provisional basis), they would be based on traits.

There are a few problems with this proposal. One is the use of too broad a definition of personality disorder, requiring only one of three criteria: inability to establish identity, work, or relationships (Krueger, Skodol, Livesley, Shrout, & Huang, 2007). However, the deeper issue is that dimensional approaches blur the distinction between traits and symptoms. That is the essential difference between normality and mental disorder.

Another suggestion to "dimensionalize" Axis II is to turn the DSM criteria themselves into a series of scores (Oldham et al., 1992). Patients with BPD would receive a number for each criterion plus a total score.

I consider this idea to be a nonstarter. If the DSM criteria are poorly drawn, or frankly wrong, there is no point in dimensionalizing them at least until we find a way to revise them properly. It would be absurd to apply scores to items that only reflect a consensus by a committee (as opposed to items based on systematic studies establishing discriminant validity).

Westen, Shedler, and Bradley (2006) have proposed still another solution, which is to sharpen the DSM categories through "prototpype matching," a procedure requiring clinicians to sort clinical features, thereby approximating the prototype of each disorder. Although this approach could have some advantages, it may be too time consuming for clinical application.

We should keep in mind that the DSM system is meant for practical use, so that clinical utility must be a primary concern (First, 2005). I find the approach of trait psychology to diagnosis to be somewhat abstract and purist. As a physician, I am trained to be pragmatic rather than theoretically consistent. Moreover, I am not convinced that self-report measures actually measure the way the brain organizes personality. That question can best be resolved by determining whether traits are correlated with genes or biological markers, and up to this point the evidence on that score is unconvincing (Paris, 2005b).

Trait psychologists also point out that dimensions convey more information than categories. That is true, but clinicians and researchers often do better with less information.

Ultimately, diagnoses should be guides to treatment. However, with a few exceptions, DSM diagnoses do not help clinicians decide about therapy. Although diagnoses of schizophrenia and bipolar disorder point to the prescription of specific drugs, that is not nearly as true for major depression or most anxiety disorders. Although the category of BPD also does not imply a specific mode of treatment, it describes a group of patients who require a nonstandard approach to psychotherapy, and that is the main reason why it should be retained.

Ultimately, categorical and dimensional approaches to diagnosis are complementary. We often use dimensions in medicine. Thus, blood pressure can vary within normal levels, until it exceeds 120/80. However, hypertension is a category of illness because the dimensional cutoff marks a qualitative jump, the point at which complications become much more likely.

Because all diagnostic categories in psychiatry have fuzzy edges, I wonder why dimensional theorists are "picking on" Axis II. One could just as easily apply dimensional diagnosis to Axis I disorders such as depression or anxiety. Even schizophrenia lies within a spectrum. The problem with dimensional approaches is that they leave clinicians uncertain whether patients fall outside the boundary with normality. Pathology begins not with extremes on a dimension but with people who are not functioning in life.

We need not expect categories to be fully distinct as long as they usefully describe how clinical phenomena cluster together. This is why clinicians use diagnoses for communicating about their patients. And clinicians, unlike researchers, do not feel comfortable with scores on multiple dimensions. Dimensional systems tend to be unwieldy in practice. That is why few clinical psychologists use the Minnesota Multiphasic Personality Inventory for diagnosis in spite of the large body of research behind that instrument. Because clinicians are always short of time, they would probably not use a dimensional approach to personality disorders that required them to score a large number of traits. In addition, the outcome of an unusable system would be that BPD would be even easier to ignore.

Dimensional systems have a real value for research. Traits have more biological correlates than any categories of disorder (see Chapter 4). They remain stable even when symptoms remit. They are markers for vulnerability to disorder, before pathology develops and after it remits. But they cannot replace categories in clinical practice.

In summary, dimensions are good at describing the traits that underlie BPD but do not account for its symptoms. And one cannot understand the disorder without understanding its trait domains. In fact, the theory to be developed in this book considers traits to be the fundamental diatheses that develop into disorder when patients are exposed to stressors.

But categories are equally essential. They tell you how trait domains cluster together and what kinds of symptom patterns to look for. For this reason, it would be premature to replace the BPD diagnosis with a dimensional profile.

IS BPD A PERSONALITY DISORDER?

BPD does not actually belong on Axis II. In principle, Axis I describes symptomatic conditions, whereas Axis II describes trait disturbances. However, even the most severe mental disorders, such as schizophrenia, reflect both. BPD is rooted in trait vulnerability but can present with as many symptoms as the major psychoses.

It would be more logical to move BPD to Axis I. Placing it on Axis II leads to the mistaken idea that this disorder has a close relation with normal personality, which it does not. In addition, disorders on Axis II tend either to be missed entirely (Zimmerman & Mattia, 1999) or not to be taken seriously.

The general definition of a personality disorder in DSM-IV-TR (American Psychiatric Association, 2000) requires long-term dysfunction in mood, impulsivity, and cognition, significantly affecting functioning, with an onset early in life. The problem with this definition is that it does not distinguish Axis II from Axis I: Patients can also develop mood and anxiety disorders early in life and be affected by them for years. This is why Livesley (2003) proposed that *all* personality disorders be moved to Axis I, reserving Axis II for trait profiles (rather than disorders). I agree with that suggestion. The distinction between Axis I and Axis II, which was intended to encourage clinicians to think about personality disorders, has backfired. Disorders like BPD are placed in an "Axis II ghetto," where they can safely be ignored.

Although I agree with Livesley about moving all serious personality pathology to Axis I, I disagree regarding whether BPD itself should remain in DSM. I suggest that the problem is the way we define the category, not whether it is valid in the first place. We need to update the almost 30-year-old definition of BPD to get it in line with current research. We should rewrite the criteria and require more symptoms to be present to make a diagnosis. One way to improve the BPD diagnosis is to base it on the domains described by Gunderson and Zanarini and to require that symptoms be present in most, if not all, of those domains. Doing so would narrow the definition of BPD and describe a more homogeneous group of patients who are likely to require the same form of treatment.

BPD IN PRACTICE AND IN THE COMMUNITY

In the practice of psychotherapy, how common are patients with BPD? Are there many cases, or does it just seem that way (if each case feels like 10)? Research sheds light on this question. A large number of patients in a variety of clinical settings meet criteria for the BPD diagnosis (as currently defined in DSM).

Most patients with BPD in practice have had hospital admissions related to suicidality (Zanarini, Frankenburg, Khera, & Bleichmar, 2001). However, their precise percentage on wards is hard to determine. In most North American hospitals, beds have been sharply cut back, and managed care discourages the admission of suicidal patients. Moreover, hospitals have different thresholds for admission, depending on number of beds and size of catchment areas. Thus, widely quoted estimates of BPD from the past, such as 25% of all inpatients at McLean Hospital (Gunderson, 1984), would not apply in the current scene.

We do have recent information about the prevalence of BPD in outpatient settings. The numbers derive from a study by Zimmerman, Rothschild, and Chelminski (2005) using a large practice affiliated with Rhode Island Hospital. Among 859 patients surveyed, 80 (9.3%) met diagnostic criteria. BPD patients are also common in primary care settings. A study by Gross et al. (2002) found that 6.4% had BPD (in a sample of 218 patients seeing a group of internists).

Needless to say, BPD patients are particularly common in the emergency room. Forman, Berk, Henriques, Brown, and Beck (2004) found that 41% of 114 repetitive suicide attempters and 15% of 39 single attempters met criteria for this diagnosis.

However, clinical cases are not necessarily representative of the frequency of mental disorders in community populations. Are there patients with similar problems who are not coming for help? If so, do they have milder or more severe symptoms? Research shows that there are more individuals whom we do not see, and that they differ somewhat from patients who present for treatment.

Psychiatric epidemiology, which measures the prevalence of mental disorders in the community, provides data that can guide research, clinical practice, and planning for mental health systems. However, until recently few studies have assessed the prevalence of Axis II diagnoses.

The Epidemiologic Catchment Area (ECA) Study (Robins & Regier, 1991) was a large-scale survey funded by the National Institute of Mental Health (NIMH) and conducted in the 1980s. It examined the prevalence and correlates of the most important Axis I disorders. However, it failed to provide information about Axis II (only antisocial personality was assessed). One reason is that the ECA instrument (the Diagnostic Interview Schedule) was designed for use by nonprofessional interviewers. Axis II diagnosis requires some clinical experience for accurate assessment. Another reason was that the research base for the validity of most personality disorders was not considered to be good enough.

One widely quoted report (Swartz, Blazer, George, & Winfield, 1990) reconstructed the diagnosis of BPD from ECA data on symptoms, but that was a questionable methodology. Unfortunately, the estimate of prevalence in their study, 1.8%, has been referenced ever since, possibly because high numbers can be used to justify research funding. In the 1990s, the next wave of NIMH-funded psychiatric epidemiology, the National Comorbidity Survey (Kessler et al., 1994), again limited itself to antisocial personality disorder (ASPD) and did not try to measure BPD.

However, in the last 10 years, several studies applied epidemiological methods to measure the prevalence of all personality disorders. A report from Oslo, Norway (Torgersen, Kringlen, & Cramer,

2001) examined the frequency of all personality disorders in that city. A second study, conducted at one of the original ECA sites in Baltimore (Samuels et al., 2002), also measured all Axis II categories. A third study, designed to assess alcohol and substance abuse in the United States (Grant et al., 2004), examined the prevalence of seven Axis II disorders (unfortunately not including BPD). A longitudinal study of university students (Lenzenweger, Johnson, & Willett, 2004) examined all personality disorders (albeit in a relatively privileged population). A prospective study of children monitored into adulthood (Crawford et al., 2005) estimated the frequency of personality disorders (albeit from self-report data rather than from interviews).

Two of the most important and comprehensive studies appeared fairly recently. In the United Kingdom, Coid, Yang, Tyrer, Roberts, and Ullrich (2006) published a study of all DSM-defined personality disorders in a representative community sample. In the United States, Lenzenweger, Lane, Loranger, and Kessler (2007) published a study using a nationally representative sample, based on the National Comorbidity Survey Replication (Kessler, Chiu, Demler, Merikangas, & Walters, 2005). Measuring the prevalence of all Axis II disorders in a large community sample became possible through the use of a research interview (the International Personality Disorders Examination) that had previously been used in a World Health Organization-sponsored comparison of Axis II disorders in six countries (Loranger, Hirschfeld, Sartorius, & Regier, 1991) and in which BPD was included.

The results of all these surveys vary somewhat, but their findings generally converge. BPD has a prevalence of about 1%. Although that figure is lower than previous estimates, it is as great as that for schizophrenia.

These studies also suggest that in the community there are patients with BPD who do not come for help. (We lack systematic data about treatment patterns in community populations.)

Like other mental disorders, BPD varies in severity. Practitioners tend to think about diagnoses in terms of the worst cases. Even in schizophrenia, many patients live in the community without being monitored in the mental health system (Harding, Brooks, Ashikaga, Strauss, & Brier, 1987). Similarly, many people with BPD have less severe symptoms, and, as Chapter 6 shows, these patients are more likely to recover. We sometimes get the mistaken impression that all cases are like the most difficult ones we treat, in which serious pathology continues unabated for years.

Gender is another reason for discrepancies between clinical practice and community prevalence. In the clinic, BPD is mostly a female disorder: Up to 80% of patients are women (Zimmerman et al., 2005). That may not be true in the community. Torgersen et al. (2001) found more women in his survey, but both Coid et al. (2006) and Lenzenweger et al. (2007) identified as many men. By and large, women are more likely to seek help than men: clinics see more females with almost any psychiatric disorder, and fewer males pursue therapy.

Some years ago, our group carried out a special study of men with BPD (Paris, Zweig-Frank, & Guzder, 1994a). However, we had to advertise to find cases. We placed our advertisement in an alternative newspaper (read by many young males). We had expected to find a large overlap with ASPD. However, although I have seen such cases in practice, none of the research participants had that comorbidity. In most respects, men with BPD were identical to women with the disorder. The one difference we noted (Paris, Zweig-Frank, & Guzder, 1995) was that, unlike females, 10% of our male sample was actively homosexual.

The most probable explanation for gender differences in clinical samples is that women are more likely to develop the kind of symptoms that bring patients in for treatment. Twice as many women as men in the community suffer from depression (Weissman & Klerman, 1985). In contrast, there is a preponderance of men meeting criteria for substance abuse and psychopathy (Robins & Regier, 1991), and males with these disorders do not necessarily present in the mental health system.

Men and women with similar psychological problems may express distress differently. Men tend to drink more and carry out more crimes. Women tend to turn their anger on themselves, leading to depression as well as the cutting and overdosing that characterize BPD. Thus, ASPD and borderline personality disorders might derive from similar underlying pathology but present with symptoms strongly influenced by gender (Paris, 1997a; Looper & Paris, 2000).

We have even more specific evidence that men with BPD may not seek help. In a study of completed suicides among people aged 18 to 35 years (Lesage et al., 1994), 30% of the suicides involved individuals with BPD (as confirmed by psychological autopsy, in which symptoms were assessed by interviews with family members). Most of the suicide completers were men, and very few were

in treatment. Similar findings emerged from a later study conducted by our own research group (McGirr, Paris, Lesage, Renaud,
& Turecki, 2007).

That men can have typical borderline pathology is illustrated by
the following case.

Case 7

Steven was a 28-year-old working part time who had recently
finished a 3-year course in theater at a community college. Steven was living with his girlfriend of 2 years. The relationship
was difficult and stormy, because Steven could be very demanding. He was assessed after going into a frightening rage following a conflict with one of his teachers.

Steven had a psychiatric history going back to age 18 and
had been admitted twice for suicidal threats. Although he never
made a suicide attempt, he often cut himself. The main problem
was rages, with threats against others and occasional destruction
of property, and a history of binge drinking. Other symptoms included "having a movie with sound and pictures" run in his
head associated with violent fantasies and chronic feelings of depersonalization and derealization.

Steven met all DSM criteria for BPD and scored 8/10 on the
DIB-R.

WHY MAKING A BPD DIAGNOSIS IS IMPORTANT

BPD is a diagnosis that makes a difference. If patients with BPD go
unrecognized, they can end up getting the wrong treatment. Even
with the diagnosis, patients may receive interventions that are misguided or counterproductive. However, *without* the diagnosis, they
are most likely to be treated with drugs of limited value. In a therapy
practice, missing BPD prevents clinicians from modifying their methods.

There are several advantages in making a diagnosis of BPD. The
first concerns the recognition of a complex form of psychopathology
with symptoms that do not occur in isolation. BPD is a construct that
can account for the co-occurrence of a wide range of affective, impulsive, and cognitive symptoms in the same patient.

The second advantage concerns prediction of outcome. BPD has
a characteristic course over time, beginning in adolescence, with symptoms peaking in early adulthood, followed by gradual recovery in

middle age (Paris, 2003). This pattern provides an important frame for therapy.

The third advantage lies in predicting response (or lack of response) to treatment. For example, pharmacotherapy for depression is less effective in the presence of any personality disorder, and patients with BPD do not consistently respond to antidepressants (see Chapter 7).

Fourth, generic forms of psychotherapy do not work well in BPD. Instead, there is good evidence that specific methods of psychotherapy are effective. If one does not make the diagnosis, patients may not be referred for these treatments.

Failure to recognize BPD leads to mistaken expectations about course and treatment response. Making the diagnosis allows us to inform and educate patients and their families.

There are problems with the BPD diagnosis, but they are hardly unique. Unclear boundaries afflict most disorders in DSM. There has always been some tendency to assume that diagnoses on Axis I must be more valid than those on Axis II. Actually, Axis I disorders, like personality disorders, are defined imprecisely, overlap with each other, and lack a clear cutoff with normality (Paris, 2008). Examples include conduct disorder, which has an unclear boundary with misbehavior, and social phobia, which fades imperceptibly into shyness. Major depression is quite fuzzy around the edges and lacks a definite boundary with normal unhappiness (Horwitz & Wakefield, 2007).

In a personal discussion regarding problems that affect categories in DSM-IV-TR, a prominent researcher in psychology suggested that after DSM-III came out in 1980, psychiatry should have supported studies to determine the validity of every criterion for every diagnosis. (Technically, this would have required measuring *discriminant validity*, i.e., assessing the correlation of each criterion with a diagnosis, and the absence of correlations with other categories). But no such studies were ever carried out. To this day, we cannot say that the criteria for major depression are the right ones or that requiring five of them to make a diagnosis is a valid procedure.

This work has also never been done in BPD—but it could be. I favor retaining the BPD diagnosis but recommend carrying out research to determine which criteria best establish discriminant validity.

In summary, there are many problems with the BPD diagnosis. Yet it would be a mistake to dismiss or eliminate this category. And there would be clinical consequences if we did so.

DEFINITIONS

CLINICAL IMPLICATIONS

- BPD is a diagnosis that describes a wide range of symptoms and that is rooted in personality traits.
- The best approach to refining the diagnosis lies in requiring more criteria and in requiring symptoms in more domains.
- Dimensional descriptions of traits are more useful for research than for clinical practice.
- There are more cases of BPD in the community than are seen by clinicians.
- The BPD diagnosis describes a group of patients who require a unique approach to treatment.

CHAPTER 2

The Boundaries of BPD

WHY BPD REMAINS CONTROVERSIAL

A certain suspicion still surrounds BPD. That comes from its history. In the past, the diagnosis was often seen as vague and based on psychodynamic theories. BPD was perceived as a holdover from the heyday of psychoanalysis, an idea so totally rooted in speculation that only Woody Allen would take seriously. One of my most esteemed teachers, Heinz Lehmann, told me not to use this category "since no one knows what it means." At the time of that conversation (1969), Lehmann was probably right.

Another problem derives from the term itself: There is no border on which one can be "borderline." Akiskal, Chen, and Davis (1985) memorably described BPD as "an adjective in search of a noun." Although other terms in psychiatry, such as schizophrenia, are equally meaningless, the current label does not help acceptance of the concept.

Forty years ago, psychodynamically oriented teachers trained me to diagnose patients as borderline cases. I was encouraged to read the then recent work of Roy Grinker (1968). Even so, I was not convinced. I remained loyal to Lehmann and refused to make the diagnosis for years. I hardly dreamed that I would someday become a researcher on BPD.

25

In the early years of my practice, however, I developed a strong interest in chronically suicidal patients. I had been trained in psychotherapy but was unhappy with concentrating these skills on treating the "worried well." After all, as a medical specialist, I should see highly disturbed people. Moreover, treating suicidal cases would provide me with a marker for success or failure: The patient would be either alive or dead at the end of therapy.

Then Gunderson and Singer (1975) showed that patients could be diagnosed using a semistructured interview, moving the diagnosis from speculation about hidden mental mechanisms to assessment of observable phenomena. Now the concept began to make sense to me. I was even helped by one of my patients, who handed me a paper by Otto Kernberg, saying "Read this—it might help." I came to realize that BPD was a diagnostic construct that described the patients who interested me most.

Once convinced of the usefulness of diagnosing BPD, I read everything I could find on the subject. I found that many writers had thoughtful and insightful things to say based on their clinical experience. Yet I was still not satisfied that I understood the problem. Very little that I read was helpful for treating patients.

Eventually I went into research to explore these questions. In this respect, I was no different from many of my contemporaries: the leaders in personality disorder research were almost all psychotherapists with research training.

Yet even today, after 30 years of serious research and decades after its acceptance into DSM-III in 1980, resistance by clinicians to making a diagnosis of BPD continues. This is a situation that requires an explanation.

COMORBIDITY AND CO-OCCURRENCE

Opposition to diagnosing BPD reflects, at least in part, difficulties in treatment. Clinicians just want to make the problem go away by attributing symptoms to another diagnosis. In psychiatry, doing so usually leads to a prescription of medication. However, that is not how the argument is usually presented. Instead, one hears that because BPD is highly comorbid with other disorders, particularly depression, one should treat the comorbidity.

There can be no doubt that BPD lacks a clear boundary: The diagnosis is associated with a wide range of symptoms and overlaps with many disorders on Axis I. Almost every time I have published a report on a clinical sample of patients with BPD, reviewers ask me to document its comorbidity. That request could be based on the assumption that Axis I diagnoses should take preference over personality disorders.

But what is the meaning of comorbidity? Is BPD really a form of another mental disorder? Are other mental disorders any more real? Given the validity problems of Axis I disorders, co-occurrence is a more neutral term than *comorbidity*, which implies the presence of two separate conditions.

The diagnosis of BPD describes a mixture of traits and symptoms: personality trait disturbances that go back many years, combined with acute symptoms related to recent life events. The most extensive co-occurrences are with mood disorders, anxiety disorders, and substance abuse (Zanarini et al., 1998a). These overlaps have been used to support the idea that BPD is a variant of other conditions.

Most of these reformulations would remove BPD from DSM by turning it into a subtype of another category. Over the years several disorders have been suggested. Schizophrenia came first. But the most frequent candidates in recent decades have been depression and bipolar disorder. There are also a few clinicians who consider BPD to be a form of posttraumatic stress disorder (PTSD).

This chapter shows that all Axis I disorders that are comorbid with BPD correspond only to one facet of the syndrome. None account for its broad range of pathology.

BPD AND PSYCHOSIS

For the most part, overlap between BPD and schizophrenia is not a serious problem for establishing a diagnosis. It might have been in the past, when schizophrenia was broadly defined and widely overdiagnosed. That was the context of Stern's original idea: that BPD lies on a border between neurosis and psychosis. His idea found a parallel in the diagnostic term *pseudoneurotic schizophrenia* (Hoch, Cattell, Strahl, & Penness, 1962), which suggested that patients with a wide variety of neurotic symptoms are latently psychotic.

Although patients with BPD have micropsychotic symptoms, personality disorders primarily affecting mood and impulsivity (like BPD) can be separated from those that primarily affect cognition, such as schizotypal personality (Spitzer, Endicott, & Gibbon, 1979).

Neither family history studies (White, Gunderson, Zanarini, & Hudson, 2003) nor biological markers (Paris, 2003) support any link between BPD and schizophrenia. In contrast, schizotypal personality disorder is clearly related to psychosis, through both family history and biological markers (Siever & Davis, 1991).

Because the frequency of cognitive symptoms in BPD is not widely appreciated, one occasionally still sees confusion about differential diagnosis. About half of all patients with BPD experience hallucinations (usually auditory but sometimes visual) as well as other cognitive symptoms, particularly subdelusional paranoid feelings and repeated episodes of depersonalization (Zanarini, Gunderson, & Frankenburg, 1990).

These are clinically important features that require specific management. Their recognition led to the introduction of a ninth criterion for BPD in DSM-IV. Unfortunately, the new criterion only mentioned paranoid and dissociative symptoms and did not address the transient, stress-related auditory hallucinations that are so common in BPD (Yee, Korner, McSwiggan, Meares, & Stevenson, 2005).

When cognitive symptoms are florid, questions of differential diagnosis with schizophrenia can arise. However, psychotic phenomena in BPD remain transient, and insight is retained. Hearing voices can seem real at the moment, but patients come to understand that they are not. Although BPD patients experience paranoid feelings under stress, they do not have fixed or bizarre delusions.

The following cases demonstrate the range of cognitive symptoms in this population.

Case 1

Bill, 25 years old, was in treatment for chronic suicidality, unstable relationships, and mood instability. He also had paranoid ideas, often thinking that his neighbors were plotting against him. However, all these thoughts were exaggerations of real situations and never involved fixed delusions, and his thoughts lacked the bizarre quality seen in schizophrenia. Bill often heard critical voices in his head when stressed, but he knew that such experiences were imaginary.

Nonetheless, Bill had been initially diagnosed with schizophrenia and treated for psychosis over 5 years with long-acting antipsychotic medication. Bill actually liked attending this clinic and getting injections, because it gave him a reason to come in every 2 weeks and to talk with a nurse. However, as his life stabilized, Bill's micropsychotic symptoms remitted (along with his other symptoms). By age 30, Bill stopped taking neuroleptics and never had a relapse of paranoid ideas or hallucinations.

Case 2

Moira, a 24-year-old student, was admitted for suicidal threats. Other problems included mood instability and stormy relationships. In the course of the intake, she reported hearing voices in her head telling her she was bad or advising her to kill herself. These experiences did not occur on a daily basis; rather, they were linked to stressful events or times when Moira felt unusually distressed. Although Moira sometimes believed her voices while they were talking to her, she knew they were imaginary once they stopped. There was no delusional elaboration of these hallucinations.

Case 3

June, 17 years old, was being treated for cutting and overdosing. She regularly heard voices and described living in an imaginary world in which friendly figures spoke to her reassuringly. Sometimes she thought that this was a real world, perhaps on another planet, and that she could enter it if she were to die. Most of the time, June was well grounded in the present but she had a very intense fantasy life. It is relevant that June had recently seen the movie *I Never Promised You a Rose Garden*, which influenced the content of her experiences.

There are also patients with schizophrenia who can be mistakenly diagnosed with BPD.

Case 4

A 25-year-old woman presented on numerous occasions to the emergency room with overdoses and cutting, leading to a presumptive diagnosis of BPD. However, a careful mental status revealed that she had auditory hallucinations on a daily basis, and that the voices consisted of two men talking to each other about her. The patient identified these as "spirits," which she believed to have been persecuting her for the last 5 years. Further supporting a diagnosis of schizophrenia, the patient had been well functioning since the age of 20, but since falling ill had become a different person, suspicious and unable to either work or return to school.

BPD, DEPRESSION, AND DYSTHYMIA

Patients with BPD often have depressive symptoms, which may be chronic, as in dysthymia, or acute, as in major depression. In fact, when patients are in crisis, they *usually* meet criteria for major depression. (It is not that difficult to do so if the main requirements are to be sad and dysfunctional for 2 weeks.)

These phenomena can lead clinicians to downplay (or ignore) accompanying personality pathology. I cannot count the number of emergency room reports I have read describing patients with BPD as having only major depression (with Axis II either ignored or deferred). However, the larger question is whether the personality disorder is "nothing but" a form of mood disorder. Years ago, Akiskal et al. (1985) proposed that BPD is a variant of depression (or dysthymia).

There were several problems with that idea. First and foremost, depression is a different phenomenon in BPD. Patients with classic depression will feel sad no matter what is going in their lives. Almost by definition, you cannot cheer up someone who is clinically depressed.

The situation is quite different in BPD. One does not see continuously low mood but rather *affective instability*. Mood can change by the day or by the hour (Gunderson & Phillips, 1991). A patient may wake up anxious, be depressed in the afternoon, feel fine in the evening, but go into a rage before bedtime. Research on affective instability in BPD shows that shifts from depression to anger are particularly common (Koenigsberg et al., 2002; Henry et al., 2001). This pattern of affective instability and environmental sensitivity has little resemblance to classic depression.

Second, antidepressants are much less effective in BPD than they are in classic depression. As Chapter 7 shows, drugs "take the edge off" BPD symptoms but almost never lead to remission (as they can in classical depression). For this reason, a diagnosis of mood disorder that ignores personality often leads to poor therapy. Treatment methods most strongly supported by evidence (specific methods of psychotherapy developed for BPD) will not be prescribed when patients are only seen as suffering from chemical imbalances and are prescribed one drug after another.

Third, the subjective experience of depression in BPD is unique. Sadness is more intense (Stanley & Wilson, 2006), and is characterized by a clinging dependency not often seen in major depressive disorder (Wixom, Ludolph, & Westen, 1993).

Because patients with BPD are so often sad, they frequently meet criteria for dysthymia (i.e., low mood more days than not, with at least two symptoms of depression, such as low mood, fatigue, or insomnia). However, although dysthymia describes a set of symptoms, it is a heterogeneous category (Chen, Eaton, Gallo, & Nestadt, 2000). In addition, although antidepressants help some patients with dysthymia, they are less consistently effective for that diagnosis than they are in full-scale depression (De Lima & Hotopf, 2003).

When patients with BPD present to emergency rooms and clinics, something has happened to make them feel sadder than usual. The diagnosis of major depression, like BPD itself, requires five of nine symptoms to be present. Someone who has felt low for 2 weeks and has four other symptoms will qualify for a diagnosis. This overly broad definition makes major depression a heterogeneous category, with symptoms ranging in severity from melancholia to nearly normal reactions to losses (Horwitz & Wakefield, 2007).

The large-scale STAR*D study (Rush, 2007), as well as other research (see review in Moncrieff & Kirsch, 2005), shows that only some patients with depression have a full response to antidepressants. Diagnosing major depression gives us an illusion of meaning but does not tell us enough to be clinically useful.

Another argument in favor of the idea that BPD is a form of major depression is the frequent presence of a family history of mood disorder (Akiskal, 1985). However, impulsive disorders such as substance abuse and antisocial personality are actually more common than mood disorders in first-degree relatives (White, Gunderson, Zanarini, & Hudson, 2003). Another argument (Akiskal, 1985) is based on commonalities in biological markers (such as REM latency, in which rapid eye movements during sleep start sooner than in most other people). Yet these biological markers are present only when BPD patients are also depressed (De la Fuente, Bobes, Vizuete, & Mendlewicz, 2001; Philipsen et al., 2005).

The perception that depression trumps a diagnosis of BPD fails to take problems with impulsivity and unstable relationships into account and simply assumes that they are secondary. However, it is difficult to see how all these long-term problems can be accounted for by mood, given that most people with depression do not have them.

Along the same lines, it has been suggested that one cannot diagnose a personality disorder in patients who are currently depressed (Farabaugh, Mischoulon, Fava, Guyker, & Alpert, 2004). It has been noted that some depressed patients appear to have personality disorder symptoms, which then disappear after treatment and remission (Farabaugh et al., 2004). But that is exactly what does *not* happen in BPD. Although some patients with refractory depression never fully recover and have symptoms resembling a personality disorder, patients with BPD have a very different course, with symptoms that start at a young age and are hardly ever fully absent. Patients with BPD are chronically depressed with acute exacerbations and are almost never euthymic, even when they no longer meet criteria for major depression. Unfortunately, a focus on depression has been used to justify prescribing antidepressant medication without bothering to investigate personality.

Finally, as discussed in Chapter 1, one sometimes hears that a personality disorder cannot be diagnosed in a single interview. Perhaps this idea masks a reluctance to do so, even when a patient has an extensive life history to justify the diagnosis. One hour is often quite sufficient to make a diagnosis of BPD, assuming the therapist dies not spend the entire time asking for details of depressive symptoms.

In summary, BPD is associated with depression but is not accounted for by it. Lowered mood does not explain why patients act out impulsively. Nor does low mood account for the troubled relationships that characterize BPD.

Case 5

Susan, a 24-year-old, was under treatment for chronic depression, with rapid shifts of mood, usually to anger and rageful outbursts. She also had a history of cutting and repetitive overdoses. Susan had been diagnosed with major depression and treated with a variety of antidepressants from several drug classes. However, none of these agents yielded any lasting effect. Every medication change led to short-term improvement for a few weeks followed by relapse to the previous state. Yet Susan was able to stop using antidepressants entirely once she became engaged in psychotherapy.

BPD AND THE BIPOLAR SPECTRUM

The latest, and currently the most influential, attempt to remove BPD from the list of mental illnesses in DSM is the proposal that these patients actually suffer from a bipolar spectrum disorder.

The concept of a bipolar spectrum has emerged in the last decade, expanding the diagnostic construct of bipolar disorder to include a wider range of syndromes (Akiskal, 2002; Angst & Gamma, 2002; Ghaemi, Ko, & Goodwin, 2002). In addition to the classic forms of illness—bipolar I (with mania) and bipolar II (with hypomania)—spectrum disorders include bipolar III (antidepressant-induced hypomania) and bipolar IV (ultra-rapid-cycling bipolar disorder). This concept also implies that the bipolar spectrum could include many cases currently diagnosed as unipolar depression, anxiety disorders, substance abuse, eating disorders, as well as personality disorders.

Mood instability of any kind has come to be seen by many clinicians as a symptom of bipolar disorder. Yet rapid mood swings are also one of the most characteristic features of personality disorders. Moreover, there are important differences between BPD and bipolar disorder (Paris, Gunderson, & Weinberg, 2007). First, mood in BPD has a different quality. Second, mood shifts occur in response to life events. Third, the temporal frame is different in that mood in BPD changes over hours, not weeks. The biological mechanisms behind this pattern could be entirely different.

Thus, mood changes in bipolar disorder are qualitatively different from those that characterize BPD. One cannot cheer up a severely depressed person or "bring down" anyone suffering a manic episode. Although changes from depression to elation distinguish bipolar II, moods in BPD are more likely to shift from euthymia to anger (Koenigsberg et al., 2002). Moreover, unlike bipolar disorder, mood changes in BPD are usually reactions to environmental events (Henry et al., 2001). When one interviews patients with BPD carefully, one almost always find triggers for changes in mood.

Temporal frames present one of the most important problems with the idea that rapid mood changes reflect bipolarity. To place patients firmly in the bipolar spectrum, they should at least have had episodes of hypomania. This is not true of the cases that have been called "bipolar IV," which actually describes the affective instability of BPD (Ghaemi et al., 2002). Unless it can be proved that the mood swings seen in BPD are related to bipolarity, the concept of bipolar IV disorder has to be questioned.

The key question that defines the boundary between BPD and bipolar II concerns the definition of a hypomanic episode. As defined in DSM-IV-TR, hypomania consists of "persistently elevated, expansive, or irritable mood, lasting throughout at least 4 days." Such episodes are rarely, if ever, seen in BPD (Koenigsberg et al., 2002; Henry et al., 2001). When interviewing patients carefully about times when they are "high," one will find that elated mood is not continuous but rather is mixed with sadness or anxiety and especially with anger. Assessment of hypomania depends on inaccurate retrospective reporting by patients of whether their mood has, in fact, been elevated, how long these changes have lasted, and whether or not they have been stable over a 4-day period. And, ratings of hypomania are often unreliable (Dunner & Tay, 1993).

My experience is that clinicians' judgments are easily biased by preconceptions. Thus, patients are not necessarily asked detailed questions about how long the elevated mood lasted, whether it was persistent, and whether it was accompanied by behavioral changes such as loss of a need to sleep, overtalking, overspending, or sexual promiscuity.

When patients do have hypomania, they will meet criteria for bipolar II disorder. Some might interpret that as an example of comorbidity. I have a different view. Because I consider these disorders to be distinct, I refuse to diagnose BPD if a patient has a classic bipolar disorder (either type I or type II). I acknowledge that to do so involves deviating from DSM instructions. However, the DSM system, which avoids exclusion criteria, is the real reason for multiple diagnoses. Moreover, major psychoses such as schizophrenia and bipolar disorders have profound effects on personality. It makes little sense to add an Axis II diagnosis when these conditions are present. One would not do so if a patient had personality changes secondary to dementia or mental retardation. Bipolar I affects the personality, as does its less severe variant, bipolar II.

Finally, do mood disturbances drive the other symptoms of BPD? Akiskal (2002) argues that impulsivity and interpersonal problems are usually secondary to mood swings. This point of view seems to consider personality itself to be an epiphenomenon of mood.

The current "mania" to see all kinds of mental disorders as mania could be described as *bipolar imperialism*. This is the latest of the many diagnostic fads that have afflicted psychiatry (Paris, 2008). In this perspective, a large range of mental disorders should be redefined as "soft bipolarity." Angst and Gamma (2002) suggest that many, if not most, cases of unipolar depression and substance abuse would be included. In addition, the diagnosis of bipolarity in prepubertal children (Biederman, 2006; Wozniak, 2005) has become very common, largely on the basis of impulsivity and mood instability. However, it is difficult to see why every aggressive or behavioral disturbance in children should be equivalent to the irritability seen in classic bipolar disorder.

At the extreme, the imperialists could move the majority of mental disorders into the bipolar spectrum. (There continue to be arguments as to how many patients with schizophrenia actually have mania.) As one of my colleagues (Patten, 2006) has asked, Is there anyone who *doesn't* have bipolar disorder?

These are not academic issues. Once patients are diagnosed as bipolar, they will be put on mood stabilizers and antipsychotic medication. Doing so has profound consequences for patients. The problem goes beyond personality disorders: If depressed patients (and virtually anyone else with mood swings) are considered to fall within the bipolar spectrum, they will receive the same treatment. However, if these medications prove to be unnecessary or ineffective, bipolar imperialism is doing real damage to patients.

Advocates of the bipolar spectrum are sincere but have not considered the evidence critically enough. One cannot wave one's hand and decide that BPD belongs in the bipolar spectrum on the basis of similar symptomatic presentations. In medicine, we do not conclude that symptoms, such as pain or inflammation, necessarily reflect the same cause or pathogenesis or require the same treatment. Advances in medical diagnosis have been based on the discovery of biological markers (blood tests or imaging findings) that distinguish between disorders on a more objective level. In the absence of biological markers, most mental disorders are at best syndromes and not truly diseases.

What kind of evidence would be needed to resolve questions about the boundary between bipolar disorders and BPD? I follow the arguments presented in our recent and extensive review of the literature (Paris et al., 2007).

The first is to determine the extent to which BPD and bipolar disorder are, in fact, comorbid (or co-occurrent). Again, comorbidity is extremely common in most mental disorders and is an artifact of a system in which similar criteria are used for different disorders. The more symptoms one has (i.e., the sicker you are), the more likely one is to have more than one disorder listed in DSM.

There is, in fact, a somewhat increased level of co-occurrence, in both directions, between BPD and bipolar disorders (Gunderson, Weinberg, et al., 2006). However these relationships are not specific to BPD, and in the vast majority of cases bipolar disorders and BPD are distinct. Moreover, all studies have been conducted in clinical samples, and no one has examined these relationships in community populations.

A second way of addressing the issue is to determine whether bipolar disorder occurs in the families of patients with BPD (or vice versa). We found no such relationship in our literature review.

A third way is to examine response to medication. As I discuss in Chapter 7, support for the efficacy of mood stabilizers in BPD is weak. No one has ever conducted a randomized controlled trial (RCT) showing that these drugs are more than marginally effective in treating patients who fall into the proposed bipolar spectrum.

A fourth approach is to examine course: to see whether patients with BPD ever develop bipolar disorder with time (or vice versa). Actually, evolution into bipolarity occurs very infrequently in BPD, which has an entirely different course. Unlike bipolar disorders, it often remits by middle age.

Finally, is there any evidence that bipolar disorders and BPD have a common cause? Although there is a genetic vulnerability to bipolar disorder, we do not know much about its mechanism. As discussed in Chapter 4, we know even less about the causes of BPD. Although evidence is rather slim, no common etiological factors have been found in genetic studies, biological studies, or neuroimaging or from psychosocial risk factors.

Our conclusion was that BPD and bipolar I are clearly distinct, but with some symptomatic overlap with bipolar II. I propose that even that overlap is an artifact of definition and of the difficulty in establishing a history of hypomania. I have seen many cases of bipolar II and consider them to be mild versions of bipolar I that usually respond to mood stabilizers. In the absence of true hypomania, one cannot even speak of bipolarity, because ultra-rapid mood swings are more suggestive of personality disorder. Again, I do not diagnose BPD when I am convinced that bipolar II is present.

The following cases demonstrate some of the problems in differential diagnosis between BPD and bipolar disorders.

Case 6

Lisa had been cutting herself since age 16 and presented to a clinic with chronic suicidal ideation, irritability, and rages.
    Bipolar II disorder was diagnosed on the basis of Lisa's mood swings as well as repeated episodes in which she impul-

sively became involved with men, sometimes flying thousands of miles to meet them after an initial Internet contact. At certain points of her illness, Lisa also showed quasi-psychotic symptoms, such as an intense fantasy that she was Jesus's sister who had been sent to earth with a mission. At one point, she talked to a statue in her neighborhood about this idea, but the statue did not talk back. Lisa had no hallucinations other than hearing her name called. Lithium, prescribed for a full year in adequate doses, had no effect on her symptoms. Instead, all these symptoms came under control within weeks once Lisa entered psychotherapy and formed a solid therapeutic alliance.

Lisa met all DSM criteria for BPD and scored 10/10 on the DIB-R.

The next two cases describe patients who were referred to me for BPD but who were better diagnosed with a primary mood disorder.

Case 7

Mona was a 30-year-old child care worker completing an undergraduate degree. Eight years previously, Mona had three admissions to the hospital for lengthy psychotic episodes in which she thought she was the object of a plot and that she had a mission in the world. Once she was discharged, Mona did not want to take medication but had several periods of therapy. Although she had not relapsed since, she thought there was a conspiracy against her. In spite of an inner state of tension and racing thoughts, she was able to do her schoolwork, did not overspend, and was not promiscuous. Mona had a history of binge drinking and had never had a lasting intimate relationship.

I gave Mona a diagnosis of bipolar I disorder. Her psychotic episodes were consistent with mania, and this is a disorder that can go into remission for many years.

Case 8

Helen was a 23-year-old woman who had been a heavy cocaine drug abuser, yet her symptoms persisted even when she stopped taking drugs. At one point, Helen thought that there would be a constitutional crisis in Canada because she had been taken off a voting list. This was associated with an idea that she was a "genius." As part of her battle, Helen called several government bodies and tried to contact the prime minister. Her current mental status showed subdelusional paranoid ideas. When interviewed, she was not psychotic but still wondered whether the phones were tapped at home or whether her doctors were plotting to make use of her mind. Helen sometimes had suicidal ideas but had made only one suicide attempt.

The prominence of grandiose ideas, absence of hallucinations, and presence of periods of normal functioning all pointed to bipolarity. Although Helen had been able to function in spite of these thoughts, her periods of hypomania supported a diagnosis of bipolar II disorder.

BPD AND POSTTRAUMATIC STRESS DISORDER

Some years ago, van der Kolk, Perry, and Herman (1991) proposed that BPD is a "complex" form of post-traumatic stress disorder (PTSD). This idea was based the assumption that we know the cause of BPD, which is child abuse.

However, in spite of research data showing that childhood trauma is common in these patients (see Chapter 5), it does not follow that adverse early experiences are the main etiological factor. Careful examination of the evidence shows that severe trauma is found in only a minority of cases. And most people exposed to child abuse in community samples develop neither BPD nor any other diagnosable psychiatric disorder (Fergusson & Mullen, 1999).

The posttraumatic theory of BPD is a misleading oversimplification that has led to a fair amount of misguided therapy. Although the disorder can be *associated* with traumatic events, it does not develop unless other risk factors are also present (see Chapter 4).

Case 9

Leila came for treatment for chronic suicidal ideation, multiple overdoses, and unstable intimate relationships. She also had transient episodes of depersonalization. A previous therapist had diagnosed PTSD. Leila did have problems resulting from sexual abuse by her stepfather between the ages of 7 and 12. It was interesting, nonetheless, to note that her older sister, who was abused in precisely the same way, had never had experienced enough psychological problems to seek treatment. Although the issue of child abuse played an important role in her psychotherapy, Leila's symptoms resolved gradually as she found regular employment and become involved in more stable, less demanding relationships.

Another mistake can occur when therapists conclude that an abuse history points to a diagnosis of BPD.

Case 10

Mary, 30 years old, who had recently been arrested for assault after an argument with her sister. She had gone to her sister's house to complain that the sister had not protected her from child abuse. Mary's history of childhood sexual abuse was by no means repressed. Her father had died when she was 6, and her mother had many different boyfriends, several of whom, once Mary reached menarche, made passes at her. On several occasions, lonely, desperate, and unable to ask for support from her mother, Mary did not protest when these men molested her. Nonetheless, Mary obtained a university degree and worked as a teacher. She never had stable relationships.

Mary met overall criteria for a personality disorder but scored 0/10 on the DIB-R. A psychologist had given her the diagnosis on the basis of a traumatic childhood, even though the patient had none of the symptoms.

A related claim, also based on the theory that BPD originates in childhood trauma, is that these patients may have a comorbid dissociative disorder (Sar, Akyuz, Kugu, Ozturk, & Ertem-Vehid, 2006). This idea can be refuted in two ways. First, as Chapter 5 shows, trauma does not cause BPD, and dissociation is a feature of the disorder whether there is a history of childhood adversity or not. Second, there is no such thing as a dissociative disorder. These conditions are artifacts of dubious therapeutic methods that actively encourage patients to dissociate (A. Piper & Merskey, 2004a, 2004b). Unfortunately, the DSM system created a separate category for these fictional conditions, with scales developed to assess them and every textbook required to have a chapter on the subject.

BPD AND ATTENTION-DEFICIT/ HYPERACTIVITY DISORDER

Another disorder that threatens to be a fad diagnosis explaining a broad range of adult psychopathology is attention-deficit/hyperactivity disorder (ADHD). It is true that, under current diagnostic criteria, some patients with adult ADHD also have BPD (T. W. Miller, Nigg,

& Faraone, 2007). However, it is not common for patients with BPD to have ADHD (Zanarini et al., 1998b). Clinicians should keep in mind such a diagnosis cannot be made without a well-established history of ADHD during childhood. And although there is a superficial resemblance between the overactive and impulsive behaviors seen in ADHD and those associated with BPD, neuropsychological studies observe major differences in cognition between these populations (Lampe et al., 2007).

WHEN COMORBIDITY IS CLINICALLY IMPORTANT

This chapter has downplayed the importance of comorbidity in BPD. Major depression is common, but the presence of that diagnosis is unenlightening for treatment planning. Dysthymia is part and parcel of the clinical picture of BPD. If bipolar II is present, we should not even make the diagnosis (but make sure that the patient has actually had hypomanic episodes, not just mood swings).

Yet some comorbidities *do* make a difference for treatment planning. Specifically, the presence of other impulsive disorders is important and can seriously interfere with therapy. If the patient has a serious substance abuse problem, that may need to be treated first. The same principle applies to the more severe forms of anorexia and bulimia, which can take over the patient's life.

Case 11

Caroline was a 44-year-old nurse whose problems included mood instability, suicidal threats, alcohol abuse with benzodiazepine dependence, sexual promiscuity, and unstable relationships with unsuitable partners (usually married men). Caroline had been in rehab programs but continued to binge and take drugs, even on days when she needed to work. During the initial consultation, she was disinhibited after taking 4 mg of clonazepam.

Caroline met DSM and DIB-R (8/10) criteria for BPD but was advised to obtain treatment for her addiction before entering therapy for her personality disorder.

Case 12

Carol, 25 years old and unemployed, developed anorexia nervosa at age 10. She had always been determined to remain thin no matter what the consequences; at the time of interview Carol weighed 99 pounds and wanted to lose 10. She sometimes had binges and forced vomiting to deal with intake. Carol used laxatives daily and was a compulsive exerciser.

Carol described mood swings as well as micropsychotic symptoms: occasional auditory hallucinations (voices she cannot make out) and visual hallucinations (of spiders). A widespread pattern of impulsivity included abuse of alcohol and benzodiazepines, sexually promiscuity, cutting, threats of suicide, and rages during which she breaks things. Intimate relationships were unstable, and she retained only a few friends. Carol met all DSM criteria for BPD and scored 8/10 on the DIB-R. However, her eating disorder had taken over her life to the extent that treatment for a personality disorder was unlikely to be helpful until her anorexia was under control.

BPD AND OTHER AXIS II DISORDERS

Many studies (e.g., Pfohl, Coryell, Zimmerman, & Stang, 1986; Nurnberg et al., 1991; Zanarini et al., 1998b) have found that Axis II disorders are highly comorbid with each other. It seems that if patients have one personality disorder, they must have two or three. This observation has been used to discredit the very idea of categorizing personality disorders, but what it actually shows is how imprecise the Axis II system is. Comorbidity on Axis II is another artifact. Because none of the categories have any required criteria, it should not be surprising that they overlap.

Sometimes, however, these overlaps have clinical relevance, most particularly between ASPD and BPD. If a patient meets criteria for ASPD, treatment is much less likely to be effective (McMain & Pos, 2007).

Case 13

David was a 37-year-old plumber who took a large overdose of pills after a breakup with his girlfriend. He had a long history of problems dating back to childhood, when he was truant from school, involved in theft and scams, and used drugs and alcohol. David became a heavy user of heroin and cocaine and was in prison twice for selling drugs. During that time, he developed a habit of cutting himself as a way to get out of trouble. David never held jobs steadily and had a history of very unstable relationships. Although the current clinical picture (chronic suicidality with mood swings and stormy intimacy) suggested BPD, the history of ASPD was more striking. David would probably not have benefited from the type of therapy often given to BPD patients, which focuses on affect regulation.

Overlaps with other Axis II disorders are not clinically meaningful. Most of the other personality disorder categories have little research behind them and have dubious validity. If patients have a well-researched diagnosis such as BPD, treatment planning should not be affected if they also meet criteria for other personality disorders that have rarely been studied (e.g., histrionic or dependent).

The main differential diagnosis for BPD on Axis II is usually "none of the above." At least half of all patients with personality disorders do not fit into any of the categories but meet the overall definition, giving them a diagnosis of personality disorder not other specified (Johnson et al., 2005; Zimmerman et al., 2005). Many patients who do not meet BPD criteria, particularly those defined more narrowly by research measures, will have a personality disorder NOS. As Chapter 6 shows, patients can recover from BPD but still meet criteria for an overall personality disorder diagnosis, in which case they will fall within the NOS category.

Case 14

George, a gay 37-year-old with a history of substance abuse (alcohol and cocaine), has had long-term problems in both work and relationships. George had never achieved a sustained relationship. He quarreled with people at work and was not able to hold a steady job. He was living alone, and his only contact with other people was on the Internet.

George met overall criteria for a personality disorder, but did not have BPD, the only feature being unstable mood with angry outbursts. On the DIB-R, he scored 5/10.

CLINICAL IMPLICATIONS

- BPD overlaps with other mental disorders, particularly depression and bipolar disorders, and there can also be confusion with schizophrenia and PTSD.
- None of these disorders account for the full range of symptoms

(affective instability, impulsivity, unstable relationships, and cognitive symptoms).

- Diagnosing BPD as a form of another disorder may lead to patients getting the wrong treatment and not receiving therapies that have been specifically been shown to be effective for BPD.

CHAPTER 3

Personality and Development

*T*he symptoms of BPD, like those of many mental disorders, first become apparent in adolescence. The mean age of first clinical presentation is 18 years (*SD* = 5–6 years; Zanarini et al., 2001). The true age of onset can often be at puberty: Adolescents who cut and overdose do not always present to mental health professionals.

An early onset of a mental disorder points to an important biological component. Even so, some children function reasonably well up to adolescence before developing symptoms.

We need to know more about what patients with BPD were like during childhood. Were they entirely normal? Did they have symptoms whose significance was unrecognized? Were they exposed to stressors that only have a full impact later?

This chapter addresses these questions in the light of a general theory. Patients with BPD have heritable trait vulnerabilities that produce symptoms under exposure to psychosocial stressors. Therefore, the disorder cannot be understood without considering its underlying trait structure. These traits, which correspond to the domains of borderline pathology described in Chapter 1, should be present before the onset of symptoms.

TRAIT DOMAINS UNDERLYING BPD

Not one but several trait dimensions underlie BPD. They correspond to three of the four domains: emotional dysregulation (or affective instability), impulsivity or disinhibition, and cognitive dysfunction. (The last domain, problems in interpersonal relationships, may be a consequence of the other domains.)

BPD is a complex syndrome that has symptoms derived from all of these domains. Although one or another of these has been thought to be primary, the evidence is not convincing. Studies using cluster analysis, factor analysis, or latent class analysis to examine which features hang together have been inconsistent, but one recent large-scale report (Clifton & Pilkonis, 2007) concluded that a single factor fitted the data parsimoniously.

Let us now examine each of the BPD domains in greater detail.

Emotional Dysregulation (Affective Instability)

Emotional dysregulation (ED) refers to an unusual intensity of emotional responses and/or a slow return to baseline following such episodes (Putnam & Silk, 2005). *Affective instability* (AI) is a similar construct, describing mood changes characterized by temporal instability, high intensity, and delayed recovery from dysphoric states (Koenigsberg et al., 2002).

In classic mood disorders, one sees a consistently lowered (or raised) level of mood. As discussed in Chapter 2, you cannot cheer up a depressed person, and you cannot "bring down" someone who is in the midst of a manic episode. But in ED or AI, emotion is far from constant, Instead, affect is highly variable and shows a rapid and intense response to environmental triggers (Gunderson & Phillips, 1991). In BPD, patients can be in a different mood every day or even by the hour.

Linehan (1993) proposed the influential theory that BPD arises primarily from ED. A large body of empirical evidence supports the centrality of this trait (defined as ED or AI) in BPD. Patients with BPD have more intense emotions to begin with, have difficulty regulating them, and rapidly shift from one emotion to another (Putnam & Silk, 2005; Henry et al., 2001; Koenigsberg et al., 2002). Livesley (2003) suggested that the borderline pattern reflects abnormalities on a broad trait of emotional regulation. Livesley et al. (1998) developed a personality inventory with a specific subscale to assesses AI.

ED and AI are constructs that describe a tendency to respond to life events with unusually strong emotions. They differ from the dimension that trait psychologists call *neuroticism,* which is a measure of negative emotionality (or in common parlance, being "thin skinned"). Neuroticism is one of the five factors in the FFM and can be assessed quantitatively using self-report questionnaires. Costa and Widiger (2001) have suggested that unusually high scores on that trait might define BPD. However, this suggestion fails to distinguish negative emotions (such as anxiety and depression) from high levels of variability in affect.

Chapter 1 noted problems associated with "reducing" BPD to its traits. Moreover, self-report measures may not be the only or the best way to measure affective phenomena. People do not always remember how unstable their mood was, particularly when they remain upset. Instead of questionnaires, researchers can assess moment-to-moment changes in mood by having patients score their reactions as they occur using either pencil and paper or a Palm Pilot. Several research groups, in Toronto, New York, Missouri, and Germany, are using this method (ecological momentary assessment [EMA]). Our own group (Russell, Moskowitz, Sookman, & Paris, 2007) found that BPD patients experienced more unpleasant emotions and also showed more variability in mood than normal controls. Similar findings have been reported by others (Ebner-Priemer et al., 2007).

Thus far, no one has identified any consistent biological correlates of ED or AI. One research method is to expose patients to experimental settings in which affectively charged images are presented, after which one can measure a range of psychophysiological responses. This method, however, has not yet identified any unique pattern in BPD (Herpertz, Kunert, Schwenger, & Sass, 1999). However, there are large discrepancies between experimental models and real-life situations, and studies using methods such as EMA convincingly demonstrate AI in daily interpersonal encounters (Russell et al., 2007).

A related approach is to ask study participants to identify various emotional states from the observation of faces. Frank and Hoffman (1986) found that BPD patients are unusually sensitive to faces and are particularly accurate in identifying negative emotions. Similarly, Wagner and Linehan (1999) found that BPD patients are hypersensitive to faces showing fear. Donegan et al. (2003) reported that patients see neutral faces as threatening, and that responses are associated with increased reactivity in the amgydala on functional magnetic resonance imaging (fMRI).

Impulsivity (Disinhibition)

Impulsivity describes a set of psychopathological phenomena that share a common biological substrate. A biopsychosocial definition of impulsivity proposed by Moeller, Barratt, Dougherty, Schmitz, and Swann (2001) describes (1) decreased sensitivity to the negative consequences of behavior; (2) rapid, unplanned reactions to stimuli before complete processing of information; and (3) lack of regard for long-term consequences. Several other terms in the literature describe much the same phenomena: *disinhibition* (Clark, Livesley, & Morey, 1997), low *effortful constraint* (Nigg, Silk, Stavro, & Miller, 2005), low *conscientiousness* (Costa & Widiger, 2001), as well as *externalizing behaviors* (Achenbach & McConaughy, 1997; Krueger, Caspi, Moffitt, Silva, & McGee, 1996). In longitudinal research, impulsive traits are stable, showing a consistent trajectory over the course of childhood and adolescence (Masse & Tremblay, 1996).

Linehan (1993) suggested that impulsive behaviors are a response to dysregulated affects. It is true that behaviors can be used to deal with unpleasant emotions, as with cutting and substance abuse. However, many patients with chronic dysphoria never carry out impulsive actions. In our own research (Zweig-Frank & Paris, 1995), we found that patients with other types of personality disorders (mainly Cluster C) had high levels of neuroticism but showed few impulsive behaviors. Also, patients with ASPD have striking impulsive behaviors without being notably dysphoric (Paris, 1996b). BPD shows a wide range of such behaviors, and it makes sense to consider impulsivity as a separate underlying trait dimension.

One problem is the ambiguous way that the term *impulsivity* has been used (Whiteside & Lyman, 2001). Some actions are not carried out on the spur of the moment; for example, cutting, particularly when addictive, can be planned in advance. Even so, the broad concept describes a tendency to carry out actions in response to stress, what therapists have traditionally referred to as "acting out."

A large body of evidence supports the centrality of impulsivity in BPD. Standard self-report measures (such as the Barratt Impulsiveness Scale [BIS]; Patton, Stanford, & Barratt, 1995) show that BPD patients score high on all aspects of this trait (Links, Heslegrave,

Mitton, van Reekum, & Patrick, 1995; Links, Heselgrave, & van Reekum, 1998; Paris et al., 2004).

Impulsivity helps to explain why patients not only *feel* suicidal but *act* on their thoughts by carrying out multiple suicide attempts (Soloff, Lynch, Kelly, Malone, & Mann, 2000). Tellingly, impulsive spectrum disorders (such as antisocial personality and substance abuse) are the most frequent disorders in first-degree relatives of probands with BPD and are much more common than mood disorders (White et al., 2003). In addition, high levels of impulsivity are the most consistent predictor of clinical outcome in BPD (Links et al., 1998).

Impulsivity can also be validated through biological correlates (Zuckerman, 2005). Neurobiological studies have found that impulsivity in BPD has a consistent association with abnormalities in neurotransmitter activity. In contrast to the absence of consistent correlates for other trait dimensions, the biological correlates of impulsivity are robust, with consistent relationships to brain systems that modulate behavioral inhibition (Moeller et al., 2001), associated with serotonergic pathways (Siever & Davis, 1991).

Serotonergic dysfunction in BPD has been demonstrated using neuroendocrine challenge tests that measure the brain's hormonal response to agents that increase serotonin activity (Coccaro et al., 1989; Paris et al., 2004). This relationship has also been confirmed by neuroimaging: positron emission tomography (PET) assessing serotonin activity in various brain regions (Siever et al., 1999; Leyton et al., 2001).

Cognitive Dysfunction

The cognitive symptoms in BPD are not accounted for by either affective instability or by impulsivity. Hallucinations or depersonalization can be triggered by periods of emotional dysregulation (Gunderson, 2001). However, patients with high neuroticism and those with other impulsive disorders, rarely hear voices.

As discussed in Chapter 2, cognitive dysfunction is not a trait in the same sense as ED or impulsivity, given that these phenomena are rarely seen in normal people. But at least half of patients meeting overall diagnostic criteria for BPD develop cognitive symptoms, and these features distinguish BPD from other personality disorders (Zanarini et al., 1990; Yee et al., 2005). On the other hand, these symptoms do not imply the presence of a frank psychosis. Patients may have paranoid feelings without interpreting them delusionally, hear voices or see visions while understanding that these perceptions are imaginary, and experience depersonalization without impaired reality testing.

Cognitive symptoms may reflect an entirely separate domain of trait vulnerability. We know little about their biological correlates or their sources in development. Yet they are key features of BPD. These are the phenomena that even today seem to place these patients on a "borderline."

TRAIT INTERACTIONS

BPD is an outcome that reflects a combination and interaction of multiple trait dimensions. Neither affective instability nor impulsivity by themselves account for the clinical features of the disorder. It is their interaction that "cooks" the disorder. Moreover, the dimensions can interact through feedback loops in which affective instability promotes impulsivity and impulsive actions can lead to further affective instability.

The criteria for clinical diagnosis describe a separate domain of unstable relationships. Although that is certainly one of the cardinal features of BPD, interpersonal problems could either be a separate domain or a secondary effect of affective instability and impulsivity.

Although intimacy is difficult for everyone, if one responds with intense emotion to every conflict, and acts out impulsively when problems arise, relationships are going to be highly unstable. In BPD patients, the way intimate relationships begin (with intense emotion and an impulsive "jumping in") reflects impulsive traits. Similarly, these traits influence the way intimate relationships end (with rage and impulsive breakups).

CHILDHOOD PRECURSORS OF BPD

Having described the trait domains underlying BPD, we can now reflect on what these patients may have been like as children. We have no evidence that patients who develop adult BPD have been seriously symptomatic before puberty. In most cases, the adolescent onset of the disorder represents a qualitative change. However, children at risk for BPD should still show an unusual trait profile, with higher levels of affective instability, impulsivity, and cognitive dysfunction.

These principles are in accordance with a large body of research on the childhood precursors of other mental disorders. For example, children who later develop schizophrenia have subtle abnormalities in childhood that can sometimes be identified by reviewing videotapes (Baum & Walker, 1995). Depression in adults may be preceded by subclinical dysphoria during childhood (Cicchetti & Toth, 1998).

We have particularly extensive data on the precursors of ASPD. Children who meet criteria for this category as adults almost always have an early onset of conduct disorder (L. N. Robins, 1966; Zoccolillo, Pickles, Quinton, & Rutter, 1992), and the requirement for a history of conduct symptoms before age 15 is included in DSM-IV-TR (American Psychiatric Association, 2000).

Unfortunately, we do not have the same kind of data about what BPD patients were like as children. The pathways to BPD are not as consistent as those leading to ASPD.

My experience is that BPD patients report many different pathways to their adult disorder. Many describe serious problems in childhood but report not having been treated. Some patients state unequivocally that their life was normal until they entered adolescence. These inconsistent patterns suggest that multiple pathways can lead to the same clinical picture.

Many of the characteristic symptoms of BPD (such as chronic suicidality) lack parallels in childhood. Although children can think about or threaten suicide (Pfeffer, 2002), attempts are uncommon before puberty (Brent, 2001). The precursors of BPD are more likely to be found in traits than in symptoms.

INTERNALIZING AND EXTERNALIZING PROBLEMS

The distinction between externalizing and internalizing problems provides a key framework for studying childhood pathology (Achenbach & McConaughy, 1997). The Child Behavior Checklist, which can be scored by parents or teachers, assesses a mixture of behaviors, problems, and symptoms. Its two basic dimensions do an excellent job of describing the range of psychopathology seen in children.

Similar traits underlie adult mental disorders (Krueger et al., 1996). Most disorders listed in DSM can be factor analyzed into domains of internalization or externalization (Krueger, 1999). Although this schema does not account for a cognitive domain, it describes a basic structure for personality and symptoms that applies to all stages of development.

Adult patients with BPD have both externalizing and internalizing symptoms: They are both impulsive and emotionally dysregulated. Children who develop the disorder may have this combination of traits (Depue & Lenzenweger, 2001; Paris, 2005a). If so, the childhood pattern for BPD would differ from ASPD, whose precursors mainly involve externalizing behaviors (i.e., conduct disorder), with very few internalizing symptoms (L. N. Robins, 1966).

We need longitudinal research in community samples as well as high-risk groups to establish which patterns of behaviors and traits precede BPD. Even so, children with these precursors may not have enough symptoms to come to clinical attention. In general, referral patterns in child psychiatry reflect disruptions caused by externalizing symptoms. Unlike children with conduct disorder, those who later develop BPD may have less prominent externalizing symptoms and more internalizing symptoms, which may not be recognized. Gender is another factor that makes it difficult to identify the developmental precursors of BPD. Girls at risk may have fewer more obvious symptoms, particularly before puberty.

Although these obstacles have thus far prevented us from coming up with a definitive answer about the precursors of BPD, a few approaches have at least begun to address the problem.

BORDERLINE PATHOLOGY OF CHILDHOOD

Another strategy is to look for children who have symptoms that resemble adult BPD. There are indeed such cases. The clinical literature on borderline children (Kernberg, Weiner, & Bardenstein, 2000; Paris, 2000a) describes a population with a mixture of impulsive and affective symptoms (behavioral problems, suicidal threats, and mood instability) as well as cognitive phenomena similar to those seen in adults with BPD (micropsychotic phenomena such as hallucinations and paranoid trends). Thus, these children have psychopathology in three of the trait dimensions affected by adult BPD. (Interpersonal relationships are also disturbed.) Our group also found this syndrome to be common among children whose mothers meet criteria for a diagnosis of BPD (Weiss et al., 1996).

Case 1

Rory was a 9-year-old boy referred to a child psychiatry clinic after being expelled from school for disruptive behavior in class. When confronted by the school principal after one of these incidents, he threatened to jump out of the window.

Rory was an angry and unhappy child with no friends and rarely enjoyed sports or games. He had said several times that he wished he was dead. He would fall into rages in which he would sometimes bang his head against walls. Rory was close to failing in school, and his behavior varied from demanding and clinging to argumentative and hostile.

Rory's father was an alcoholic who left the mother early on and had since played no role in child care. The mother was a chronically depressed woman who had been a client of several social agencies and had also received psychiatric consultation. At age 3 Rory was placed in a foster home, where he lived for 2 years, until his mother reclaimed him. Rory had a vague manner and described himself as "spaced out." He described a vivid and intense fantasy life. He sometimes believed himself to be in contact with a foster brother, James, whom he had not seen in 4 years. He regularly heard James's voice in his head talking to him, although he was not actually sure whether this was his imagination.

Our group conducted a formal study of a cohort of children with borderline pathology (Guzder, Paris, Zelkowitz, & Marchessault, 1996; Guzder, Paris, Zelkowitz, & Feldman, 1999). We used an instrument specifically developed to assess the clinical picture, modeled on structured interviews for diagnosis developed for adult BPD, the Child Diagnostic Interview for Borderlines (C-DIB; Greenman, Gunderson, Cane, & Saltzman, 1986), with subscales that assess multiple dimensions of pathology, impulsivity, depression, and suicidality as well as micropsychotic symptoms.

Other groups of researchers have studied similar groups of children but used different terminology to describe them: "multiple complex developmental disorder" (Cohen, Paul, & Volkmar, 1987; Lincoln, Bloom, Katz, & Boksenbaym, 1998), or "multidimensionally impaired disorder" (Kumra et al., 1998). These are children with micropsychotic symptoms, daily periods of emotional lability, impaired interpersonal skills, and deficits in information processing. Kumra et al. (1998) monitored 26 patients to a mean age of 15 years, and although most showed remission of psychotic symptoms, many developed features of a chronic mood disorder (Nicolson et al., 2001). However, because chronic depression in adolescence is associated with Cluster B personality disorders (Pepper et al., 1995), these children might also be at risk for BPD.

However, the relevance of borderline pathology in childhood to BPD is not clear. Like many childhood diagnoses, it overlaps with other categories (Bemporad, Smith, Hanson, & Cicchetti, 1982; Petti & Vela, 1990). And most cases involve boys, not girls.

Lofgren, Bemporad, King, Lindem, and O'Driscoll (1991) monitored 19 of these children. By age 18, the cohort had developed a wide range of personality disorders in all the DSM clusters (and not Axis I diagnoses such as schizophrenia or bipolar mood disorder), but there were no cases of BPD. We obtained similar results from our own follow-up (Zelkowitz, Guzder, Paris, Feldman, & Roy, 2007), with many patients doing poorly in adolescence but with only 20% meeting criteria for a BPD diagnosis.

Borderline pathology in childhood might, therefore, be a general precursor for adult personality disorders rather than for BPD itself. Nonetheless, several groups have found that psychosocial risk factors associated with the syndrome strikingly parallel those described by adults with BPD: neglect, abuse, family dysfunction, and parental mental disorder (Goldman, D'Angelo, DeMaso, & Mezzacappa, 1992; Goldman, D'Angelo, & DeMaso, 1993; Guzder et al., 1996; Guzder, Paris, Zelkowitz, & Feldman, 1999; Feldman et al., 1995; Paris, 2000a). Borderline pathology of childhood is also associated with the neuropsychological abnormalities seen in adult BPD (Petti & Vela, 1990; Lincoln et al., 1998; Paris, Zelkowitz, Guzder, Joseph, & Feldman, 1999), reflecting defects in "executive functioning" associated with impulsive personality traits.

In summary, we have only suggestive evidence about the childhood precursors of BPD. It would, of course, be of great practical importance to identify potential patients before symptoms appear. Then we could target a high-risk group and develop methods of prevention.

BPD IN ADOLESCENCE

Many mental disorders—schizophrenia, bipolar disorder, and substance abuse—begin in adolescence. There are major changes in brain structure at that stage of development (Cicchetti & Rogosch,

2002). Puberty is associated with elevated levels of hormones that help to sculpt these new neural circuits, leading in turn to behavioral changes. Variation in the timing of interactions between hormones and the adolescent brain produce individual differences in behavior as well as differences between boys and girls.

However, adolescence is also accompanied by numerous psychosocial challenges. The psychosocial challenges of this phase of development may be particularly difficult for those who are vulnerable on the basis of personality profiles. This is a time when one sees an increase in many impulsive behaviors, particularly addictions (Schuckit & Smith, 1996).

The emergence of clinically significant levels of impulsivity and suicidality is also related to developmental timing. After puberty, trait vulnerability and stressful events can reach a "tipping point," when patients begin to develop wide mood swings and a wide variety of impulsive behaviors, including cutting, overdoses, and substance abuse, precisely the clinical picture found in BPD (Depue & Lenzenweger, 2001; Paris, 2003).

To understand these relationships, we need, once again, to take gender into account. ASPD (primarily a male disorder) and BPD (mainly a female disorder) have similar childhood precursors and psychosocial risk factors (Paris, 1997a). However, the developmental patterns are different. Girls with conduct symptoms in adolescence often develop a range of personality disorders (including BPD) in young adulthood (Rey, Singh, Morris-Yates, & Andrews, 1994; Goodman, Hull, Clarkin, & Yeomans, 1999). Gender differences also affect the timing of conduct symptoms, in that aggressive behavior starts earlier in boys than in girls (Crick & Zahn-Waxler, 2003). This sequence, in which impulsive symptoms emerge only after puberty, parallels the adolescent onset of impulsive disorders such as substance abuse (Chambers, Taylor, & Potenza, 2003) and eating disorders (Garner & Garfinkel, 1980).

Longitudinal data have shed light on the adolescent precursors of BPD as well as what symptoms predict its continuance into young adulthood. Crawford, Cohen, and Brook (2001a, 2001b) found that among adolescents with Cluster B personality disorders, externalizing symptoms predicted continuing psychopathology in males, whereas a combination of externalizing and internalizing symptoms predicted continuing symptoms in females.

To determine prepubertal predictors of BPD, one can retrospectively assess adolescents for childhood histories of psychological symptoms. Those with a diagnosis of Cluster B personality disorders report a history of conduct problems (Bernstein, Cohen, Skodol, Bezirganian, & Book, 1993) as well as depression and anxiety (Pepper et al., 1995; Lewinsohn, Rohde, Seeley, Klein, & Gotlib, 2000). Again, precursors of these problems could have been present earlier in development (Caspi, Moffitt, Newman, & Silva, 1996), even if they do not bring children to clinical attention.

Many of these researchers have been conservative about making a full diagnosis of BPD, concentrating on symptoms. However, many studies have documented typical cases of BPD in the adolescent years (Ludolph, Westen, & Misle, 1990; Block, Westen, Ludolph, Wixom, & Jackson, 1991; Garnet, Levy, Mattanah, Edell, & McGlashan, 1994; Mattanana, Becker, Levy, Edell, & McGlashan, 1996; Becker, Grilo, Edell, & McGlashan, 2002). At this point, one begins to see the characteristic behavioral features of the disorder (suicide attempts and cutting) as well as accompanying features (e.g., sexual promiscuity and substance abuse).

However, personality disorder diagnoses in adolescence are not necessarily stable when patients are monitored into young adulthood (Bernstein et al., 1993; Garnet et al., 1994; Mattanana et al., 1996). This kind of diagnostic instability should not be understood as recovery. Behavioral patterns can shift enough to move the patient from one personality disorder category to another or to personality disorder NOS. Diagnostic instability probably reflects the fact that personality disorders are comorbid with each other, so that patients do not retain one stable diagnosis on Axis II (Grilo, Becker, Edell, & McGlashan, 2001). These observations probably reflect more about the imprecision of our classification system than about the underlying nature of psychopathology (Kernberg et al., 2000).

It is not known whether patients with an onset earlier in adolescence have a better or worse course and prognosis than those who present later. It was once thought that "adolescent turmoil" does not carry a risk for adult psychopathology, but current evidence suggests it does (Cicchetti & Rogosch, 2002).

Thus, personality pathology in adolescence is not a transient phenomenon. Most adolescents with this pattern continue to have serious difficulties in early adulthood (Bernstein et al., 1993). In a prospective community follow-up (Johnson et al., 2005; Kasen, Cohen, Skodol, Johnson, & Brook, 1999), adolescent personality disorders predicted a wide variety of symptoms in young adulthood that were associated with Axis I and Axis II disorders as well as suicidality. For this reason, we should not be reluctant to make a diagnosis of BPD in adolescent patients.

Case 2

Dora was a 14-year-old living with her single mother, who had immigrated to a large city and who had poor social supports. In spite of these disadvantages, Dora had done well in school until she reached an early puberty (age 10). By age 13, she was involved with a pathological peer group, taking drugs, cutting herself regularly, and running away from home. After child protection authorities were called in, Dora was sent for evaluation at a psychiatric clinic. She scored 8/10 on the DIB-R and met all DSM-IV criteria for BPD.

LATE-ONSET BPD

At the other end of the developmental spectrum, a few patients present with the symptoms that characterize BPD only in adulthood or even in early middle age. However, we have to question whether a diagnosis can be made at that point in life. After all, DSM-IV-TR requires that personality disorders begin in adolescence or young adulthood. This important guideline narrows the construct of PD to intrinsic and long-term problems of early onset rather than later failures of adaptation to life's vicissitudes. Patients who have functioned well for many years and do not recover from a depression should not be diagnosed as BPD, even if they have similar symptoms.

Nonetheless, patients who are at risk for the disorder may only show mild, subclinical features (Zanarini et al., 2007). Some may be protected from developing more symptoms by culture and circumstance. A change of culture or circumstances could precipitate symptoms corresponding to a classic clinical presentation, which usually occurs much earlier in life.

Case 3

Joan was a 40-year-old model who had been competent and successful for most of her life. Her symptoms, which began in her later 30s, included wrist slashing, suicidal threats (without real overdoses), binge eating, and mood swings. Joan often heard voices, such as her ex-boyfriend insulting her. Her relationships with men had always been poor, with infidelity and physical violence. Joan described her life as a "shambles."

Joan lived for 12 years with a man who was the father of all three of her children; she left him because of his infidelity. She lived with her next boyfriend for 7 years, but he beat her, insulted her, and also was unfaithful.

Joan met diagnostic criteria for borderline personality disorder: all nine criteria on the DSM-IV and a score of 9/10 on the DIB-R.

An onset of BPD in early middle age is unusual, and Joan might have been labeled histrionic if seen 10 years previously. A strikingly beautiful woman with elegant clothes, her good looks had attracted enough attention to meet many narcissistic needs. However, as Joan aged and as disappointments with intimacy mounted, she became unable to continue working, losing the main source of her self-esteem. Although Joan was a mother, she was limited in her capacity to parent and derived little real pleasure from time with her children.

Case 4

Lalith was a 25-year-old graduate student who had been educated in her home city in India. Although Lalith reported always having been unhappy, as long as she lived at home, academic progress was steady and she had a supportive circle of friends. Yet when she moved to North America, all that changed. Without family and community, Lalith felt lost. She fell into a unproductive love affair with a local man, had an abortion, and began to take recurrent overdoses.

This patient, whatever her problems, would almost certainly not have developed BPD in a different environment. (The social dimension of the disorder is examined in Chapter 4.)

Whether personality traits are functional or dysfunctional often depends on the environment. There is a niche for almost everyone: Each personality type will do well in settings in which their traits work for them rather than against them (Paris, 1997b). Even affective instability is not necessarily a problem if a containing environment limits its extent. Then the individual will only be described as "emotional," not at all a bad thing. Similarly, impulsivity, if contained, only means that people respond rapidly to challenges. That trait can be good or bad depending on circumstance and context.

CLINICAL IMPLICATIONS

- BPD is a disorder of development, rooted in traits that reflect a biological vulnerability.
- BPD, like other mental disorders, usually begins in adolescence.
- Borderline pathology during childhood does not develop into adult BPD, but symptoms in adolescence are not transient, and one should not be hesitant to make a diagnosis.
- A later onset of BPD may either reflect a different pathological process or be due to social protective factors.

PART II

Causes

CHAPTER 4

Risk Factors

Like other mental disorders, BPD can only be understood in a broad etiological model. We need to take biological, psychological, and social risk factors, as well as their interactions, into consideration. In the next chapter, I propose an integrated theory. In this chapter, I first review research about all risk factors associated with the disorder.

LESSONS FROM BEHAVIOR GENETICS

Behavioral genetics has produced some of the most important (and surprising) scientific findings in the history of psychology. This method separates heritable from environmental influences on psychological traits or mental disorders. Data are usually drawn from questionnaires administered to samples of identical and fraternal twins (there are also some adoption studies). If monozygotic (MZ) twins are more similar to each other than dizygotic (DZ) twins, the trait under study is heritable. The extent of that heritability can be calculated, giving a percentage of the total variance accounted for by genetic similarity.

It turns out that for almost any trait one can think of, about half the variance is genetic. Quantitatively, the level of heritable influence on personality usually lies between 40 and 50% (Plomin, DeFries, McClearn, & Rutter, 2000), and the heritability of trait dimensions increases with age (Jang, Livesley, & Vernon, 1996).

These findings are not a complete surprise. Almost everyone agrees that genes have an influence on personality. But the universality of heritable factors affecting psychopathology is striking. The same roughly 50–50 split applies to almost every mental disorder listed in DSM-IV (Paris, 1998; Kendler & Prescott, 2007).

Although these findings leave a crucial 50% for nongenetic factors, the nature of these environmental influences is a shocker. The variance affecting personality traits is almost entirely "unshared" (i.e., not related to factors that make people more similar; Plomin et al., 2000). Thus, being brought up in the same family does not mean that children will have similar traits. In fact, your sibling may be no more similar to you in personality than a perfect stranger. For that reason, research in behavior genetics presents a serious challenge to the assumption that parenting plays a primary role in personality development or in mental disorders.

Twin studies of personality disorders have demonstrated much the same pattern. In a Norwegian study (Torgersen et al., 2000), 221 twins (92 MZ and 129 DZ pairs) were identified in which at least one had a personality disorder; in about 20% of cases, the diagnosis was BPD. The heritability of most personality disorders was about 50%, and that of BPD was 60% (given the small sample size, this number is not in any way precise). In a study conducted in three countries (Belgium, The Netherlands, and Australia), Distel et al. (in press) examined the heritability of BPD in large twin samples using a self-report instrument to identify its features. The results showed that 42% of the variance was accounted for by heritable factors and 58% by nonshared environmental factors.

Traits most associated with BPD, such as affective instability, have a similar heritability: 40 to 50% (Livesley et al., 1998; Jang, Livesley, Vernon, & Jackson, 1996). Thus, personality disorders show about the same level of genetic influence as their underlying trait dimensions.

The findings from behavioral genetics are supported by results from family history research. Although family studies cannot separate heredity from environment, they document the prevalence of mental disorders in first-degree relatives. When we apply this method to BPD, we do not often see relatives with the same diagnosis. However, first-degree relatives tend to have subsyndromal pathology

(Zanarini et al., 2007). When they have diagnosable disorders, these most often fall in the impulsive spectrum: substance abuse and antisocial personality (White et al., 2003). To a lesser extent, relatives can suffer from major depression (related to the internalizing symptoms of BPD). By and large, what is inherited lies on the trait level rather than a specific diagnostic category.

Thus, behavior genetics tells us that personality and personality disorders are influenced by heritable factors. However, it does not explain how genes affect behavior.

THE NATURE OF GENETIC INFLUENCE

Once a heritable pattern is identified, the next logical step is to look for aberrant genes. However, it is very rare in medicine for one gene to cause a disease. Thus, research has not found any gene to be associated with any of the most important mental disorders (depression, bipolar disorder, schizophrenia). The genetic factors behind mental illness reflect a pattern of "complex inheritance," in which many genes interact to produce heritable influences on risk (Morton, 2001).

Genes are generally associated with traits rather than with categories of disorder. And even broad personality dimensions (such as neuroticism) are not associated with single genes. This is why we need to examine the biological mechanisms behind overt symptoms, what have been called "endophenotypes" (Gottesman & Gould, 2003).

Research concerning impulsive disorders (antisocial personality, substance abuse, and bulimia nervosa) shows a consistent relationship between brain serotonin activity and impulsivity (Siever, Torgersen, Gunderson, Livesley, & Kendler, 2002). These differences should have genetic correlates. One research group (Ni et al., 2006) found a significant association between the short form of the serotonin transporter gene, a common but somewhat less efficient allele, and BPD. The same group (Ni et al., 2007) also reported an association between BPD and a variant of the monoamine oxidase A gene. However, as is the case with most genetic associations, each of these relationships explained only about 1% of the variance.

The link between impulsivity and serotonin is not simple. If it were, then selective serotonin reuptake inhibitor (SSRI) antidepressants would be more helpful than they are in BPD (see Chapter 7).

Brain function is, in any case, too complex to be explained by "chemical imbalances." The same transmitter can have different effects on different receptor sites, and multiple pathways, interacting with each other, determine how signals are transmitted in the brain. We know little about the relationship between neurotransmission and the trait domains that underlie BPD. Although researchers have been trying for decades to explain the causes of mental disorders through abnormalities in neurochemistry, they have not succeeded.

Searching for specific genes may also not be productive without considering context. Genes interact with each other and are turned on and turned off by the environment (Rutter, 2006). We can only understand their effects by studying interactions between genetic vulnerability and life stressors (Caspi et al., 2002, 2003).

In summary, genes do not determine behavior in any direct way. They bend the twig but do not tell you the eventual shape of the tree.

In recent years, the neurosciences have made great progress. All mental disorders have been the subject of biological research. The hope is to understand the mind through genetics and biology. However, in spite of all the hype, we are very far from that goal. By and large, research has told us more about how the brain works than about the causes of mental illness or its treatment (Paris, 2008).

Searches for genetic markers, specific neurotransmitter abnormalities, or changes in functional brain imaging have produced many suggestive findings, but little specific to disorders. Biological measures are more strongly associated with trait dimensions than categories. The absence of direct relationships is not really surprising when one considers the complexity and wide range of symptoms associated with psychopathology.

Finally, genetic and temperamental vulnerabilities, by themselves, do not cause mental disorders, because traits can be compatible with normal functioning when the environment is benign. Thus, not everyone with trait vulnerability develops a mental disorder. As suggested in Chapter 3, biological markers can be clinically useful ways of identifying risk; however, environmental factors often determine whether disorders develop. For this reason, biological reductionism is an oversimplification, and a research agenda based on neuroscience alone is bound to fail. It is likely that many of the findings in the literature reflect effects of disorder rather than causes. Neuroscientists, in their haste to reduce symptoms to genetic and cellular mechanisms, have not looked carefully enough at interactions between biological and environmental risk factors.

BIOLOGICAL CORRELATES OF BPD

With these general principles in mind, let us examine what is known about the biological correlates of BPD. Because traits are more related to markers than are disorders, a research strategy needs to dismantle BPD into its affective, impulsive, cognitive, and interpersonal components.

The most consistent correlates of BPD are related to impulsivity, a trait that has been consistently linked to deficits in central serotonergic functioning. The concept of impulsive aggression describes these traits (Coccaro & Kavoussi, 1997). A number of research strategies have been used to establish the link.

Neurotransmitters

Serotonin is a neurotransmitter used by most organs in the body. For this reason, it can be measured in blood platelets with a technique called "paroxetine binding." Our research group (Ng, Paris, Zweig-Frank, Schwartz, Steiger, & Nair, 2005) found abnormal paroxetine binding in a sample of BPD patients (compared with normal controls).

It is more precise to measure serotonin activity in the brain itself. One method consists of neuroendocrine challenge. That procedure involves administering a drug that stimulates central serotonin activity. Several studies have used either fenfluramine (a diet pill) for this purpose or meta-chlorphenylpiperazine (m-cpp). Because serotonin stimulates the hypothalamic–pituitary–adrenocortical axis, one can measure the release of hormones such as prolactin and cortisone after administering the challenge.

In a much-quoted study, Coccaro et al. (1989) found that patients with impulsive aggression, many of whom also had BPD, failed to respond in a normal way to fenfluramine challenge. This phenomenon is called "prolactin blunting"; if the hormonal response is flat, the serotonin system must be deficient.

Our group (Martial et al., 1997) initially confirmed this finding but in a larger sample (Paris et al., 2004) obtained somewhat different results. Using m-cpp challenge, we observed that serotoninergic responses were more rapid (and possibly less effective) than in normal controls. Only individuals with high impulsivity showed the blunting that Coccaro et al. (1989) had reported. Rinne, Westenberg, den Boer, and van den Brink (2000) also observed prolactin blunting (in response to m-cpp) in highly impulsive BPD patients. Thus, research findings may vary with the nature of the sample.

Moreover, the serotonin system works differently in males and females. Coccaro et al. (1989) studied men in a Veterans Affairs hospital, but prolactin blunting is not seen in women with BPD (Soloff, Meltzer, Becker, Greer, & Constantine, 2005).

Another method to measure serotonergic activity in the brain is to give people a diet deficient in tryptophan, the amino acid that the body uses to manufacture serotonin. Among patients treated for depression, tryptophan depletion leads to relapse (Moskowitz, Pinard, Zuroff, & Annable, 2003). Our research group is conducting a pilot study to determine the feasibility of this method in a sample with BPD.

Again, if low brain serotonin were the main biological problem behind BPD, one would expect that SSRIs should reverse its symptoms. Because that is not the case, the neurochemical variations associated with BPD are not likely to be simple.

Brain Imaging

PET measures activity at sites in the brain after administering a radioactive agent that is taken up and metabolized in various regions. In BPD, because research has focused on serotonin, the agonist used has usually been a precursor of that neurotransmitter. These studies (Siever et al., 1999; Leyton et al., 2001) have suggested that serotonin activity is lower at multiple sites in BPD. However, these findings are also seen in other diagnoses and are not specific to the disorder.

It should also be kept in mind that there are many different receptors for serotonin, each of which has a different function. Although some research methods examine serotonin activity as a whole, PET studies (e.g., Soloff et al., 2007) can focus on only one type of receptor.

A less expensive method is fMRI, which has been widely used in research. This technique allows us to see which brain areas are "lighting up" and to relate increased levels of activity to specific circumstances. Völmm et al. (2001) as well as Donegan et al. (2003) found increases in amgydala activity in BPD. Because the amygdala is the main center for fear and emotional activation in the brain, these results could be related to the high anxiety and dysphoria seen in this disorder.

In another study, Völmm et al. (2004) reported abnormal levels of activity in the orbitofrontal cortex when patients were asked to carry out a neuropsychological test requiring planning. That region is associated with "executive function" (i.e., planning ahead, the opposite of impulsivity). Another group of researchers (Beblo et al., 2006) have examined which brain areas light up when patients think about traumatic life events, finding higher levels of activation in both the amygdala and prefrontal cortex.

Volumetric studies using standard MRI methods examine whether patients with mental disorders have smaller (or larger) brain structures. There has been particular interest in the hippocampus (involved in memory and learning) as well as in the amygdala and prefrontal cortex. However, the evidence thus far is drawn from small samples (it is difficult to recruit BPD patients to sit in brain scanners).

Some of these data suggest decreased volume of the prefrontal cortex (Strakowski et al., 2002; Lyoo, Han, & Cho, 1998), with a specific decrease in the size of the anterior cingulate (Hazlett et al., 2005), a region related to decision making and control of impulsivity. One study found a decrease in the size of parietal cortex in BPD (Irle, Lange, & Sachsse, 2005)

Several MRI studies point to decreases in the volume of the hippocampus as well as the amygdala (Lyoo et al., 1998; Driessen et al., 2000; Tebartz van Elst, Hesslinger, et al., 2003; Tebartz van Elst, Ludaescher, et al., 2003; Schmahl, Vermetten, Elzinga, & Bremner, 2003; Brambilla et al., 2004). Another study found that reductions in hippocampal volume in BPD are related to high levels of aggression (Zetzsche et al., 2007). Again, it is possible that a smaller amygdala might be less effective for emotion regulation.

Still another method involves the measurement of event-rated potentials (ERPs), a form of electroencepholograpy that examines how brain potentials respond to stimuli over time. One such study (de Bruijn et al., 2006) described "reduced action monitoring" (i.e., problems in controlling impulsivity).

Taken as a whole, all these findings are suggestive in that they indicate that BPD patients have higher levels of emotional activation without sufficient control and modulation from higher cortical structures. However, all such results are ultimately correlations that may not be specific or explanatory. It is also not known whether changes in brain activity and volume precede BPD, in which case they would be markers for biological vulnerability, or whether they develop as a result of the disorder.

Neuropsychological Testing

Another way to measure biological factors in BPD is through neuro-psychological instruments (such as the Wisconsin Card Sorting Test, the Continuous Performance Test, or the Go/No-Go Task) that assess the ability of patients to plan and to control their impulses. These measures also assess executive function: behaviors and cognitions related to activity in the prefrontal cortex. On all these measures, patients with BPD show abnormalities in executive function that resemble those seen in ASPD (O'Leary, 2000; Leyton et al., 2001).

We can now summarize what neuroscience and cognitive science tell us about BPD and what we still need to find out. By and large, the findings of biological research parallel much of what we already know about the disorder. Genetic and biological variations drive the traits that underlie BPD. However, much more is unknown than known about relationships between brain function and abnormalities in mood, behavior, and cognition. At this point, research on impulsivity is most advanced, but we know next to nothing about the biology of affective instability. The same is true for the cognitive symptoms of BPD.

Thus, biological factors do not provide an explanation for the disorder, but they shape the traits that underlie symptoms. People who develop BPD have temperamental variations that are genetically influenced and associated with changes in brain chemistry and structure. Even so, these trait differences need not lead to psychopathology, but can become problematic when people are challenged by environmental stressors.

PSYCHOLOGICAL THEORIES OF BPD

It was long believed that BPD had almost exclusively psychological origins, and that the disorder was rooted in problematic family experiences. Therapists often blamed parents when children developed BPD.

Psychodynamic theories were fueled by assumptions about the childhood origins of adult psychopathology. The analytic paradigm also assumed that the more severe the adult pathology, the earlier in life it must have originated. The symptoms in BPD were sometimes thought to reflect problems in the toddler phase or even in infancy.

These ideas were never scientific. They were based on theory, armchair speculation, and a superficial relationship between the behavior of patients with BPD and small children. Moreover, psychoanalysts were generalizing from a very small population of patients seen in therapy. In principle, all these ideas *could* be tested empirically. However, it took years for researchers to become interested in studying them.

Even though psychodynamic theories of BPD have no research support, they continue to exert a certain influence. I still have to warn psychiatric residents not to jump to the conclusion that every patient with this disorder must have had difficulties early in childhood.

Let us now consider some of the main theories. Masterson and Rinsley (1975) suggested that because patients with BPD had problems with separation, they must have failed to master separation–individuation in childhood (the toddler phase). These authors also suggested that mothers were to blame for BPD, in that they did not want their children to separate (i.e., that they were overprotective).

Gerald Adler (1985) had a different theory about BPD. He thought the intense feelings of aloneness these patients describe had their roots in emotional neglect during childhood by their mothers. (No data were brought forward to support this hypothesis.)

A more sophisticated version of the neglect hypothesis has had greater influence. Attachment theory is now the dominant strain in psychoanalysis and is a model that has stimulated a large body of research (Cassidy & Shaver, 1999). The basic theory derives from the assumption that abnormal attachments to caretakers during childhood can shape psychopathology later in life.

Applying this theory to BPD, Fonagy, Target, and Gergely (2000) suggested that abnormal patterns in childhood (insecure and disorganized attachment) are behind the difficulties that patients have with interpersonal relationships. K. N. Levy (2005) as well as Bradley and Westen (2005) have also suggested that early problems in attachment are related to adult BPD.

Attachment theory is a promising line of investigation; however, it remains more descriptive than explanatory. Attachment behaviors are not just a result of parenting but also reflect genetically influenced personality traits, and there are major discontinuities between patterns in childhood and adulthood (Rutter, 1995; Paris, 2000b).

Although some researchers on attachment have explicitly disclaimed parent blaming (Bateman & Fonagy, 2006), it is hard to see how one can avoid such an implication. Moreover, even if patients with BPD have abnormal attachments (part of the definition of the disorder), it does not necessarily follow that problems were caused by experiences in early childhood.

Otto Kernberg (1976) was one of the first psychoanalysts to buck the long tradition of holding parents accountable for BPD. Kernberg argued that BPD is rooted in a constitutional vulnerability, conceptualized as an abnormal level of aggression that interferes with cognitive development. Although the science of the 1970s was unable to measure the biological correlates of impulsivity, recent research suggests that Kernberg has been (at least partially) vindicated.

Let us now examine some of the research methods used to study psychological risks for BPD.

METHODS OF EMPIRICAL RESEARCH

Retrospective Studies

Retrospective research is a straightforward approach that involves asking adults with BPD to describe their childhood. However, interpretation of these kinds of data has several pitfalls.

The most important problem is that reports of childhood symptoms reflect *recall bias* (i.e., the tendency of people who are currently ill to remember events earlier in their life in a negative way; Schachter, 1996). Patients with BPD can have particularly distorted perceptions of both current and distant life events.

A second pitfall is confusion between severe and mild trauma: Most patients with BPD do not report the events that are most likely to produce sequelae (Paris, 1994; Zanarini, 2000).

Third, associations in clinical samples do not represent what community studies show about the long-term effects of childhood adversity. Children who suffer mild trauma, and even those who suffer severe trauma, may not develop mental disorders (Paris, 2000b; Fergusson & Mullen, 1999).

With these limitations in mind, retrospective research on the relationship between childhood adversities and BPD describes frequent and fairly consistent relationships between trauma or neglect in childhood and BPD in adulthood. However, in view of the pitfalls of the method, these relationships can only be considered as hypotheses that need to be confirmed in prospective research.

Prospective Studies

Prospective follow-up studies of children drawn from community samples offer a better way of understanding relationships among adversity, personality, and psychopathology. When one performs prospective research, one does not have to depend on unrepresentative clinical samples or unreliable memories.

Thus, well-designed studies in large-scale community samples have the potential to avoid all these problems. Unfortunately, such research (e.g., Caspi et al., 1996; Cohen, Crawford, Johnson, & Kasen, 2005) has been rare.

Even so, prospective research has its own limitations. First, the method is better at examining outcomes that occur commonly than those that are relatively rare. The precursors of high-prevalence disorders such as depression, delinquency, and substance abuse have been illuminated by longitudinal community studies (Tremblay, 2006). However, disorders like schizophrenia (or BPD), with a prevalence of less than 1%, are much more difficult to find in the community.

A second problem is that even with the best intentions, the people most likely to drop out of a study may well be those with the most serious psychopathology. Keeping track of all participants is not always practical, and even trying to do so makes this kind of research very expensive.

A third problem is that prospective studies have not always measured temperament early in life. Although a few studies have made use of birth cohorts, many began their follow-up only during middle childhood.

Fourth, this research still has difficulty separating genetic from environmental effects to observe their interaction. The ideal study would monitor identical and fraternal twins over time.

Finally, only a few large-scale prospective studies have examined personality disorder as an outcome. The best data thus far have come from the Children in the Community Study (Cohen et al., 2005), which has been monitoring a cohort of children from the Albany–Saratoga area of New York State for 30 years. However, the study has identified very few patients who actually have a diagnosis of BPD, and its reports about personality disorders use number of symptoms, not full diagnosis, as an outcome variable.

In summary, although prospective studies yield suggestive findings that could shed light on how personality disorders develop, we lack a study that controls for genetics and temperament and that monitors a large group of children from early childhood to adult-hood.

High-Risk Studies

The impact of psychological adversity on mental disorders can also be studied by carrying out *high-risk studies*: following up children known to be exposed to pathogenic experiences. One might, for example, monitor children with a history of early neglect and trauma to determine whether they are at higher risk for BPD. Although this type of study would be important, research has rarely been carried out, largely because of the practical and ethical difficulties.

The main exception derives from the work of a group headed by Catherine Widom of John Jay College in New York, one of the few researchers in the world to collect prospective data on the outcome of childhood trauma. Widom (1999) identified a sample gathered from records of documented court cases of childhood abuse and neglect, interviewed the individuals about 20 years later, and compared them with a matched control group who did not experience abuse or neglect (Horwitz, Widom, McLaughlin, & White, 2001; Widom, 1999; Widom, Dumont, & Czaja, 2007). Abused and neglected women had higher rates of dysthymia, ASPD, and alcohol problems than controls, although physical abuse was more predictive of negative sequelae than sexual abuse (Widom et al., 2007). Notably, this cohort also showed a high rate of resilience (Widom & Kuhns, 1996), and only a minority developed symptoms.

Although abused and neglected women had higher rates of dysthymia, ASPD, and alcohol problems than controls, these relationships were no longer significant when recent life stressors were considered, and the cohort had a high rate of resilience (Widom & Kuhns, 1996).

A lack of consistency in the relationship between trauma and long-term sequelae is common in studies of children at risk (e.g., Werner & Smith, 1992). There could be two reasons for the discrepancy. First, vulnerability factors determine the response to adversity. Second, cumulative risk arises from multiple adversities during childhood as well as continued exposure to new adversities in adolescence and young adulthood.

Finally, relationships between childhood environment and adult outcome could also be accounted for by common heredity. Fathers who are alcoholic or criminal are likely to have children with impulsive symptoms, whether or not they are involved in raising them (Rutter, 2006). Patients with BPD may have fathers with ASPD and substance abuse (White et al., 2003). Without genetic controls, twin studies, and prospective designs, we cannot conclude that family adversity by itself causes pathology.

RETROSPECTIVE STUDIES OF PARENTING

In the 1980s and 1990s, empirical studies tested psychodynamic theories about the relationship between parenting and BPD. Systematic data on childhood experiences in patients with BPD have documented reports of all kinds of psychological adversities (Zanarini, 2000).

Some of the earlier reports, including publications from our research group (Frank & Paris, 1981; Paris & Frank, 1989; Zweig-Frank & Paris, 1991), found that patients with BPD report having been emotionally neglected (consistent with the ideas of Adler) as well as overprotected (consistent with the ideas of Masterson). Our group used a standard measure, the Parental Bonding Instrument (PBI; Parker, 1983), that retrospectively asks adults to assess the quality of parenting on two dimensions: affection versus neglect and autonomy versus overprotection. One might imagine scenarios in which parents fail to meet the emotional needs of their children while preventing them from finding alternate attachments elsewhere. This might well interfere with mechanisms of resilience.

Yet looking back, I must raise questions about our findings. (I remember being told by the journal editor to put the word "recollections" in the title of the paper. I only later realized how right he was to insist!) Validity depends on the accuracy of retrospective report in patients who are currently ill. Reports of neglect and overprotection in childhood were probably influenced by severity of illness. Another issue concerns comparison groups. When we compared our cohort with patients with milder disorders such as depression, the individuals with BPD described almost everything about their childhood as worse. In later studies (Paris, Zweig-Frank, & Guzder, 1994a, 1994b), we compared patients with BPD and a group with other personality disorders and found fewer differences. Reports of parental neglect and overprotection may not be particularly specific, because they are seen in all patients with depression (Parker, 1983).

A third issue concerns whether perceptions of parental mistreatment are stable over time. In a later study (Zweig-Frank & Paris, 2002), we administered the PBI to recovered patients at age 50. The results showed that scores on parental neglect were not elevated, although overprotection scores were still high. It is possible that recovery from BPD may have influenced this cohort to see their parents in a better light. Although we did not give the PBI to the same cohort at different points in time, one sees similar phenomena in therapy: As patients get better, they have more good things to say about their families.

This is not to say that all findings about emotional neglect should be discounted. They may have specific effects on vulnerable populations. As Linehan (1993) suggested, families could have difficulty validating the unusually strong feelings of children at risk for BPD. In other words, we could be looking at a gene–environment interaction. If so, problems in parental bonding could be a risk factor for BPD, even if they do not, by themselves, cause the disorder.

CHILD ABUSE AND TRAUMA

The most striking finding of research on the childhood of patients with BPD is how many report traumatic events, particularly sexual and physical abuse. Such experiences are generally more common in patients than in nonpatients. However, rates among patients with BPD are unusually high; the majority of patients report some form of child abuse (Herman, Perry, & van der Kolk, 1989; Ogata, Silk, Goodrich, Lohr, Westen, & Hill, 1990; Paris, Zweig-Frank, & Guzder, 1994a, 1994b; Zanarini, 2000). The prevalence is also significantly higher than in neighboring disorders (several studies compared BPD with depression or other personality disorders).

These findings had a great impact on the clinical community. They were widely interpreted as supporting psychological theories that account for BPD as a response to childhood adversity (e.g., Herman & van der Kolk, 1987), associated with the idea that the symptoms of BPD are reenactments of childhood experiences or even that the disorder itself could be redefined as "complex PTSD" (see Chapter 2).

However, such ideas are examples of linear thinking, vastly oversimplifying complex relationships. The association between childhood trauma and adult psychopathology can only be understood in light of community studies. The patients whom therapists see do not represent the larger population of people who have had traumatic experiences during their childhood, only those who have enough symptoms to seek help. And the patients we see do not even represent all those who meet criteria for a diagnosis of BPD.

It is true that most adult patients with BPD report childhood adversities or trauma, including sexual and physical abuse, parental neglect, and familial dysfunction (Zanarini, 2000). However, these findings have been widely misunderstood. When severe and extended abuse is separated from milder incidents (e.g., a single event involving molestation by a stranger), the number of cases is reduced to about a third (Ogata et al., 1990; Paris et al., 1994a, 1994b). Moreover, there is no specific relationship between risk and outcome. Trauma is a risk factor for many mental disorders (Paris, 2000b), and BPD can develop without any trauma history (Paris, 1994).

Community studies of the long-term sequelae of childhood adversities (Malinovsky-Rummell & Hansen, 1993; Browne & Finkelhor, 1986; Fergusson & Mullen, 1999, Rind & Tromovitch, 1997; Rind, Tromovitch, & Bauserman, 1998) consistently show that only a minority of children who have been exposed to sexual or physical abuse ever develop mental disorders. Similarly, although childhood neglect and parental separation are risk factors for psychopathology, they do not necessarily lead to mental disorders (Paris, 1994, 2000b).

The gap between risk and outcome can be explained by the fact that personality traits mediate responses to adversity (Paris, 2003). These individual differences in temperament, personality, and vulnerability have a strong genetic component (Plomin et al., 2000). Thus, the long-term outcome of adversity in childhood depends on interactions between genes and environment (Kaufman, 2006; Rutter, 2006).

Most children have a high degree of resilience to all but the most severe and prolonged environmental insults (Rutter, 2006). Predisposing factors help to explain why some eventually develop symptoms and others do not. Those with emotional dysregulation and impulsivity are more likely to develop BPD symptoms when negative life events occur. In contrast, those with a different trait profile may be at risk for other forms of pathology but not for BPD.

In summary, retrospective studies of childhood adversity are useful but have been interpreted in a misleading way. To study this relationship properly, researchers need to carry out high-risk or prospective research. Ideally, high-risk studies, in which large groups of abused children are followed up into adulthood, should be able to determine how frequently adversities lead to mental disorders and, if so, which disorders.

Again, such research is rare. It is expensive to perform, and it would be ethically problematic to monitor abused children without intervening to prevent sequelae.

What we *do* know about the long-term effects of abuse comes from community studies. These are door-to-door surveys of the general population that identify groups who report having been exposed to either childhood sexual abuse or physical abuse. About 20% of those who report childhood abuse will have measurable psychopathology in adulthood (Browne & Finkelhor, 1986; Fergusson & Mullen, 1999). However, although 20% is a high number, it is striking that 80% of those exposed develop no mental disorders. Thus, although trauma is a risk factor, it does not consistently lead to pathology. Resilience is the rule.

This research, demonstrating the ubiquity of resilience, is not sufficiently known in the clinical community. Therapists tend to assume that patients must have been abused if they are sick and that patients who are sick may have been abused. Also, when patients report child abuse, there is a tendency to attribute *all* their symptoms to these experiences rather than to concurrent risks.

Interestingly, when findings of research that points to resilience *have* come to public attention, they have sometimes led to controversy. Some people are concerned that resilience can be interpreted as proving that abuse is not really bad for children. (Of course, no one would claim that is the case.) A research psychologist, Bruce Rind, author of two of the major studies, was censured on the floor of the U.S. Congress in 1998 for publishing surveys showing that most people recover from childhood sexual abuse. (The resolution was sponsored by that noted exemplar of ethical conduct, Congressman Tom DeLay.) Instead of complaining about valid scientific findings, one might have thought that everyone would be pleased with research showing that most children bounce back from adverse experiences.

The clinical community is right to be concerned about the impact of childhood sexual abuse: These experiences are hurtful. The question is whether or not they lead to mental illness. All adverse life experiences have *some* impact, but they do not necessarily lead to mental disorders. Although childhood sexual abuse increases the risk for a variety of adult diagnoses (Kendler & Prescott, 2007), few people are permanently affected. This is a "good news story."

A large literature demonstrates the ubiquity of resilience. For example, in a well-known study of children exposed to poverty and severe family dysfunction, Werner and Smith (1992) found that the majority of children growing up in these circumstances emerged as well-functioning adults, although some first had to weather a stormy adolescence. Another famous research project that monitored children into adulthood, the Isle of Wight Study (Rutter, 2006), yielded similar findings.

In summary, although childhood adversity is not a *cause* of any mental disorder, it is a *risk factor* for many disorders. If you are vulnerable, adversity may tip you over, and you will develop symptoms. If you are resilient, it may not.

Thus, two general principles emerge from the research literature on trauma. One is that children who lack genetic vulnerability do not develop psychopathology. The other—and this is a major source of misunderstanding about the effects of trauma—is the importance of the *parameters* of abuse. Childhood sexual abuse and physical abuse cannot be thought of as homogeneous single risks. The type of abuse makes it more or less likely that children will eventually develop psychopathology. Single incidents of sexual molestation by strangers should not be confounded with years of parental incest. Occasional hitting by parents should not be confounded with physical abuse causing injuries on many occasions.

Community studies (Browne & Finkelhor, 1986; Fergusson & Mullen, 1999) show that the most important parameters for childhood sexual abuse are the identity of the perpetrator and the nature of the act. First and foremost, childhood sexual abuse has a different impact depending on who is responsible. Father–daughter incest is the most pathogenic kind of childhood sexual abuse. If the perpetrator is a close family member, the effects also tend to be worse, whereas if it is a stranger, the impact is much less. The second important issue is what happened. If intercourse with a child has taken place, the effects are worse. If inappropriate touching has occurred, the impact will be less.

Other factors are less crucial but worth noting. How long and how often did abuse take place? If molestation went on for years, effects could be greater, but if abuse happened only once, there may be no effects at all. One also needs to know whether abuse was associated with a threat of violence.

These parameters must always be considered when patients report histories of childhood sexual abuse. Similarly, the most important parameters of physical abuse are related to severity (beatings leading to physical injury). Failure to make these distinctions has led to misleading statements that two-thirds (or more) of patients with BPD have been abused as children.

In our own study (Paris et al., 1994a, 1994b), only about one-third of our cohort had experienced the types of abuse (from caretakers, incidents of sexual intercourse, and multiple events) that lead to long-term sequelae in community populations. Another one-third had experienced milder incidents (usually single molestations from nonrelatives). Another one-third had never been abused at all. It is in the one-third of patients who report serious childhood sexual abuse that these adversities are most likely to be important risk factors for the disorder. The findings for physical abuse were very similar.

The most important parameter of childhood sexual abuse remains the identity of the perpetrator. In a careful review of the literature, Zanarini (2000) noted that about 25% of patients with BPD describe abuse in childhood from a caretaker. This kind of abuse is a breach of trust.

When you take parameters into account, it is not surprising that the relationship between childhood sexual abuse and BPD is less than consistent. Fossati, Madeddu, and Maffei (1999) conducted a meta-analysis showing that the association has a moderate (but not large) effect size. Child abuse is only one of several pathways to the disorder.

Nonetheless, abuse is a risk factor for BPD. And patients with BPD with these histories have more severe psychopathology (Soloff, Lynch, & Kelly, 2002). The relationship between childhood maltreatment and adult symptoms has been confirmed in prospective longitudinal studies. Thus, the Albany–Saratoga study (Cohen et al., 2005) found an association between trauma and psychopathology, of which personality disorder symptoms were one of several outcomes (Johnson, Cohen, Brown, Smailes, & Bernstein, 1999). In this prospective cohort of children followed up into young adulthood, childhood adversities, including neglect, physical abuse, and sexual abuse, were associated with a higher number of personality disorder symptoms, including BPD criteria (Kasen et al., 1999; Johnson et al., 1999; Johnson, Cohen, Chen, Kasen, & Brook, 2006). (However, as already noted, too few participants had a diagnosable disorder, so the researchers had to use a symptom count rather than clinical diagnosis.)

The clinical point that emerges from all this research is that therapists should not assume that every patient they see with BPD has been abused. They also need to consider childhood adversities in a larger context.

One important question concerns whether abuse itself does the damage, or whether long-term effects derive from a climate that allows abuse to happen. In one study, family dysfunction accounted for the outcome variance associated with childhood sexual abuse (Nash, Hulsely, Sexton, Harralson, & Lambert, 1993). When children are abused, they may not have been protected by or securely attached to their parents. Conte, Wolf, and Smith (1989) studied pedophiles and found that they know how to identify their prey: lonely girls who are obviously in need of attention.

There is also no such thing as a symptom that can be used as a marker for child abuse. It has been claimed that because BPD patients who dissociate and mutilate themselves often have histories of sexual abuse, these symptoms develop in response to such experiences (van der Kolk, Perry, & Herman, 1991). However, our research group examined the relationship between trauma and symptoms by comparing BPD patients with and without childhood sexual abuse and physical abuse. Whether or not abuse histories were present, BPD patients were more likely than a comparison group (with other personality disorders) to have high scores on the Dissociative Experiences Scale (Zweig-Frank, Paris, & Guzder, 1994a, 1994b, 1994c, 1994d). Thus, dissociation occurs in BPD whether or not patients are abused. We also found that patients with BPD mutilate themselves whether or not they have been abused. These findings also applied to defense mechanisms, which were the same in abused and nonabused individuals (Bond, Paris, & Zweig-Frank, 1994). All these problems are intrinsic to BPD, not to any particular life experience.

It has also been claimed that if patients do not remember abuse, they may have repressed the memory of such events (Herman, 1992). Unfortunately, the evoking of recovered memories in therapy has been one of the greatest scandals in the history of psychotherapy. The idea that traumatic events tend to be repressed turns out to be entirely wrong (McNally, 2003). Therapies based on this theory involve a misguided procedure in which patients are encouraged to produce such stories (A. Piper & Merskey, 2004a). And many of the victims have been patients with BPD.

Again, we should not forget that reports of trauma and neglect are retrospective and open to recall bias. If you ask seriously ill adults about their childhood experiences, it is inevitable that memories will be colored by current states of mind (Schachter, 1996). When patients with BPD present negative perceptions of their parents, it is worth remembering that they tend to see anyone who gets close to them rather critically, including their therapist. If therapists agree with patients that parents are at fault, they run the risk of supporting their tendency to blame other people for their problems as opposed to encouraging ownership and responsibility.

For therapists too, the good news is still resilience. Children are tougher than we think: They have to be!

In an earlier book, I called the idea that early experiences explain adult symptoms one of several "myths of childhood" (Paris, 2000b). Even when early adversity is prominent in the history, one cannot assume causality. The patients who therapists treat are more vulnerable to life events than people in the community who do not come for help.

In summary, psychological risks for BPD are ubiquitous but far from specific. Every patient can have a different pathway to the disorder. Some will have been exposed to many risks, whereas others may report none at all. And there is no predictable relationship between life adversity (whether in childhood or adulthood) with BPD or with any of its component symptoms. Finally and crucially, the impact of adversity must be understood in terms of genetically influenced personality traits that mediate vulnerability.

SOCIAL FACTORS

Mental disorders exist in a social context. Although everyone has a trait profile that could be associated with vulnerability to one illness or another, it is the environment that determines whether traits become disorders. As clinicians, we usually think of environment in terms of current and past psychological risks. These factors are specific to individual patients. However, there are also adversities that affect everyone, because they exist on a societal level.

Psychological symptoms and mental disorders are strongly influenced by the society in which people live. Some disorders may only present under certain cultural conditions (Prince & Tseng-Laroche, 1990). For example, eating disorders are not universal but appear in societies in cultural transition in which food is abundant (Klein & Walsh, 2003).

Some of the most common mental disorders, such as major depression (Waraich, Goldner, Somers, & Hu, 2004) and substance abuse (Helzer & Canino, 1992), vary greatly in prevalence across cultures. The precise nature of symptoms is affected by how a culture allows distress to be expressed. Although other mental disorders, such as schizophrenia, have a fairly similar prevalence around the world, they are more common in some ethnic groups than others, and prognosis and outcome can vary (Murphy, 1982).

BPD is a disorder that arises only under specific social conditions. In the historical literature, it is difficult to find evidence that this clinical picture existed in the past. One does not read in the Bible or in Shakespeare about repetitive overdoses or mutilation. Although religious fanatics can cut themselves deliberately, that behavior has an entirely different motivation (Favazza, 1996).

The modern world began in the Renaissance, but social change accelerated greatly in the 19th century. One of my colleagues provided me with a description of cutting by Lady Caroline Lamb, mistress of Lord Byron and wife of a British prime minister. But 200 years ago, such behavior must have been rare. One does not find cases of BPD described in the early psychoanalytic literature, even though one author (Blum, 1974) tried to reformulate Freud's famous case of the "Wolf Man" as an example.

Before BPD had appeared on the clinical scene, the personality traits that underlie the disorder must have existed. The structure of personality is about the same across all cultures (McCrae & Terracciano, 2005). Given the biological roots of traits, they should not vary historically. However, distress will not always express itself in the same way.

Shorter (1997), a leading historian of psychiatry, introduced the concept of a "symptom bank," meaning that psychological distress occurs at all time and all places, at any given historical moment or in any social context, and the environment shapes symptoms by offering specific options to express distress. This hypothesis closely parallels the idea of social contagion, in which symptoms are spread through personal contact or through the media (Rodger, Rowe, & Buster, 1998). Some patients with BPD learn to cut their wrists through this mechanism.

The historical determinants of psychological symptoms are exemplified by the observation that conversion disorder was more common in the 19th century than it is today (Merskey, 1997). Conversion hysteria was the focus of dramatic aspects of demonstrations at the Salpêtrière Hospital in Paris by the famed neurologist (and Freud mentor) Jean-Martin Charcot. These symptoms are also common in traditional societies (Nandi, Banerjee, Nandi, & Nandi, 1992).

In traditional societies, presenting with physical symptoms as an expression of distress was sometimes the only way for women in these societies to mobilize family and community to deal with their difficulties. However, when societies modernize, the pattern may change. In India, when researchers returned to the rural site where 15 years earlier conversions were very common, such symptoms had become less frequent, but the incidence of overdosing with pills was increasing (Nandi et al., 1992).

Behaviors associated with BPD are drawn from a symptom bank specific to modern or modernizing societies. Linehan (1993) suggested that modern society makes emotional regulation more difficult because of the absence of consistent social supports. The context of modernity also promotes the identity diffusion seen in BPD. We live in a world that promotes radical individualism, social isolation, and personal angst. These trends may be particularly conducive to developing behaviors that are self-destructive, such as cutting and overdosing. Most people express their distress in other ways (e.g., by becoming depressed or abusing substances), but those symptoms are also becoming more common in modern societies, along with those of other externalizing disorders (Millon, 1993).

The strongest evidence for sociocultural factors in mental disorders comes from epidemiological research demonstrating such changes in prevalence. When the frequency of a disorder increases over short periods of time, the explanation is almost always social.

Research from prevalence and cohort studies, as well as from cross-cultural research, shows that impulsive disorders have increased in prevalence since World War II. Although we have no specific findings related to BPD, converging evidence from other sources suggests that the disorder is becoming more frequent (Millon, 1993; Paris, 1996b). For example, a number of impulsive symptoms in adolescents and young adults (e.g., substance abuse, antisocial behavior), as well as depression among adolescents and young adults, have increased, both in North America and Europe (Rutter & Smith, 1995). Moreover, since the 1960s, there have been notable increases in the prevalence of suicide attempts (Bland, Dyck, Newman, & Orn, 1998) as well as completed suicides among young adults (Maris, Berman, & Silverman, 2000).

A second line of evidence supporting the role of social factors in mental disorders comes from cross-cultural studies. Social scientists (e.g., Lerner, 1958) have long distinguished traditional societies, which have high social cohesion, fixed social roles, and intergenerational continuity, from modern societies, which have lower social cohesion, fluid social roles, and less continuity between generations. Throughout history, most social structures have been traditional. There are few societies left in the world that can still be described in that way, although some are more traditional than others.

Thus far, no cross-cultural community studies have specifically examined the frequency of BPD. We do have data on antisocial personality, which greatly increased in prevalence in North America between 1950 and 1980 (Robins & Regier, 1991). ASPD is quite rare in traditional societies such as Taiwan (Hwu, Yeh, & Change, 1989). Impulsive disorders like BPD and ASPD are less common in these societies probably because behavior is more closely monitored, young people have social roles provided to them, and some degree of intimacy is provided through arranged marriages, extended families, and a tightly knit community.

In a study sponsored by the World Health Organization, BPD was shown to be diagnosable in multiple clinical sites across the world (Loranger et al., 1994). There are clinical reports that BPD is readily identifiable in India (C. Pinto, Dhavale, Nair, Patil, & Dewa, 2000) and in China (Zhong & Leung, 2007). However, we do not know how common such cases are, because community prevalence has not been studied. Nor do we know whether BPD is more frequent in urban settings (as one might expect from a hypothesis in which the disorder is brought on by rapid social change). This is an area that could greatly benefit from further research.

BPD: A SOCIALLY SENSITIVE DISORDER

Let us now consider mechanisms by which social factors could affect the development of BPD. I hypothesize that this disorder varies greatly in prevalence depending on social conditions and that it reflects, at least in part, responses to rapid modernization.

Mental disorders whose prevalence changes with time and circumstance can be described as *socially sensitive*. Disorders that have a more stable prevalence across cultures and time (such as schizophrenia) can be described as *socially insensitive* (Paris, 2004). Many socially sensitive disorders (e.g., substance abuse, eating disorders, antisocial personality, borderline personality) are characterized by externalizing symptoms. Impulsive traits, which tend to be contained by structure and limits and amplified by their absence, may be particularly responsive to social context. However, disorders characterized by internalizing symptoms (e.g., unipolar depression, anxiety disorders) can also be socially sensitive, because these traits can be either contained or amplified by social supports.

Traditional societies, such as Taiwan (Hwu et al., 1989) and Japan (Sato & Takeichi, 1993), have a low prevalence of substance abuse and antisocial personality. The increasing prevalence of these same disorders among young adults in Western societies points to stressors in contemporary society. Even if many, or most, young people thrive under our culture's intense modernity, a vulnerable minority are at risk for impulsive disorders.

Socially sensitive disorders begin in adolescence and youth. Although puberty is universal, adolescence as a separate developmental stage is in part a social construction (Furstenberg, 2000). Throughout most of history, young people assumed adult roles earlier in life. Traditionally, people lived in extended families, villages, and tribes and rarely traveled far. Those who did not fit in to social structures left early and searched for a niche elsewhere. The majority stayed put, doing the same work as their parents and their grandparents. Most people did not have to search very far to find intimate relationships. Marriage was arranged early in life, with partners chosen from the same or neighboring communities.

Adolescence is a stressful time for those who are vulnerable to stress. It became a stage of life only in modern societies, which expect the younger generation to postpone maturity in order to learn complex skills and to develop a unique identity. Not everyone is cut out for that challenge. In traditional societies, young people are provided social roles and networks. In modern societies, adolescents give up the protection of assigned roles and networks. They must spend many years learning how to function as adults. Instead of identifying with family and community values, they are expected to find their own, developing a unique identity. Young people rarely do the same work as their parents and must learn necessary skills from strangers. Families may not even understand the nature of their children's careers. Finally, young people are expected to find their own mates. Because there is no guarantee that this search will be successful, the young need to deal with the vicissitudes of mistaken choices, hurtful rejections, and intermittent loneliness.

In contemporary Western culture, we value individualism, and most of us would be thoroughly miserable in a traditional society. However, the situation is different for those who are temperamentally vulnerable. Mental disorders may become more common with high rates of social change, family breakdown, and loss of social cohesion and when social roles are less readily available (Paris, 1996b). Decreases in social support, interfering with a normal process of buffering, may amplify impulsivity (Millon, 1993) as well as affective instability (Linehan, 1993). Rapid social change makes mental disorders more likely. Conversely, stable social structures and attachments buffer the effects of biological and psychological risk factors, making disorder less likely to develop.

This model of social sensitivity fits existing epidemiological data fairly well, but requires empirical confirmation through surveys that specifically examine the prevalence of BPD under different social conditions.

CLINICAL IMPLICATIONS

- BPD evolves in the presence of biological vulnerability, psychological adversity, and social stressors.
- No single factor accounts for the disorder. BPD cannot be understood without considering a broad range of risks.
- One cannot assume that patients with a typical clinical picture will have a specific pattern of risk.
- One cannot assume that patients with a specific pattern of risk will develop BPD.

CHAPTER 5

A General Model

*B*PD is a complex disorder with a complex cause. Each of its domains develops through a unique pathway. Yet as we have seen, BPD is associated with an overall heritability. Thus, patients who develop this disorder must have at least one, if not several, forms of biological vulnerability. However, that does not mean that BPD is simply the result of being born with a different brain. Rather, people who carry trait vulnerabilities can develop normally if the environment is favorable.

The frequency of childhood adversities in BPD suggests that the disorder can develop as a response to environmental stressors. However, life events by themselves do not cause symptoms, unless the individual is biologically vulnerable.

The observation that cohort effects over time can raise the prevalence of suicide attempts shows that social forces influence the development of disorder. However, these risks only affect those who are biologically and psychologically vulnerable; society is not to blame for BPD.

All these factors play a role in different proportions in different patients. Whether biological, psychological, or social, risks are multiple and interact with each other.

In summary, research does not support any direct relationship between any risk factor and outcome. Rather, the data are most consistent with models of gene–environment interaction.

Stress–diathesis theory is the most useful way to think about the cause of mental disorders (Monroe & Simons, 1991; Paris, 1998). The concept is that biological diatheses determine the form that disorder takes, and the threshold for developing disorder is determined by stressful events. Current theory takes a more sophisticated view of the relationship between stress and diathesis, considering recent evidence that genes can be "turned on" or "turned off' by environmental influences (Rutter, 2006).

These interactions explain why individuals who are genetically vulnerable can be at greater risk for a mental disorder. However, if the environment is favorable, vulnerability may never cross the threshold to disorder. Similarly, although stress puts individuals at greater risk for a mental disorder, it may never develop without biological diatheses.

This principle also applies to disorders thought to be mainly genetic. For example, schizophrenia is only 50% concordant in identical twins (Gottesman, 1991), showing that there must be undiscovered environmental factors that raise the risk for disorder. The principle also applies to disorders thought to be purely environmental. For example, in PTSD, traumatic events do not necessarily produce symptoms: only 20% of those exposed to severe life events ever develop PTSD (Yehuda & McFarlane, 1995; Paris, 2000c). Moreover, behavioral genetic research has shown that all PTSD symptoms are under genetic influence (True et al., 1993).

Avshalom Caspi, a psychologist working in Madison, Wisconsin, and London, England, leads a group conducting research on gene–environment interactions in a longitudinal community sample drawn from a New Zealand birth cohort. Two reports published in the journal *Science* (Caspi et al., 2002, 2003) have been among the most quoted research in behavioral science over the last 10 years. The results showed that neither genetic vulnerability nor environmental adversity were predictive, by themselves, of outcomes such as depression or antisocial behavior. But when *both* were present, individuals were significantly more likely to develop these symptoms.

The same principles almost certainly apply to BPD, which is not explained either by chemical imbalances or bad parenting. People with trait vulnerabilities tending toward affective instability and impulsivity may be emotional and quick to react, yet never develop BPD. People exposed to psychological adversities during childhood are affected by these experiences but may never develop a mental disorder (Paris, 2000b, 2000c). Psychopathology appears when both are present: It takes both genes and environment to "cook" a case of BPD.

THE BIOLOGICAL–PSYCHOLOGICAL INTERFACE

Biology explains variability in personality but is not a consistent predictor of mental disorders. We are all wired differently, and every brain has a slightly different mix of neurotransmitters. Such variations usually fall within a normal range and are correlated with individual differences in personality traits. Even when trait profiles are extreme, people do not necessarily fall ill. These variations reflect changes in brain anatomy or chemistry. Yet, although everyone has traits, only some develop disorders.

If we consider the three major domains of BPD, variations in each can be compatible with normality. Although affective instability is a problem at the extreme, it is not always a bad thing to be highly emotional. In some ways, people who respond to life events with strong feelings are often interesting and appealing. And although impulsivity can be a problem at extreme levels, it need not be a bad thing. There are many situations in life in which one does better to react quickly. Even the cognitive domain of BPD should not be thought of as totally negative. The capacity for fantasy can be associated with creativity.

By and large, traits are most likely to be dysfunctional when they are associated with dysfunctional behaviors and are applied indiscriminately to all situations. Moreover, trait domains interact in ways that can either neutralize each other or amplify each other. Patients with both affective instability and impulsivity are likely to develop feedback loops reinforcing both characteristics.

The importance of parenting in relation to inborn traits has been described as "goodness of fit" (Chess & Thomas, 1984). Every child has a unique temperament. The task of parents is to recognize individuality. This is what Linehan (1993) was referring to when she hypothesized that invalidation of strong emotions could be a major environmental factor in BPD.

These interactive effects may be more important than the dramatic life events that have received so much attention in BPD. Exposure to trauma, neglect, and family dysfunction is bad for you, but it does not necessarily make you sick. Children are resilient to adverse events for good reason: Life is full of them. Whatever traumas are associated with development in the contemporary world, it is worth considering the human past, in which it was not uncommon for parents to die or for families to starve.

Let us consider why the effects of psychological adversity are different for people who are temperamentally vulnerable. Suppose you are unstable in your emotions and somewhat impulsive. If your life goes well, you may only turn out to be an "interesting person," someone who is highly expressive and a little turbulent. (We all have friends like that.) Now suppose that your life does not go well. A series of adverse events (not just one but many) amplifies your personality traits. The more bad things happen to you, the more unstable your emotions are and the more likely you are to do something impulsive. If this process goes too far, you will develop a mental disorder. One possibility would be BPD.

The relationship between genes and environment is even more complex, because genes affect the kind of life adversities to which people are exposed (Rutter, 2006). If you are overemotional and impulsive, you may actually seek out life experiences that are bad for you. (Consider, for example, risk-taking behaviors during adolescence, such as drug abuse.) These characteristics may also lead other people to reject you or treat you badly. And if you have parents with the same traits, they may not be able to calm you down or may make things worse by reacting badly.

THE BIOLOGICAL–SOCIAL INTERFACE

Consider now another scenario. You are living in a traditional society. Adolescents will not necessarily stay in school, because they need to work to help support their families. There is no adolescent peer culture to support danger and temptation. No one you know takes drugs. If you misbehave, your teachers and neighbors will immediately tell your parents, who will punish you. Moreover, society has taught you to honor your parents and to plan a similar way of life. In a setting like this, the only way to be a rebel would be to leave entirely. Very few will do so.

Under these conditions, one cannot create a case of BPD. People who are unusually emotional and impulsive will be contained by powerful social structures. If young people do act out, their offenses will be minor.

Growing up in modern society presents just the opposite scenario. Everything encourages you to try to separate from your parents and to plan a different life. Your peer group is of paramount importance. If your friends are experimenting with drugs and sex, you will want to do so too. If you are not too neurotic and a bit introverted, this process may not go very far. But if you are emotional and impulsive, you may be trapped in a feedback loop that runs out of control.

These interactions help to explain why serious problems in patients with BPD usually only begin in adolescence. During childhood, children are, for better or for worse, more attached to their families than to peer groups. Adolescence is a time when both biology and psychology change rapidly. At this stage, moodiness and impulsivity are increased. This happens at the same time as adolescents begin the long processes of separating from their families.

Adolescence is a time when children (at least in our culture) are exposed to (and attracted to) dangerous temptations, just as parents have difficulty maintaining close, trusting relationship with their children. For most, problems will not be that severe. As shown many years ago by Offer and Offer (1975), the majority sail through the teenage years without major crises.

However, for those who are temperamentally vulnerable, life may spiral out of control. Moodiness and impulsivity can lead to suicidality as well as the wide range of acting out seen in adolescents with BPD. Moreover, temperamental factors make it more difficult for young people to pull things together after a stormy adolescence, so that problems tend to endure in the young adult years.

THE PSYCHOLOGICAL–SOCIAL INTERFACE

Consider again two scenarios. In the first, you have grown up in a highly dysfunctional family. Your father was an alcoholic who beat you and failed to respect sexual boundaries. Your mother was overwhelmed and depressed. However, you live in a good neighborhood and go to a good school. Your teachers take an interest in you, and you make friends. After a while, you realize that the best strategy is to spend as much time as possible outside the home, either in after-school activities or at someone else's house. With the support of others, you work hard and succeed. You do not develop BPD or any other mental disorder.

In the second, alternative scenario, you have grown up in a working-class family that is not particularly dysfunctional, but your hard-working parents have little time to spend with you. Moreover, you feel estranged from their values and search for some other identity. The quality of your school is low, and you do not find encouraging teachers. You find an identity by joining a peer group that is deep into drugs. You also meet young people who cut themselves when they feel upset. When you try doing the same thing, you find that it works to reduce distress. Moreover, your relationships are not that stable. When you break up with your first boyfriend, you take an overdose of pills. Your friends are in no way shocked or surprised. But you already have BPD.

These examples illustrate the complex relationship between the family and the larger social environment. Although resilience depends in part on genetically influenced personality traits, it also depends on the quality of schools and neighborhoods (Rutter, 2006). This is probably why disorders like BPD are more common in socially disadvantaged groups (Coid et al., 2006).

A MULTIDIMENSIONAL VIEW OF BPD

Putting all these pieces together, it becomes obvious why searching for a simple explanation of BPD is futile and misleading. Only a bio-psychosocial or stress–diathesis model can even begin to do justice to the data. Moreover, not every case of BPD is the same. Some carry a higher biological load, others a higher psychosocial load. Like most mental disorders, BPD is an outcome that can be reached from many different pathways.

About 15 years ago, I wrote a book outlining this model (Paris, 1994). Since then, psychopathological theory has developed, and theorists are more likely to embrace complexity. However, therapists, faced with suffering patients, are still likely to be attracted to simplicity. And there is a more general reason why clinicians cling to models in which disorders have single causes. It is difficult for the human mind to get past linearity. One cause, one effect—how tempting! Unfortunately, there are few relationships like that in the real world.

When I began my research career 20 years ago, I decided to upgrade my knowledge of statistics. I quickly discovered that the univariate tests I had learned as an undergraduate in psychology (*t* tests and chi-squares) were no longer routinely used and had been overtaken by multivariate models (multiple regression, logistic regression, path analysis, and model fitting). If the sample is large enough, these powerful methods can allow us to study the effects of 10 or 20 risk factors on the same outcome. That is how the relationship between cause and effect really works. I have come to realize that the *world* is a multiple regression.

IMPLICATIONS OF THE MODEL FOR TREATMENT

Just as there is no single cause of BPD, there is no single modality of treatment for patients. In the rest of this book, I show why concentrating on only one aspect of the disorder leads to poor treatment. A purely biological view leads to many prescriptions (and few remissions). A purely psychological view encourages patients to externalize and blame others for their problems (identifying themselves as victims of trauma without really improving their lives). A purely social view would preclude diagnosis.

Research provides a corrective for these errors. Biology has provided few clues to methods of therapy, and no drug specifically targets the biological underpinnings of the disorder (see Chapter 7). However, we may have something better to offer in the future. In the meantime, therapists should stop blaming families for causing BPD.

If future research could identify biological markers that are specific to BPD, diagnosis would be more precise, and therapists of the future might be able to monitor the effects of psychotherapy with such measures. Although that goal is still a long way off, there is evidence that psychotherapy changes brain circuitry (Goldapple et al., 2004).

The interactions between biological and psychological factors are directly relevant to practice. Genetic vulnerability helps to explain why classic methods have not been notably successful for BPD patients, who need specifically designed therapy programs. Talking about childhood experiences will not cure BPD if adversities are not causes but contributing factors. It should not be surprising that "interpreting" current behavioral problems as reenactments of childhood is not that effective.

I am *not* saying that one should not explore childhood adversities in therapy. Patients with BPD have a need for validation. They will not listen to therapists unless they feel understood. Acknowledging difficulties in childhood is part of that validating approach. However, doing so does not mean that one needs to spend months (or years) working through the events of childhood. This is where many previous therapists interested in BPD have gone wrong. We need to understand the past but not dwell on it. Getting people better means moving forward, not backward. Patients with BPD need to join or return to the workforce and participate in society. These are people who need to "get a life."

And that is where research on social factors in BPD comes in. The vulnerability to BPD is brought on by circumstances in which young people have difficulty finding a role or an identity, pointing to the direction in which adults patients need to move. The more connections patients make, the more they will be protected from mood swings and impulsivity. Patients will be more likely to succeed if they have a secure social network. They are often best advised to hold off on falling in love until they have such a network, because intimacy is a main area of trouble in BPD.

Even more important, patients with BPD need a social role to which they can commit themselves. The more that patients can find meaning through work or advance themselves through education, the more quickly they will get better. Achievement in the real world (and not a slick formula) is what raises self-esteem. Conversely, chronic unemployment and lack of productivity are recipes for chronic illness. Lack of a job leads either to the breakdown of social networks with resulting isolation or to continued attachments to pathological peer groups.

CLINICAL IMPLICATIONS

- BPD emerges from interactions between multiple risk factors.
- Multidimensional disorders need multidimensional treatment.
- Although we have no way of changing the vulnerabilities that underlie BPD, we can modify their effects by helping patients to find a life niche consistent with their traits.

PART III

Treatment

CHAPTER 6

Outcome

*T*hirty years ago, I was one of the organizers of a conference entitled "BPD across the Life Cycle." The program consisted of a series of presentations on how the disorder might present in childhood, in adolescence, and in adulthood. I was assigned to talk about BPD in older adults. I thought it might be instructive to look up what was known about this subject. BPD patients are usually young. Why don't we see old patients? Do they die, disappear, or get better?

To my surprise, I found nothing whatsoever in the literature. Nobody had ever studied this question. I was reduced to sharing my lack of knowledge with the audience and telling a few amusing stories.

After the conference, I met with my co-organizer (Dr. Ron Brown), and we decided we should do our own research. We were working at a hospital with a strong interest in BPD. Surely we could find out what happened to all these people.

We obtained seed money to carry out the study, and the results were published a few years later (Paris, Brown, & Nowlis, 1987). What we did not know is that several other groups were asking precisely the same question and monitoring their own cohorts. This convergence was a classic example of scientific serendipity.

This was actually not the first time that research groups had examined the outcome of BPD. But no one in the past had monitored them long enough to find out whether they stayed the same, recovered, or killed themselves.

EARLY STUDIES

The first person to write about the outcome of BPD was Melitta Schmideberg, daughter of the famous psychoanalyst Melanie Klein. In a memorable phrase, Schmideberg (1959) described the course of these patients as "stably unstable." But that was only a clinical impression, not a conclusion based on data.

Roy Grinker was the first to conduct serious research on the outcome of BPD. His group systematically followed up a group of 51 patients who had been treated at Chicago's Michael Reese Hospital (Grinker, Werble, & Drye, 1968). This cohort had been admitted to a psychodynamically oriented inpatient ward that specialized in long-term psychotherapy. Although follow-up assessment was somewhat informal, the main findings supported Schmideberg: After 5 years, most patients had changed little.

Similar findings emerged when Harrison Pope studied 33 patients who had been admitted to McLean Hospital in Boston (Pope, Jonas, & Hudson, 1983). After 5 years, the cohort had not recovered and had not developed other mental disorders.

That was the level of knowledge prior to the 1980s. The real questions remained unanswered: For a chronic disorder like BPD, 5 years is too brief a period to determine outcome.

OUTCOME STUDIES FROM THE 1980s

Tom McGlashan, who is prominent in the study of first-episode schizophrenia, practiced for many years at a hospital in Maryland called Chestnut Lodge. Although now closed, The Lodge was a famous institution in its time. This is the hospital where Frieda Fromm-Reichmann worked, inspiring the semifictional story of the popular novel and movie *I Never Promised You a Rose Garden* (Joanne Greenberg, the patient who described her treatment, went on to become a successful writer and make a sustained recovery).

The Chestnut Lodge study (McGlashan, 1986) monitored a

large number of patients and had a solid methodology. Applying the then-new DSM-III criteria, a reliable baseline diagnosis was established. The follow-up assessment was quite comprehensive, and the BPD sample was large ($N = 87$). Of particular importance, McGlashan was able to locate almost 90% of his cohort, making use of a credit agency to contact people all over the country. He reported that no one was offended or upset about this procedure, and that one person even said to him "Oh yes, Chestnut Lodge—I was wondering when you would call." These patients had spent several years of their youth living at Chestnut Lodge, and most were grateful for their treatment.

The results of the study showed that, 15 years after the beginning of their therapy, most patients had improved greatly. The mean global assessment of functioning (GAF) score was 64, in the range of mild impairment. Only 4 (3%) of the patients had committed suicide. These findings contrasted with the follow-up of another cohort of patients with schizophrenia, who did not recover.

A second study was conducted at Austen Riggs, another famous psychoanalytically oriented private hospital located in the Berkshires (Erik Erikson worked there for a number of years). Unlike Chestnut Lodge, Austen Riggs is still open, surviving the managed-care era by offering shorter hospitalizations and more day treatment.

Erik Plakun was the leader of the Austen Riggs study (Plakun, Burkhardt, & Muller, 1985). The methodology was not as rigorous as in the Chestnut Lodge study; follow-up was by questionnaire rather than telephone interview, only one-third of the patients were located, and there were no data on suicide. Nonetheless, the results after 15 years were very similar. Most patients had improved, and the mean GAF score after 15 years was 67.

Both of these studies were limited by the nature of their clientele. Although extended hospitalization was once considered de rigueur for BPD, it was only available to people from very wealthy families. Would the results have been the same in less expensive settings?

The Department of Psychiatry at Columbia University is located in a large state-funded hospital, New York State Psychiatric Institute (PI), where treatment is largely free. One of the wards specialized in BPD. However, the patients who were admitted to that facility came from higher socioeconomic levels. Referral patterns favored young intelligent patients (some of them VIPs) who received intensive psychotherapy over an extended period on a ward, which was, at the time, a gold standard for treatment.

Michael Stone is a psychiatrist who had worked at PI for many years. Stone (1990) conducted a follow-up study, and he did so without a grant. His advantage was that he knew many of the patients and their families personally. Using his own telephone with great tenacity, Stone obtained data on 90% of the cohort (more than 225 patients), even though in some cases he had to depend on information by family members rather than direct contact. His sample was large, with 200 patients meeting DSM criteria for BPD at baseline. The mean follow-up period was 15 years.

Again, results were encouraging, if a bit more sobering. Most patients recovered, with a mean GAF at a similar level (63). But Stone found a suicide rate of 9%.

The Chestnut Lodge, Austen Riggs, and Columbia studies all came up with similar findings. But the samples did not resemble community profiles of BPD, which included patients with low educational and socioeconomic levels. That is where our own Montreal study made a unique contribution. We monitored a cohort of patients treated at an urban general hospital for a mean of 15 years. Most fell in the lower socioeconomic classes (IV or V). Another difference was that our patients had not had long hospital admissions or extensive follow-up therapy but rather brief admissions (sometimes with no further treatment).

We could not find as many patients as Stone or McGlashan. I identified 300 charts of patients who met criteria for BPD, but only located half of the cohort, and in the end interviewed only 100 individuals. This group resembled the original 300 on all parameters, and we also knew that 50 others were alive. But we cannot say what happened to those whom we never found (quite a few were transients who were almost impossible to locate).

Ours was the only group to rediagnose recovered patients using DSM-III criteria. We found that only 25% still had BPD. The mean GAF score was 63. These results suggest that BPD patients get better even if they are not well educated and wealthy. On the other hand, the suicide rate (8.5%) in our cohort was similar to that reported by Stone.

In summary, despite differences in samples and methodology, four studies published in the 1980s of the 15-year outcome of borderline patients obtained virtually identical results. Mean scores for global functioning fell within a mild range of impairment. In all cohorts, rehospitalization was uncommon after the first few years, and by the time of follow-up, most patients were working and had some kind of social network. All domains of BPD (dysphoria, impulsivity, disturbed relationships, and cognition) showed improvement over time. Suicide rates were similar in two of the three studies that measured them.

In spite of the long-term risk of completed suicide, 15-year studies documented much greater improvement than had been seen in earlier 5-year studies. In many cases, recovery requires more time, perhaps 10 years or more after first presentation (although some patients recovered at earlier or later points).

The results of all these studies are summarized in Table 6.1.

TABLE 6.1. Naturalistic Long-Term Follow-Up Studies of Patients with BPD

	Chestnut Lodge[a]	Austen Riggs[b]	Columbia[c]	Montreal: 15-year follow-up[d]	Montreal: 27-year follow-up[e]
Site	Private hospital	Private hospital	State hospital	General hospital	General hospital
Mean years	15	15	15	15	27
% located	86	27	91	32	25
Mean age	47	37	40	39	51
Male/female	16/84	38/62	48/52	20/80	19/81
Socioeconomic status	High	High	High	Low	Low
BPD diagnosis	DSM-III	DSM-III	DSM-III	DIB	DIB
% still BPD	Not assessed	Not assessed	Not assessed	25	8
Mean GAF	64	67	63	63	63
% early death	Unknown	Unknown	13	4	8
% suicide	3	Unknown	9	9	10
Age at suicide	Unknown	Unknown	30	30	38
% married	70	Unknown	Females: 52 Males: 29	59	59
% with children	48	Unknown	Females: 25 Males: 15	59	59

Note. GAF, Global Assessment of Functioning; DSM-III, *Diagnostic and Statistical Manual of Mental Disorders*, 3rd edition; DIB, Diagnostic Interview for Borderlines.
[a]McGlashan (1986); [b]Plakun et al. (1985); [c]Stone (1990); [d]Paris et al. (1987); [e]Paris & Zweig-Frank (2001).

PREDICTING OUTCOME

BPD patients have a wide range of variability in outcome. Several researchers have attempted to identify predictive factors for how well patients function in the long term. McGlashan (1985) reported that the strongest correlates of a positive outcome were higher intelligence, lower levels of affective instability, and shorter length of previous hospitalization (although none accounted for a large percentage of the variance). Stone (1990) found substance abuse to be a predictor of negative outcome. Our group (Paris, Nowlis, & Brown, 1989) found very few predictors of any kind at 15 years. However, in a longer follow-up, we reported that patients who were doing well at the 15-year mark continued to improve, whereas those who were not doing well did not improve as much (Zweig-Frank & Paris, 2002).

A few researchers have tried to determine whether early developmental experiences have any relationship to long-term outcome. Our own study reported a small correlation between a chart review-derived measure of problems with mothers during childhood and poorer outcome scores (Paris, Brown, & Nowlis, 1988). We later compared a group of women who had recovered from BPD with those who had not and found that childhood sexual abuse was more frequent in those who remained symptomatic (Paris, Zweig-Frank, & Guzder, 1993). That finding was consistent with a later report by Soloff et al. (2002), who found that child sexual abuse is associated with more suicidality in BPD. Stone (1990) reported a relationship between "parental brutality" and outcome in the PI cohort that accounted for 7% of the outcome variance. (However, Stone carried out all assessments himself as opposed to an independent observer unaware of outcome.)

None of these findings are strong or consistent enough to be clinically useful. There is too much variability in outcome in BPD to make predictions about the prognosis of any individual patient.

LONG-TERM OUTCOME AND SUICIDE

Suicide completions are the downside of the outcome story. The findings are not totally consistent. There was a discrepancy between a higher rate in two cohorts (PI and Montreal) and a lower rate in the Chestnut Lodge group that is difficult to explain. (It is possible that patients at Chestnut Lodge were an unusual group, sifted through referrals from other hospitals). However, high suicide completion rates for BPD have also been described in two other settings: 8% in a Norwegian study (Kjelberg, Eikeseth, & Dahl, 1991) and 10% in an unpublished study of 70 patients from Toronto (Silver & Cardish, 1991). These findings from naturalistic studies suggest that the risk for completed suicide in BPD patients is significant, but, as is discussed later, suicide rates in prospective studies are lower.

Research has failed to identify clinically useful predictors for suicide. The problem is not unique to BPD: Even in very large samples of psychiatric patients, a large number of false positives prevents risk factors, even when statistically significant, from being of real practical value (Paris, 2007). Although the number of previous attempts has some relationship to completion in BPD (Paris et al., 1988; Stone, 1990; Kullgren, 1988), most patients with multiple attempts never complete suicide. In the PI cohort (Stone, 1990), substance abuse was statistically associated with completion, but there were many false positives. Our own study (Paris et al., 1987) found that patients with higher education were more likely to complete suicide. But none of these predictors account for enough of the variance to be useful clinical markers.

Psychological autopsy studies have the advantage that they can examine BPD suicides that never present clinically. Lesage et al. (1994) studied people between the ages of 18 and 35 who committed suicide. (As already noted in Chapter 1, about one third of this cohort had BPD, and many of the suicides were men who were not in treatment.) This study reported a correlation between higher rates and separation or loss early in life and completion. However, in a much larger study (120 patients with BPD, of whom 70 committed suicide), our group (McGirr et al., 2007) did not confirm that finding. Instead, we noted that substance abuse was a predictor of completion, a finding also reported by Stone (1990). We also found (McGirr et al., 2007) that completers had lower levels of affective instability and cognitive symptoms; impulsivity seemed to be the key factor. But these findings did not provide support for the concept of predicting and preventing completion. Patients who completed suicide had a history of fewer previous attempts and less treatment and were mostly men. Because many of these findings differ from what has been observed in clinical samples, patients with BPD who kill themselves may not resemble the women we see who attend clinics and threaten suicide repeatedly.

What implications can we draw for practice? Suicidality is

frightening, and concern might seem to be justified by a 10% completion rate. Yet 90% of BPD patients do not die by suicide. Even those who make multiple threats and attempts usually survive. Moreover, one cannot predict which individuals will eventually complete suicide. In Chapter 12, I suggest that therapists need to give up on the idea of preventing suicide in this population and concentrate on other issues.

This conclusion is supported by the findings of our 27-year follow-up study (Paris & Zweig-Frank, 2001). The overall rate of suicide completion in this cohort increased to 10.3% (35% among males and 65% among females. The mean age at suicide was 37.3 (SD = 10.3). Thus, completions occur late in the course of illness, whereas few occur among patients in their 20s, when attempts are so common. These results were similar to those obtained by Stone (1990), who found a mean age of 30 for suicide completions (and might have observed later suicides if he had also followed the cohort for another 12 years).

The key clinical point is that patients with BPD do not kill themselves early in the course of their illness, when they are in their early 20s, even if this is the age when these patients are most likely to terrify us with suicidal threats and attempts. Rather, they committed suicide much later in their course, usually after many failed attempts at treatment. Thus, the patients who died by suicide were the ones who failed to recover.

In summary, outcome research on BPD offers a degree of reassurance about the danger of completion. Suicide usually occurs late in the course of the illness and not in younger patients, who alarm therapists the most. Suicide in BPD does not occur in the midst of a crisis. It happens in patients who fail to recover and when treatment has failed.

OUTCOME OF BPD AT AGE 50

The mean age of all the cohorts studied after 15 years was close to 40. But what happens after that? Do patients continue to improve, or do they get worse?

McGlashan (1986) found that some of the older participants in the Chestnut Lodge cohort showed diminished social functioning in spite of initial improvement, possibly because of continued sensitivity to stressors at midlife. McGlashan encouraged me to carry out a longer follow-up of our own cohort.

Our group eventually carried out a 27-year follow-up of patients with BPD (Paris & Zweig-Frank, 2001; Zweig-Frank & Paris, 2002). By and large, the results were reassuring. Rather than suffering relapses, most patients continued to improve as they grew older.

Data were obtained on 81 patients of the cohort of 100 that we had studied after 15 years. In the intervening years, five had died from natural causes, and there were three suicides. Nine patients known to be alive did not accept follow-up. In the end, 64 individuals (12 men and 52 women) who had reached a mean age of 51 were interviewed.

Mean GAF scores had not changed, probably because of a ceiling effect (i.e., most patients never stopped having mild symptoms). However, only 8% of the cohort now met criteria for BPD. As measured by the DIB-R, the most striking improvement between the two follow-up points was in quality of relationships. Similarly, social adjustment, as measured by a standard scale, was close to normative values.

On Axis I, only 5% had major depression or substance abuse. However, 22% of the cohort still had a diagnosis of dysthymia. These mild depressive symptoms, associated with affective instability, are the most persistent aspect of BPD. (When I interviewed female patients, they often attributed them to menopause, although I knew that they had experienced very similar symptoms in their youth.) Early-onset dysthymia is highly comorbid with BPD and is one of the most common Axis I comorbidities in BPD. In addition, affective lability changes more slowly over time than does impulsivity.

As noted, the strongest predictor of 27-year outcome was level of functioning at the 15-year follow-up. In contrast to our earlier reports, childhood experiences, as measured by self-report scales concerning parental neglect or abuse histories, had no relationship to current functioning.

I have already commented on the significance of the age at which suicide completions occurred. However, in addition to a 10% suicide rate, our cohort had an unusually high rate of early death (7.9%), a finding also reported by Stone (1990). In total, 18.2% of the original sample had died, either from natural causes or from suicide, a much higher rate than would be expected for a population of this age. This high level of long-term mortality tells us that BPD is life threatening in more than one way. These are not patients with a healthy lifestyle, and longevity is affected accordingly.

PROSPECTIVE STUDIES OF BPD OUTCOME

The 15-year follow-up studies of BPD all used what has been called a "follow-back" method. Researchers searched for patients who were identified by chart review. Although neither Austen Riggs nor my own group found most of the potential participants, the studies that did (Chestnut Lodge and PI) obtained very similar results. This similarity was reassuring. Results were not greatly invalidated by missing patients, who might have done either much worse or much better than those who were located.

However, outcome research benefits greatly from prospective designs, in which patients are assessed and monitored over years. That method provides more reliable baseline data, allowing outcome predictors to be identified more accurately. If researchers can minimize attrition, keeping track of most of their sample, prospective research has real advantages.

All the same, there are limitations to the method. How many patients with BPD are likely to sign up for prospective studies? Patients who agree to be followed over time probably have unusual characteristics, such as higher compliance, that make them somewhat different from the populations seen by clinicians. Moreover, to reduce attrition, prospective studies of BPD ensure that patients have access to long-term management, which could confound treatment effects with naturalistic recovery. In the real clinical world, BPD patients are impulsive and do not necessarily stay in treatment. In our own naturalistic cohort, only a minority had any regular therapy at all.

Thus, prospectively followed patients with BPD tend to be somewhat healthier at baseline than those whom we only see in an emergency room or in crisis clinics. Such cohorts can be expected to have a better prognosis. If patients who enroll in prospective studies are unusually agreeable, that characteristic could also make them more likely to improve over time, as opposed to the difficult and noncompliant patients we see in practice.

For this reason, we should not dismiss follow-back studies of outcome in favor of prospective data. Naturalistic studies suggest a much more chronic course, consistent with the DSM-IV definition of personality disorders, whereas prospective studies give a more optimistic picture.

The first major prospective study of BPD was conducted at McMaster University in Hamilton, Ontario (Links, Heslegrave, & van Reekum, 1998). A research group led by Paul Links studied a cohort of 130 former inpatients, 88 of whom had a diagnosis of BPD and 42 of whom had "borderline traits." At the 7-year follow-up, there was attrition, with the loss of one third of the original cohort. Two patients had died of natural causes and six had committed suicide.

The results showed a pattern similar to that seen in follow-back research. After 7 years, about half of the cohort still met criteria for BPD and a similar percentage showed symptomatic remission. Although this level of recovery was less than that observed at 15-year follow-up, it might have been more similar if the study had gone on longer. Similarly, the suicide rate was 7%. The study found that severity of initial pathology was the best predictor of outcome, accounting for 17% of the variance. Patients with serious substance abuse (about one quarter of the sample) had a worse outcome. The main limitation of this study was that 7 years is not long enough to observe recovery or establish a definitive suicide rate.

We now have much more data on outcome from two major studies prospectively following BPD patients. The largest study of BPD outcome is the NIMH Collaborative Study of Personality Disorders (CLPS; Skodol et al., 2005), conducted at several sites (Harvard, Columbia, Yale, and Brown Universities). It has been tracking 155 patients with BPD (as well as comparison groups with three other Axis II disorders) for 10 years.

The results of this research (Skodol et al., 2005; Grilo et al., 2004) show that most BPD patients had reduced symptoms within 2 years, and that about half no longer met diagnostic criteria by that point. This surprisingly rapid rate of recovery was very encouraging. On the other hand, the mean GAF scores for this cohort remained stable, suggesting that patients did not improve functionally as much as they did symptomatically. Thus, even though patients stopped overdosing and cutting, they continued to have interpersonal problems. Because these problems continued to affect functioning, one might say that these patients "graduated" from BPD to a diagnosis of personality disorder NOS.

Although patients in the CLPS study have been monitored now for almost 10 years, almost all the published results concern only 2-

year outcome. Gunderson, Daversa, et al. (2006) reported that the strongest predictors of 2-year outcome were low functioning at baseline, poor current relationships, and childhood trauma. In another report, Skodol et al. (2007) noted that positive childhood experiences were predictors of recovery in BPD.

A second prospective follow-up study of BPD has been carried out over 10 years at McLean Hospital (Zanarini, Frankenburg, Hennen, Reich, & Silk, 2005). A previously admitted cohort of 290 patients with BPD was compared with 72 patients who had other Axis II diagnoses. By 2 years, almost 40% of patients no longer met criteria for the disorder, and by 10 years the remission rate was 88%. Moreover, these patients only rarely relapsed (6%) once recovered. After 6 years, psychosocial functioning was rated as good in 60% of cases, suggesting an even greater improvement than in the CLPS study. (However, the study did not specifically report how many patients were working regularly or in stable relationships.) The 10-year outcome has now been examined, and the strongest predictors of improvement were younger age as well as the absence of childhood sexual abuse, family history of substance use disorder, and comorbid anxious cluster personality disorder. Other predictors were work experience, low levels of neuroticism, and high levels of agreeableness (Zanarini, Frankenburg, Hennen, Reich, & Silk, 2006).

Both research groups (Skodol et al., 2005; Zanarini et al., 2005) concluded from their data that BPD is a mixture of traits and symptoms. Although problematical traits remain stable over time (accounting for residual dysfunction), symptoms tend to remit.

Other studies have also confirmed the temporal instability of BPD and other Axis II categories. Lenzenweger, Johnson, and Willett (2004), who have followed a large group of university students over time, described declines in all features of personality pathology.

All the studies are summarized in Table 6.2.

Thus, prospective findings raise doubts about the validity of the definition in DSM, which implies that personality disorders must necessarily be chronic. In addition, as discussed in Chapter 1, problems derive from the way these disorders are defined. Even in the more encouraging prospective studies, we do not see full recovery, even if patients have fewer symptoms.

However, whatever their implications for diagnosis, outcome research on BPD has enormous clinical implications. With all their limitations, we have to be encouraged that both follow-back and prospective studies have shown that most patients improve with time. It

TABLE 6.2. Prospective Studies of BPD Outcome

	Hamilton[a]	CLPS[b]	McLean[c]
Site	General hospital	Multisite, general hospitals	Psychiatric hospital
n	88	155	290
Diagnosis	DIB	DSM-IV	DIB and DSM-III-R
Years follow-up	7	2	10
Mean age at baseline	34	18–45 (range)	27
Male/female	15–85	25–75	23–77
Socioeconomic status	Low	Wide range	Wide range
% still BPD	47%	42%	12%
% suicide	7.7%	Not reported	4%
Employed	58%	Not reported	Not reported
Married	37%	Not reported	Not reported

Note. DIB, Diagnostic Interview for Borderlines; DSM-IV, *Diagnostic and Statistical Manual of Mental Disorders*, 4th edition, DSM-III-R, DSM, 3rd edition, revised.
[a]Links et al. (1998); [b]Skodol et al. (2005); Grilo et al. (2004); [c] Zanarini, Frankenburg et al. (2005).

used to be thought that a diagnosis of BPD doomed patients to a life of misery. We now know this is not true. On the contrary, therapists should be comfortable in telling their patients that no matter how distressed they feel in the present, they can expect to get better in the future.

MECHANISMS OF RECOVERY

Several mechanisms lie behind the recovery process in BPD. In long-term follow of studies of community populations, impulsivity tends to decrease with age, a process that could reflect biological maturation (Vaillant, 1977). Thus, patients with BPD recover in much the same way as those who suffer from other impulsive disorders: alcoholism (Vaillant, 1995), ASPD (Black, Baumgard, & Bell, 1995), and bulimia nervosa (Keel, Mitchell, Miller, Davis, & Crow, 1999).

A second mechanism involves social learning. Although patients with BPD are slow to learn from experience, they can increase their skills over time. Improvement could also come from finding supportive relationships and choosing less pathological partners. Many patients drop out early from school, have difficulty establishing a career, experience periods of unemployment, and have problems finding stable friendship. Yet patients who recover eventually overcome most of these difficulties. Most patients in follow-up cohorts eventually obtained employment and established social networks. As is discussed in later chapters, this finding has implications for therapy. Patients with BPD need to commit themselves to work, where structure helps contain their pathology and where personal rejection is somewhat less likely.

Follow-up research also points to another mechanism for improvement: avoidance of intimacy. For most of us, intimacy is the most difficult thing in life to achieve. Patients with BPD find remaining close to another person without conflict particularly hard. Only half ever settle down in an intimate relationship permanently, but many recovered patients find satisfaction in less demanding relationships.

In the PI cohort (Stone, 1990), only 52% of the women ever married and only 25% ever had children; for men the rates were 29% and 15%, respectively. Among those who did marry, the divorce rate was one third, not excessive compared with national averages; but when marriages broke down, only 10% remarried, much less than national averages. In our cohort (Paris & Zweig-Frank, 2001), the rate of marriage was 67%, with a 36% rate of divorce. However, at 27-year follow-up, only 42% were currently living in a stable relationship and 41% remained childless.

If patients do have a long-term relationship, its success will depend, at least in part, on the personality characteristics of the partners they choose (Paris & Braverman, 1995). Some women with BPD are attracted to narcissistic men who find them initially attractive and later become abusive or abandoning. Caretaking partners may be more stable, although in my clinical experience such dyads can also run into trouble if there is insufficient limit setting.

Although I lack systematic data to confirm my hypothesis that patients with BPD improve by avoiding intimacy, clinical interviews with recovered patients often elicit descriptions of learning *not* to fall in love. Highly charged relationships create numerous problems for these patients. Over time, they learn that intimacy is dangerous. Being comfortably alone and finding other, less conflictual, ways of establishing social networks and support makes serious difficulty less likely. Less intimate friends, extended family, community organizations such as churches, as well as the presence of a pet can fill gaps left by the absence of intimacy.

Although some patients do achieve stable intimacy with time, therapists should not press patients to have relationships they cannot manage. On the contrary, they should encourage patients with BPD to be careful about falling in love. I advise young people to "take a break" from intimacy and reinforce alternatives to intimacy in older people. Successful treatment is not measured by the attainment of this kind of relationship. Therapy need not end with a piece of wedding cake.

There has been little research on the effects of parenthood on women with BPD. A surprising number remain childless. Parenthood also requires the management of intimacy, and some mothers seem to develop "borderline relationships" with their children. In our own study (Weiss et al., 1996), the children of mothers with BPD were highly symptomatic, and family life was dysfunctional (Feldman et al., 1995).

However, my clinical experience has been that patients with BPD who become mothers (in or out of a marriage or stable relationship) tend to give up impulsive behaviors, largely because they want to protect their children. (Some mothers have told me that they do not want to expose the next generation to the kind of experiences they had growing up.) Thus, mothers who have had BPD tend to give up cutting, no longer overdose, and stop using drugs. Women who do not make these changes in behavior end up being involved with the child protection system, and some lose custody. However, even when patients with BPD are less impulsive, they may retain problems in work and interpersonal functioning. Like the improved patients in prospective studies, they tend to "graduate" to a DSM diagnosis of personality disorder NOS.

TREATMENT AND RECOVERY

BPD is chronic but remits with time. Thus, response to treatment needs to be assessed in the context of recovery. Successful therapy has to do better than the healing effects of time and maturity. When patients improve after years of treatment, we do not usually know whether the outcome is the result of therapy or of "waiting out" the pathology.

This question was addressed in a meta-analysis of treatment studies of patients with personality disorders (Perry, Banon, & Ianni, 1999). The authors estimated from long-term outcome data that 3.7% of patients with impulsive personality disorders remit each year, and, based on estimates from studies of cases in psychotherapy, a mean of 25.8% patients a year are likely to recover. Although these figures seem encouraging, they are too optimistic. The problem is that this meta-analysis was drawn from a small base of data (including uncontrolled or partially controlled studies of varying provenance). Moreover, we now know that the rate of naturalistic recovery is actually much higher (Skodol et al., 2005; Zanarini et al., 2005).

To assess the long-term impact of therapy, patients need to be monitored over time. Most treatment studies last for a year or less, sufficient for major depression but not for BPD. Although research has demonstrated short-term symptomatic improvement, mainly in relation to impulsivity (in response to both drugs and psychotherapy), we do not know whether improvements are stable over time. For example, Linehan, Armstrong, Suarez, Allman, and Heard's (1991) cohort of patients treated with dialectical behavior therapy conducted in the 1980s was only followed up for 1 year.

Nonetheless, the prognosis of BPD is relatively good, with an outcome that is much better than for other major mental disorders. It has been suggested, semijocularly, that patients should be told not to commit suicide, because they only need to wait a few years before feeling better. As Chapter 8 documents, psychotherapy may help them to improve even faster.

CLINICAL IMPLICATIONS

- Most patients with BPD improve with time.
- Complete remission is less likely than gradual improvement followed by a plateau of stability.
- Patients can be told that whatever else they have heard about BPD they will probably get better.

CHAPTER 7

Pharmacotherapy

More and more, the treatment of patients with mental disorders has come to center on drug therapy. In some respects, this represents an advance. Over the years psychopharmacology has had many triumphs. A large number of drugs have a strong evidence base for efficacy. Schizophrenia can be controlled—even if not cured—by neuroleptics. Lithium is effective for treating bipolar disorder as well as for preventing recurrences. The treatment of depression is far from universally effective, but antidepressants help many patients, and anxiety disorders, particularly panic attacks and obsessive–compulsive disorder, respond to the same drugs.

BPD is a major mental disorder, in the same way as these other disorders. It might, therefore, seem logical to treat it with medication. However, the data do not clearly support doing so. The thrust of this chapter is to show that drugs are being overprescribed for BPD.

The main reason is that the drugs at our disposal were developed for other purposes. We can prescribe antipsychotics, but patients with BPD do not have true psychosis. We can prescribe antidepressants, but patients with BPD do not have classic depression. We can prescribe mood stabilizers, but the affective instability of BPD is not the same as the symptoms of bipolar disorder.

The biological mechanisms associated with BPD symptoms may

be entirely different from those of other major mental disorders. That is why using the drugs we already have to treat this disorder does not work too well. The analogy that comes to mind is the situation that faced psychiatrists before the development of neuroleptics. They had to find a way to calm agitated psychotic patients. One way to achieve that end was to prescribe sedative drugs like barbiturates. However, these agents had no effect on the underlying psychotic process.

The situation need not be permanent. When we understand the biological vulnerability behind BPD, we may be able to develop entirely new drugs to treat these patients, as different from what we have now as neuroleptics were from barbiturates. But we need to stop fooling ourselves by assuming that we already have effective drugs for patients with BPD.

I have presented these views at conferences and in writing. Some people are reassured by what I have to say: They can stop worrying about missing some magic cocktail combining the latest pharmaceuticals. Others have criticized me. Some colleagues complain I am encouraging clinicians to deny patients the benefit of modern drug therapy. My answer is: *Prove it to me.* The evidence for the efficacy of pharmacotherapy in BPD is very weak, as this chapter shows.

This is not to say we should not prescribe at all. Drugs that are currently available have a useful, if marginal, role in the treatment of BPD. Although none have much effect on the core pathology behind the disorder or produce a remission, drugs can "take the edge off" symptoms. That is certainly worth something.

The most serious criticism of contemporary practice is the ubiquity of polypharmacy. It has long been a principle in medicine that physicians should treat diseases, not symptoms. When we prescribe multiple drugs to patients with BPD, we forget that we do not understand what we are treating. Moreover, drugs from entirely different groups produce very similar effects in patients with BPD. For this reason, one drug for symptomatic relief is usually enough.

After reaching these conclusions, I was reassured to obtain support from a highly reputable source. The Cochrane Report is a website based in the United Kingdom that publishes regular and expert reviews of medical treatment. In contrast to other reviews, Cochrane requires the highest level of proof to make a clinical recommendation. Case reports and open trials are not even considered. RCTs are almost always required. When samples are small, Cochrane is unimpressed. If single RCTs without replications are all that is available, Cochrane will still be unimpressed. In accord with the principles of evidence-based medicine, Cochrane requires multiple studies or meta-analyses to support its recommendations.

A Cochrane report on the psychopharmacological treatment of BPD was published in 2006. Its conclusion was that the evidence is too weak to recommend any drug for these patients (Binks et al., 2006a).

All the same, many if not most BPD patients today are, for better or worse, receiving multiple medications. As Zanarini et al. (2001) have documented, many are given four or five different agents. Let us begin by examining the data on each of the groups of drugs that are being so readily prescribed. We then return to the issue of drug combinations. I concentrate on the results of RCTs. See Table 7.1 for a summary.

In evidence-based medicine, RCTs are the gold standard. It must be acknowledged that, although clinical trials generally provide the best evidence for drug efficacy, patients recruited into them are often unrepresentative of clinical populations, who tend to be much sicker than the individuals who participate in research (Westen & Morrison, 2000). Nonetheless, the superiority of RCTs to open trials or clinical opinion is overwhelming.

NEUROLEPTICS

In line with the idea that BPD lies on a border with psychosis, neuroleptics have long been prescribed for these patients. However, their effects are not specific to this population.

Antipsychotic drugs have been used for a number of "off-label" purposes, particularly for controlling behavioral problems (as in dementia and mental retardation). Early clinical reports have suggested that patients with BPD tend to calm down and become less impulsive when treated with these agents (Gunderson, 1984). As we see, there is some support from clinical trials for these effects.

The problem with prescribing neuroleptics involves cost and benefit. "Typical" neuroleptics such as chlorpromazine or haloperidol often cause an extrapyramidal syndrome and can also produce tardive dyskinesia (TD). Any drug that leads to this irreversible neurological condition needs to be avoided if possible. And TD is only the most worrying of a long list of side effects. When treating schizophrenia or mania, one has to accept these risks. But cost–benefit is

TABLE 7.1. RCTs of Pharmacotherapy for BPD

Trial	Study subjects and outcome measures	Study arms and duration	Results	Comments	Funding source
Cowdry & Gardner (1988)	*Subjects:* 16 women ages 23–42 yr referred by private psychotherapists *Outcome measures:* clinical change rated by physicians and patients using modified Bunney–Hamburg rating scale and 7-point scale similar to CGI; changes in dyscontrol, assessed from physician and patient reports of angry outbursts, physical violence, self-damaging behavior, and suicide threats and attempts	• Alprazolam 1–6 mg/d • Carbamazepine 200–1200 mg/d • Trifluoperazine hydrochloride 2–12 mg/d • Tranylcypromine sulfate 10–60 mg/d • Placebo *Duration:* 2 wk of dose adjustment, 4 wk of treatment, 1 wk of tapering, and ≥ 1 wk drug free before starting next drug	Physicians rated patients as significantly improved relative to placebo while receiving tranylcypromine and carbamazepine. Patients rated themselves as significantly improved relative to placebo only while receiving tranylcypromine.	Given the large number of comparisons in this study, the finding of some statistically significant differences is not unexpected.	U.S. National Institute of Mental Health
Links Steiner et al. (1990)	*Subjects:* 17 patients (16 women) ages 18–45 yr recruited from psychiatric services *Outcome measures:* depression (HAM-D, CSD), anger and suicidal components of SADS–Change questionnaire; therapist assessment of drug therapy	• Lithium, mean dose 986 mg/d • Desipramine, mean dose 162 mg/d • Placebo *Duration:* total 22 wk (3 cycles, each composed of 2-wk dose adjustment, 4 wk of treatment, 1 wk of tapering, 1 wk drug free before starting next cycle)	No statistically significant changes in scores for each study drug relative to placebo. Therapists rated lithium significantly superior to placebo.	Fewer than 14 subjects completed at least 1 of the crossover trials.	Ontario Ministry of Health and Long-Term Care

| Soloff et al. (1989) | Subjects: 90 inpatients (76% women)

Outcome measures: global functioning (GAS, SCL-90); depression (HAM-D, BDI); psychoticism (IMPS); schizotypal symptoms (SSI); hostility (BDHI); impulsivity (Ward Scale, BIS, STIC) | • Amitriptyline ($n = 30$)
• Haloperidol ($n = 31$)
• Placebo ($n = 29$)

Duration: 5 wk | All groups improved on global functioning, depression, and cognitive/schizotypal symptoms. Haloperidol was significantly superior to placebo for improving global functioning, depression, hostility, schizotypal symptoms, and impulsive behaviors. Amitriptyline was significantly superior to placebo only on depressive symptoms, verbal hostility, and STIC score. | Excluded patients who did not receive a minimum of 2 wk worth of medication ($n = 5$) | U.S. National Institute of Mental Health |
| Soloff et al. (1993) | Subjects: 108 inpatients (76% women) ages 16–36 yr (42 with BPD and 66 with BPD and schizotypal personality disorder)

Outcome measures: Depression (HAM-D, BDI); global severity (GAS, SCL-90); anxiety, anger–hostility (SCL-90, IMPS, BDHI); psychoticism (SSI, SCL-90, IMPS); impulsivity (Ward Scale, BIS, SRTIC); symptoms of ADD (derived from ADDS) and borderline psychotherapy (BSI) | • Phenelzine 60 mg/d ($n = 38$)
• Haloperidol 4 mg/d ($n = 36$)
• Placebo ($n = 34$)

Duration: Washout wk followed by 5 wk of treatment and 16 wk of continued treatment for patients responding to medication | All groups improved on measures of depression, anxiety, anger–hostility, and impulsivity. Some statistically significant differences between the three arms were found for some of the multiple outcomes tested. | High dropout rates in all groups, especially among patients who experienced neuroleptic side effects (hypersomnia and leaden paralysis). Given the multiple outcomes measured, the finding of some statistically significant differences is not unexpected. | U.S. National Institute of Mental Health |

(continued)

117

TABLE 7.1. (*continued*)

Trial	Study subjects and outcome measures	Study arms and duration	Results	Comments	Funding source
Nickel et al. (2004)	*Subjects*: 31 women ages 20–35 recruited through general practitioners who met criteria for BPD and had "feelings of constantly increasing anger." *Outcome measures*: Anger (STAXI)	• Topiramate 50–250 mg/d ($n = 21$) • Placebo ($n = 10$) *Duration*: 8 wk— Topiramate was titrated to a dose of 250 mg/day in the 6th week and then stayed constant.	Significant changes (improvement) in scores on 4 of the 5 STAXI scales in topiramate group (anger-out, anger-control, trait anger, and state anger); no statistically significant difference in the anger in scale; no changes in placebo group.	Significant weight loss in experimental group; authors did not use intention-to-treat analysis, but only two people dropped out from experimental group, none from control group. Potential subjects with comorbid major depression, substance abuse, or concurrent medication were excluded.	None
Nickel et al. (2005)	*Subjects*: 44 men recruited through physicians and newspaper ads who met criteria for BPD and had "feelings of constantly increasing anger." *Outcome measures*: anger (STAXI)	• Topiramate 50–250 mg/d ($n = 22$) • Placebo ($n = 22$) *Duration*: 8 wk— Topiramate was titrated to a dose of 250 mg/d in 6th wk and then stayed constant.	Significant changes (improvement) in scores on 4 of the 5 STAXI scales in topiramate group (anger-out, anger-control, trait anger, and state anger); no statistically significant difference in the anger in scale; no changes in placebo group.	Significant weight loss in experimental group; authors did not use intention-to-treat analysis, but only two people dropped out from control group, none from treatment group. Potential subjects with comorbid major depression, substance abuse, or concurrent medication were excluded.	None

Study	Subjects	Intervention	Results	Limitations	Funding
Nickel et al. (2006)	*Subjects*: 52 subjects (43 women) with BPD ages 16 and older *Outcome measures*: global symptom severity (SCL-90-R); depression (HAM-D); anxiety (HAM-A); anger (STAI)	• Aripiprazole 15 mg/day (*n* = 26) • Placebo (*n* = 26) *Duration*: 8 wk	Study group had a significantly greater rate of change than placebo group on all measures, except Somatization scale of SCL-90-R.	Low dropout rate (*n* = 5)	None
Kavoussi & Coccaro (1998)	*Subjects*: 10 outpatients 25–54 yr old (20% female) meeting DSM-IV criteria for at least 1 personality disorder who failed a trial of SSRIs *Outcome measures*: impulsive aggression, irritability (OAS-M)	• Divalproex sodium 500–2,000 mg/d (*n* = 10) *Duration*: 8 wk	6 of 8 completers showed significant improvement on both aggression and irritability scores; mean OAS-M scores at 8 wk significantly lower than baseline.	No control group; two patients did not complete trial. Three cases are presented in detail.	Abbott Laboratories
Hollander et al. (2001)	*Subjects*: 16 outpatients meeting BPD criteria *Outcome measures*: global outcome (CGI-I, GAS), aggression (AQ, OAS-M), depression (BDI), irritability, and suicidality	• Divalproex sodium 250 mg/d, increased to dose necessary to maintain blood valproate level at 80 μg/mL (*n* = 12) • Placebo (*n* = 4) *Duration*: 10 wk	Subjects who completed divalproex treatment (*n* = 6) improved on both GAS and CGI-I. None of the differences in outcomes between placebo and divalproex groups were significant when intent-to-treat analyses were performed.	Small sample size, high dropout rate (only six of the subjects, all in divalproex group, completed treatment).	U.S. National Institute of Mental Health; Abbott Laboratories; National Center for Research Resources, National Institutes of Health; Seaver Foundation; and PBO Foundation *(continued)*

119

TABLE 7.1. (*continued*)

Trial	Study subjects and outcome measures	Study arms and duration	Results	Comments	Funding source
Frankenburg & Zanarini (2002)	*Patients*: 30 women ages 18–40 yr with BPD and bipolar II recruited through newspaper ads *Outcome measures*: SCL-90 scales measuring interpersonal sensitivity, anger–hostility, and depression; OAS–M	• Divalproex, dose adjusted to achieve serum level between 50 and 100 mg/L ($n = 20$) • Placebo ($n = 10$) *Duration*: 6 mo	Based on last completed endpoint measure, there were greater changes in outcome scores in divalproex group than in placebo group.	Only 7 patients in divalproex group and 4 in placebo group completed the study. Based on the data for patients completing study, results show no difference between groups.	Abbott Laboratories
Hollander et al. (2005)	*Subjects*: 52 patients (54% women) with BPD, history of aggression, and score 15 on Aggression scale of OAS-M *Outcome measures*: aggression (OAS-M); impulsivity (BIS); affective stability (YMRS); HAM-D)	• Divalproex 500–2250 mg/d ($n = 20$) • Placebo ($n = 32$) *Duration*: 12 wk	Significant improvement on aggression in divalproex group; greatest improvement in patients with high baseline impulsivity or high baseline aggression scores who took divalproex. Patients with low baseline impulsivity/aggression did not show significant improvement. Baseline affective symptoms did not influence treatment outcome.	Small number of subjects in secondary analyses; was interested in interaction between pretreatment clinical characteristics and drug effect.	Abbott Laboratories

Study	Method	Results	Limitations	Funding
Zanarini & Frankenburg (2001)	*Subjects*: 28 women ages 18–40 yr recruited through newspaper ads who met criteria for BPD *Outcome measures*: SCL-90 subscales measuring anxiety, depression, paranoia, anger-hostility, and interpersonal sensitivity	• Olanzapine 2.5 mg (*n* = 19) • Placebo (*n* = 9) • Doses adjusted in both groups according to perceived response and side effects *Duration*: 6 mo	Olanzapine group showed statistically significant improvement on all components of SCL-90 scale except Depression	Authors did not use intention-to-treat analysis. Only eight subjects in olanzapine group and one subject in placebo group completed the study.	Eli Lilly
Bogenschutz & Nurnberg (2004)	*Subjects*: 40 patients (25 female) ages 18–60 yr recruited from community and outpatient clinics *Outcome measures*: CGI-BPD and global CGI; impulsive aggression (OAS-M and AIAQ); depression (HAM-D); anxiety (HAM-A); global symptom severity (SCL-90); global functioning (GAF); alcohol use (ASI); movement disorders (AIMS, BAS, SAS)	• Olanzapine 2.5–20 mg as titrated over time (*n* = 16) • Placebo (*n* = 19) *Duration*: 12 wk	Olanzapine group showed significantly greater improvement than placebo group on CGI-BPD and global CGI; secondary measures did not show significant difference at endpoint, although some (GAF, AIAQ, and HAM-D) showed significant differences at 8 wk.	Only 23 patients completed the trial. Results for global scale presented only in graphs, without confidence intervals. No intention-to-treat analysis.	Eli Lilly

(*continued*)

TABLE 7.1. (*continued*)

Trial	Study subjects and outcome measures	Study arms and duration	Results	Comments	Funding source
Salzman et al. (1995)	*Subjects*: 22 patients recruited through newspaper ads *Outcome measures*: Global mood and functioning, anger and depression (HAM-D, GAS, PDRS, POMS, OAS-R)	• Fluoxetine 20 mg/d titrated to maximum of 60 mg/d (*n* = 13) • Placebo (*n* = 9) *Duration*: 13 wk	Both groups showed some improvement. Secondary analyses showed clinically and statistically significant decrease in anger in fluoxetine group.	Multiple secondary analyses done despite the finding of no significant differences between study groups in primary outcome measures except self-reported mood.	Not stated
Coccaro & Kavoussi (1997)	*Subjects*: 40 patients recruited by outpatient referral or self-referral through public service announcements *Outcome measures*: Aggression and Irritability subscales of OAS-M; physician-rated CGI-I and patient-rated AIAQ	• Fluoxetine 20–60 mg/d (*n* = 27) • Placebo (*n* = 13) *Duration*: 2-wk single-blind placebo lead-in phase followed by randomization and 12-wk follow-up	Sustained reduction in scores on OAS-M Aggression and Irritability subscales with fluoxetine relative to placebo; fluoxetine was superior to placebo in proportion of subjects showing improvement on CGI-I; no difference between groups in self-reported AIAQ measures.	Of 64 patients entered in 2-wk placebo lead-in phase, only 40 were eligible for randomized treatment phase. Only 14 patients in fluoxetine group and 9 in placebo group completed the trial. No intention-to-treat analysis.	U.S. National Institute of Mental Health and Eli Lilly

Study	Subjects/Methods	Results	Comments	Funding
Simpson et al. (2004)	*Subjects:* 25 women with BPD (mean age 35 yr) recruited from 5-day dialectical behavior therapy program involving partial hospitalization *Outcome measures:* BDI, STAI, OAS-M, DES, STAXI, GAF	• Fluoxetine 40 mg/d ($n = 12$) • Placebo ($n = 13$) • All patients received dialectical behavior therapy *Duration:* 12 wk	No statistically significant difference between groups in any outcome measure	Multiple primary outcomes	Brown University Medical School and Eli Lilly
Zanarini, Frankenburg, & Parachini (2004)	*Subjects:* 45 women ages 18–40 yr recruited through newspaper ads who met criteria for BPD *Outcome measures:* Depression (MADRS) and impulsive aggression (OAS-M)	• Fluoxetine 10 mg ($n = 14$) • Olanzapine 2.5 mg ($n = 16$) • Fluoxetine 10 mg plus olanzapine 2.5 mg ($n = 15$) *Duration:* 8 wk	Olanzapine was more effective than fluoxetine in treating both symptom areas studied. Combination treatment was also superior to fluoxetine but not to olanzapine.	Results presented using regression models. All groups improved over time on both outcome measures.	Eli Lilly

(*continued*)

123

TABLE 7.1. (*continued*)

Trial	Study subjects and outcome measures	Study arms and duration	Results	Comments	Funding source
Rinne, vandenBrink et al. (2002)	*Subjects*: 38 women ages 18–50 yr recruited from outpatient clinics, community mental health centers, newspaper and Internet ads *Outcome measures*: subscales (Rapid Mood Shift, Impulsivity, and Aggression) of BPD Severity Index	• Fluvoxamine 150 mg/d (*n* = 20), titrated to maximum of 250 mg/d after wk 10 • Placebo (*n* = 18) *Duration*: 6 wk	No statistically significant differences between groups except for subscale of rapid mood shift	Of 125 subjects screened, 78 met diagnostic criteria; only 38 were entered in trial. The authors did not use intention-to-treat analysis.	De Geestgronden Institute of Mental Health Care, Stichting tot Steun of Vereniging Bennekom, National Fund for Mental Health, and Solvay Pharma
Zanarini & Frankenburg (2003)	*Subjects*: 30 women ages 18–40 yr recruited through newspaper ads who met criteria for BPD *Outcome measures*: OAS-M, MADRS	• E-EPA (an omega-3 fatty acid), 1,000 mg/d (*n* = 20) • Placebo (*n* = 10) *Duration*: 8 wk	Improvement from baseline in both outcome measures significantly greater in E-EPA group than in placebo group	Low dropout rates	Not stated

| Tritt et al. (2005) | Subjects: 24 women ages 20–40 yr, recruited through family doctors' ads and who met criteria for BPD and had "feelings of constantly increasing anger." Outcome measures: anger (STAXI) | • Lamotrigine 50–200 mg/d (n = 18) • Placebo (n = 9) Duration: 8 wk—Lamotrigine dose increased throughout study: 50 mg in 1st 2 weeks, 100 mg in 3rd week, 150 mg in 4th and 5th weeks, 200 mg/day in weeks 6–8 | Significant changes (improvement) in scores on 4 of the 5 STAXI scales in lamotrigine group (anger-out, anger-control, trait anger, and state anger); moderate changes on the anger-in scale; no changes in placebo group. | Very strict exclusion criteria: Substance abusers and those with other comorbid disorders, including major depression, were excluded. | Not stated |

Note. ADDS, Atypical Depression Inventory; AIAQ, Anger, Irritability and Assault Questionnaire; AIMS, Abnormal Involuntary Movement Scale; AQ, Aggression Questionnaire; ASI, Addiction Severity Index; BAS, Barnes Akathisia Scale; BDHI, Buss–Durkee Hostility Inventory; BDI, Beck Depression Inventory; BIS, Barratt Impulsiveness Scale; BPDSI-IV, Borderline Personality Disorder Severity Index (4th version); BSI, Borderline Syndrome Index; CGI, Clinical Global Improvement; CGI-BPD, Clinical Global Impressions Scale modified for Borderline Personality Disorder; CGI-I, Clinician Global Impression Rating of Improvement; CSD, Carroll Scale for Depression; DES, Dissociations Experiences Scale; E-EPA, ethyle-icosapentaenoic acid; GAF, Global Assessment of Functioning Scale; GAS, Global Assessment Scale; HAM-A, Hamilton Rating Scale for Anxiety; HAM-D, Hamilton Rating Scale for Depression; IMPS, Inpatient Multidimensional Psychiatric Scale; MADRS, Montgomery-Asberg Depression Rating Scale; OAS-M, Modified Overt Aggression Scale; OAS-R, Overt Aggression Symptom Checklist; PDRS, Personality Disorder Rating Scale; POMS, Profile of Mood States; PTSD, posttraumatic stress disorder; SADS, Schedule for Affective Disorders and Schizophrenia; SAS, Simpson–Angus Scale; SCL-90, Symptom Checklist-90; SRTIC, Self-Report Test of Impulse Control; SSI, Schizotypal Symptom Inventory; STAI, State–Trait Anxiety Inventory; STAXI, State–Trait Anger Expression Inventory; STIC, Self-Report of Impulse Control; Ward Scale, Ward Scale of Impulse Action Patterns; YMRS, Young Mania Rating Scale.

different in the treatment of nonpsychotic patients who can just as easily be offered less toxic drugs. One should not take a chance with drugs that can damage the brain unless there is a very good reason for prescribing them.

The newer, or "atypical," neuroleptics, such as risperidone, olanzapine, and quetiapine, were developed as better alternatives to older drugs such as chlorpromazine and haloperidol. Many physicians have the false impression that newer drugs are always safer than older ones. That is true in some respects (atypicals are less likely to produce TD). However, atypicals can also be problematic because they can produce striking weight gain accompanied by a "metabolic syndrome" that brings on diabetes mellitus (Newcomer & Haupt, 2006). This serious side effect is particularly likely with olanzapine, one of the most frequently used atypicals.

Atypicals should never be prescribed lightly. However, physicians have been lulled into complacency by the received wisdom that they are safe. I keep hearing about these drugs being used to control anxiety or insomnia. This is an irrational practice, given the existence of less toxic alternatives.

On a short-term basis, neuroleptics can be used to treat micropsychotic phenomena. Although there have been no clinical trials to document this practice, these drugs target psychotic symptoms associated with many forms of mental disorder, and my experience is that they work well for this purpose in BPD. However, once a patient is on a neuroleptic drug, physicians are often afraid to take them off the drug. This might make sense in schizophrenia, in which relapse often follows withdrawal of antipsychotic medication. It does not make sense in BPD, in which psychotic symptoms are either transient or mild.

The other, and more common, use for neuroleptics derives from their overall calming effect, reducing impulsive symptoms (Soloff et al., 2000). However, for the reasons discussed previously, atypicals should not be the first choice. One can try something less toxic first, such as an antidepressant.

Although clinical trials of neuroleptics have been published, they do not compare atypicals with other options. Paul Soloff of the University of Pittsburgh carried out the earliest studies of the efficacy of neuroleptics in BPD (Soloff et al., 1993). The trial concerned haloperidol, then the most commonly prescribed neuroleptic. However, this drug was never good for outpatients. Given its high potency, it is most useful for emergencies in psychotic patients. But it is associated with a very high frequency of extrapyramidal symptoms, even at very small doses, making it a less than optimal choice for maintenance. It was, therefore, not really surprising that Soloff et al. found that patients often stopped taking haloperidol. Moreover, short-term effects (reductions in impulsive behaviors such as cutting and overdosing) were not maintained on 6-month follow-up for those continuing to take this agent.

In spite of their wide usage in current practice, almost all the literature concerning atypical neuroleptics in BPD consists of case reports or open-label trials (Grootens & Verkes, 2005). Only olanzapine has undergone an RCT (Zanarini & Frankenburg, 2001). The results, at least in the short term, were positive, but the sample was small and the follow-up period short. Moreover, BPD is a chronic illness, and none of the patients in this study actually showed a remission. There is also one study (Soler et al., 2005) suggesting that patients receiving dialectical behavior therapy might benefit from adding olanzapine to the regimen.

By and large, antipsychotics should be considered an option for BPD patients who do not respond to antidepressants. And even if effective, these agents should not be taken long term. No one has ever studied the effects of using antipsychotics over several years in personality disorders, and there is evidence that effects do not last (Soloff et al., 1989). As noted, once antipsychotics are prescribed, physicians leave patients on the same drugs for fear of what might happen if they are withdrawn. This results in even more side effects. And patients who become obese when taking atypicals will have additional problems in rehabilitation, not to mention effects on their general health.

SPECIFIC SEROTONIN REUPTAKE INHIBITORS

SSRIs have been widely used for patients with BPD. Yet their efficacy is not impressive.

A large body of research suggests that patients with personality disorders of any category respond less well to antidepressant drugs than do patients who have no personality disorder. Although this conclusion has been challenged (Mulder, 2004), a large-scale meta-analysis (Newton-Howes, Tyrer, & Johnson, 2006) confirmed it.

It is worth questioning why this might be so. One reason is that major depression, as defined by DSM, is not really all that major.

Rather, it is a poorly defined entity describing a heterogeneous group of patients. In the melancholic subtype, one sees a life-threatening illness that can literally come out of the blue. However, most patients fall into the category of major depression simply because they have symptoms of low mood and associated dysfunction for more than 2 weeks. (One wonders how many people have *never* experienced a major depression defined in that way.) Thus, depression is not one thing but many things.

In this light, it should not be that surprising that antidepressants do not always work when people feel depressed, even for those who do *not* have a comorbid diagnosis of personality disorder. One large-scale study (STAR*D) found that only about half of patients with any form of depression have a good response and that even less will attain full remission (Trivedi et al., 2006; Rush, 2007).

Research on patients with BPD shows an even more inconsistent response that fails to match the effects of antidepressants in classical depression. It is not even clear whether these drugs act on mood itself or break cycles that lead to depression through their calming and anti-impulsive effects.

In fact, research suggests that SSRIs (e.g., fluoxetine, paroxetine, sertraline) are most effective in reducing anger and impulsive symptoms in patients with BPD (Salzman et al., 1995; Coccaro & Kavoussi, 1997). High doses (e.g., 60–80 mg fluoxetine) can sometimes produce specific effects on self-injury, although patients have difficulty tolerating these levels (Markowitz, 1995). A direct effect on depression in BPD has not been demonstrated, although one study (Rinne, van den Brink, Wouters, & van Dyck, 2002) reported that mood swings were somewhat stabilized, which could be a secondary effect of reducing impulsivity.

The best thing about SSRIs in BPD is that it is very difficult to commit suicide with them. Potential lethality on overdose is a serious consideration in patients who repeatedly use pills to attempt suicide. For this reason, whatever their merits, neither tricyclic antidepressants nor monoamine oxidase inhibitors (MAOIs) have been popular in the treatment of BPD. Moreover, many patients dislike tricylics because of their anticholinergic side effects, and some MAOIs require a special diet.

Since SSRIs became popular, a number of new antidepressants have arrived "on the block." There is little reason, other than marketing, to believe that they are more effective than the drugs we had before. Although venlafaxine, mirtazapine, and bupropion, among others, are being widely prescribed, none of these drugs has ever been studied in BPD using an RCT or shown to do anything that SSRIs cannot also do.

Psychiatrists and other physicians have taken up the practice of searching for "the right antidepressant," switching from one agent to another or adding them on to each other. As the STAR*D study showed (Rush, 2007), this strategy works only for a minority of patients. It is unlikely to help patients with BPD. Unfortunately, we see many patients who have been through this "merry-go-round," running through every antidepressant on the market. If patients remain on one drug, one cannot tell whether it was effective or whether the prescription was given when the patient was feeling better for other reasons. Given the unstable mood associated with BPD, placebo effects are particularly likely to occur.

It is unusual today to see a patient with BPD who is not on an antidepressant. This practice remains more a matter of clinical lore than of evidence from controlled trials. Antidepressants may "take the edge off" symptoms of BPD, but they do not treat the disorder and never produce remission. Nonetheless, if patients need to be on one drug, I would recommend an SSRI as the least toxic alternative.

MOOD STABILIZERS

BPD patients have highly unstable moods, and this phenomenon has sometimes been interpreted as evidence of bipolarity (see Chapter 2). One might readily imagine that drugs that stabilize mood in bipolar disorder could be equally effective in other conditions.

In fact, research on the use of mood stabilizers in BPD has shown equivocal and unimpressive results. In spite of their name, these drugs have little effect on AI. This supports the concept that AI derives from different mechanisms than mania and hypomania.

The only controlled study of lithium in BPD failed to demonstrate efficacy (Links, Steiner, Boiago, & Irwin, 1990). In any case, few clinicians would wish to use a drug that is so dangerous on overdose. Carbamazepine, one of the early alternatives to lithium, has been examined in one study, albeit in a small sample (Cowdry & Gardner, 1988), and seemed to have some value in reducing impulsivity. But this drug is toxic (and dangerous on overdose).

The most popular mood stabilizer today is valproate. Although many patients with BPD are taking this agent, a preliminary controlled trial found only marginal efficacy (Hollander et al., 2001). A more extensive multicenter trial (Hollander, Swann, Coccaro, Jiang, & Smith, 2005) found that valproate has some value in reducing impulsive aggression. Nonetheless, effect sizes were quite small and many patients dropped out of the study. The most positive results for valproate (Frankenburg & Zanarini, 2002) were found in patients with BPD comorbid for bipolar II disorder (i.e., those with clear-cut hypomanic episodes). These findings can hardly be generalized to the population with BPD as a whole, and I wonder whether comorbidity with bipolar II actually shows that patients do not have BPD.

There are now several other mood stabilizers on the market. Small clinical trials have suggested that lamotrigine (Tritt et al., 2005) and topiramate (Nickel et al., 2005; Loew et al., 2006) also reduce anger, impulsivity, and anxiety, much in the same way as valproate. But neither of these drugs produces a remission of BPD.

So why are results not better? The most likely reason is that the emotional dysregulation seen in BPD is an entirely different phenomenon from mood swings in bipolar spectrum disorders. If you can achieve the same result with a less toxic agent, such as an SSRI, why give patients drugs that are more likely to create problems? At this point, I do not see much of a role for mood stabilizers in BPD, and I do not prescribe them.

OTHER OPTIONS

Zanarini and Frankenburg (2003) reported that omega-3 fatty acids were effective for BPD symptoms of anger and depression. This study was conducted in a small sample of patients recruited by advertisement and does not provide sufficient evidence to recommend a salmon oil diet for patients.

Patients with BPD may also receive pharmacological agents that have never been specifically tested in this population. The most frequently prescribed are benzodiazepines (Zanarini et al., 2001). Although it is true that many BPD patients also suffer from anxiety disorders, SSRIs are known to be effective for these symptoms. And although benzodiazepines are often used for insomnia, because their effects tend to wear off with time, they are probably not ideal for chronic problems with sleep.

POLYPHARMACY

No pharmacological agent has ever been shown to produce a clinical remission of BPD. Although short-term benefits can be seen, patients remain ill. Moreover, one can never be sure whether the improvements one sees are placebo responses (particularly likely in this group of notably suggestible patients). Patients with BPD on medication frequently remain unstable in mood, impulsive actions, and relationships. The result is that patients are tried on a second or a third drug, usually without removing any of the others.

Failure by clinicians to recognize the limitations of drug therapy in BPD leads to the practice of polypharmacy. Multiple drug prescriptions, although not evidence based, makes it ever more likely that patients will suffer from multiple side effects. As noted, patients with BPD are often on four to five drugs, with at least one from each major group (Zanarini et al., 2001).

Unfortunately, polypharmacy has been supported by algorithms for drug treatment in BPD included in the American Psychiatric Association guidelines (Oldham et al., 2001). These algorithms are not based on RCT evidence and, if followed, lead almost inevitably to multiple prescriptions.

CLINICAL IMPLICATIONS

- The evidence base for pharmacological treatment of BPD is slim. Yet almost all patients today are being prescribed drugs. This practice is doing harm to patients, who are taking drugs for years (and enduring serious side effects) to little purpose.
- Although some BPD patients are not suitable for psychotherapy, it is usually worth trying.
- Because the evidence for psychotherapy is much better than for any drug, the role of medication in the treatment of BPD is adjunctive. Drugs can be used to control symptoms for short periods of time (months, not years).
- If one had to choose one drug for BPD, it should be an SSRI. Second choice would be a neuroleptic in the lowest possible dose. There is insufficient evidence to consider using anything else.

CHAPTER 8

Psychotherapy

*P*sychotherapy, like any other intervention, can and should be scientifically tested to determine its efficacy. The highest standard of proof is the same as for drugs—an RCT.

Using this method, we now know that several methods of therapy are effective for patients with BPD. However, it does not follow that almost *any* form of therapy will be good enough. Specific methods have been developed to treat BPD, and these are the approaches that have undergone clinical trials. I present the empirical evidence for each type of therapy. (See Table 8.1 for a summary.)

DIALECTICAL BEHAVIOR THERAPY

Marsha Linehan is a psychology professor (and cognitive–behavioral trained therapist) at the University of Washington in Seattle whose research has focused on attempted suicide. In the 1980s, Linehan developed and tested a method of treating chronically parasuicidal patients (whom she later recognized as having a diagnosis of BPD). She called her method dialectical behavior therapy (DBT). (The "dialectic" refers to the relationship of acceptance and validation to the expectation that the patient will be committed to change.)

DBT is an adaptation of cognitive-behavioral therapy (CBT) that

TABLE 8.1. RCTs of Psychotherapy for BPD

Trial	Study subjects and outcome measures	Study arms and duration	Results	Comments	Funding source
Linehan et al. (1991)	*Subjects*: 22 women ages 18–45 yr treated with DBT; 22 matched controls receiving TAU *Outcome*: frequency of parasuicidal behaviors, hospitalization. Beck scales for depression, hopelessness, suicidal ideation	12 mo of DBT included individual and group sessions	Subjects receiving DBT had reduced parasuicidal behaviors and hospitalizations. No difference in measures of depression, hopelessness, suicidal ideation.	Low dropout rate in DBT (< 10%).	U.S. National Institute of Mental Health
Linehan et al. (1999)	*Subjects*: 28 women ages 18–45 yr who met criteria for BPD and substance use disorder *Outcome*: drug use (urinalysis); self-reports (time line follow-back assessment); treatment received (THI); parasuicide history (PHI); global adjustment (GAS); social adjustment (GSA); anger (STAXI)	• DBT (*n* = 12) • TAU (*n* = 16) *Duration*: 12 mo (assessments every 4 mo), plus follow-up 4 mo after end of treatment (16 mo)	DBT subjects had greater reduction in drug abuse than TAU group in both interviews and urinalyses, but only statistically significant at certain time points. Both groups improved on GAS, GSA throughout the year; at 16-mo follow-up, DBT group had significantly better social and global adjustment. Subjects as a whole had fewer parasuicidal episodes and improvement in anger.	High dropout rate—only 9 participants completed full year of therapy (6 DBT and 3 TAU). Many analyses found results in the treated sample but not in intent-to-treat analyses.	

(continued)

TABLE 8.1. (*continued*)

Trial	Study subjects and outcome measures	Study arms and duration	Results	Comments	Funding source
Linehan et al. (2002)	*Subjects:* 23 women ages 18–45 yr with BPD and current opiate dependence *Outcome measures:* drug use (urinalysis; self-reports, time line follow-back assessment); parasuicidal behaviors (PHI); global adjustment (GAS); global social adjustment (GSA); general psychiatric symptomatology (BSI)	• DBT (*n* = 11) • CVT-12S (*n* = 12) *Duration:* 12-mo RCT plus follow-up evaluation at 4 mo posttreatment (16-mo assessment)	Subjects in both groups had declining opiate use until 8-mo point, when CVT-12S subjects showed increasing opiate use while DBT subjects maintained treatment gains. No significant between-condition difference at 16-mo assessment (both groups had reduced opiate use). Both groups significantly improved on GAS and BSI.	All participants also received opiate agonist therapy in addition to psychosocial treatment. 4 DBT subjects dropped out; there were no drop-outs from CVT-12S.	U.S. National Institute on Drug Abuse, National Institute of Mental Health
Linehan et al. (2006)	*Subjects:* 101 women ages 18–45 yr with recent suicidal and self-injurious behavior *Outcome measures:* suicidal behaviors (SAS-II, SBQ), emergency services use depression (HAM-D)	• DBT (*n* = 52) • CTBE (*n* = 49) *Duration:* 1-yr RCT plus 1 yr posttreatment follow-up	DBT group improved more than CTBE. Both groups improved significantly on suicide ideation, reasons for living, depression.	Significantly more participants in CTBE dropped out of therapy (*n* = 21, vs. *n* = 10 in DBT).	U.S. National Institute of Mental Health
Koons et al. (2001)	*Subjects:* 20 women veterans ages 21–46 yr with BPD *Outcome measures:* symptom scales	• DBT (*n* = 10) • TAU (*n* = 10)	DBT group had greater decrease in suicidal ideation, hopelessness, depression, anger expression.	Very small sample	

	Subjects / Design	Results	Notes	Funding source
Verheul et al. (2003)	*Subjects:* 58 women with BPD; mean age, 35 yr *Outcome measures:* symptom scales • DBT (*n* = 29) • TAU (*n* = 29)	DBT resulted in better retention rates and greater reductions of self-mutilating and self-damaging impulsive behaviors.	Confirms Linehan et al. (1991)	
Giesen-Bloo et al. (2006)	*Subjects:* 86 participants (93% women) ages 18–60 yr with BPD diagnosis referred by community mental health institutes *Outcome measures:* BPD severity (BPDSI-IV); quality of life (EuroQol Thermometer, WHOQOL); general psychopathologic dysfunction; measures of SFT/TFP personality concepts • SFT (*n* = 44) • TFP (*n* = 42) *Duration:* 3 yr, sessions 2x/week	Both groups improved significantly from baseline on all measures; SFT group showed significantly greater improvement than TFP group.	High dropout rates (12 SFT, 22 TFP); effectiveness of treatment became apparent after 12 mo.	Dutch Health Care Insurance Board
K. N. Levy et al. (2006)	*Subjects:* 90 patients (93% female) ages 18–50 yr who met BPD criteria *Outcome measures:* attachment organization, attachment coherence, resolution of loss, resolution of trauma (all from AAI); mentalization and RF (RF coding scale) • TFP (*n* = 31) • DBT (*n* = 29) • SPT (*n* = 30) *Duration:* 1-yr outpatient treatment, with assessments at 4-mo intervals	Significantly more people in TFP group had secure attachment at T2 compared with T1 and with other groups; TFP group also significantly improved in attachment coherence and RF; no differences across groups in resolution of loss and resolution of trauma.	Did not use intent-to-treat analysis; only 60 participants (22 TFP, 15 DBT, 23 SPT) completed the 12 mo of treatment; sought to examine mechanisms of change, not success of treatment.	U.S. National Institute of Mental Health; International Psychoanalytic Association; Kohler Fund of Munich; Borderline Personality Disorder Research Foundation

(*continued*)

135

TABLE 8.1. (*continued*)

Trial	Study subjects and outcome measures	Study arms and duration	Results	Comments	Funding source
Spinhoven et al. (2007)	*Subjects:* 78 patients (92% female) ages 18–60 yr, with BPD diagnosis referred by community mental health institutes *Outcome measures:* BPD severity (BPDSI-IV); therapeutic alliance (WAI); relationship with therapist (DDPRQ-10); core beliefs/schemas (YSQ); personality (IPO)	• SFT (*n* = 44) • TFP (*n* = 34) *Duration:* 3 yr of biweekly therapy	Improved BPD severity (reduced scores on BPDSI) in both groups across time; therapeutic alliance greater in SFT than TFP, and therapist frustration (DDPRQ) decreased in SFT and increased in TFP. Time-to-treatment dropout dependent on quality of therapeutic alliance. In both groups, dissimilarity of personality between patients and therapists (YSQ, IPO) increased therapeutic alliance from patient's point of view (WAI-P).	Excluded patients who did not complete 3 mo of therapy (*n* = 8, all in TFP group); included all others, even those who did not complete therapy	Dutch Health Council
Clarkin et al. (2007)	*Subjects:* 90 patients (92% female) ages 18–50 yr who met BPD criteria *Outcome measures:* negative effect, effortful control, BPD pathology; conceptualization of self and others	• TFP • DBT • Supportive psychotherapy *Duration:* 1-yr outpatient treatment, with assessments at 4-mo intervals	Improvement in all groups on anxiety, depression, global functioning, and social adjustment. Both TFP and DBT led to decreases in suicidality and decreases in impulsivity. TFP reduced anger and irritability.	Number and length of sessions per week differ between groups: TFP, two 50-min sessions/week; DBT, one 1-hr session and one 1.5-hr group session/week; supportive psychotherapy, one 50-min session/wk	Borderline Personality Disorder Research Foundation

Study	Subjects / Outcome measures	Treatment / Duration	Results	Comments	Limitations
Stevenson et al. (2005)	*Subjects:* 30 outpatients (63% women) *Outcome measures:* DSM checklist, symptom checklist (Cornell Index); morbidity budget: number of hospital admissions; time spent as inpatient; number of outpatient visits to medical facility each month; quantity of drugs used daily (prescribed and nonprescribed); self-destructive behavior and outwardly directed violence (number of episodes); time away from work	• Psychotherapy based on Hobson's conversational model (*n* = 30) *Duration:* 1 yr, 2x/wk; follow-up 1 yr, 5 yr after end of treatment	Patients retained gains made at 1-yr follow-up on all measures; comparison with other subjects showed this improvement to be unrelated to aging/natural time course of BPD.	No intention-to-treat analysis (48 patients started therapy); analysis based on data of 30 subjects who completed therapy and responded at 1-yr follow-up; all 30 were recontacted. Used assessment data from 150 patients on 1st presentation to clinic as a comparison group to determine effects of aging on outcome measures.	None indicated
Korner et al. (2006)	*Subjects:* 60 persons (55% female) either in therapy or on wait list between 1994 and 2001 *Outcome measures:* BPD diagnostic criteria; global functioning (GAS); self-harm, emergency room presentations	• Conversational model therapy (*n* = 29); twice weekly 50-min sessions • TAU (*n* = 31) *Duration:* 12 mo	Treatment group had improvement of GAS scores from baseline after 12 mo, decrease of symptom severity; decrease in self-harm and emergency room presentations. TAU group did not change on WSS or GAS, had increase in emergency room presentations and self-harm	Replication of earlier study with control group; used DSM-III-R BPD criteria; comparable results	None stated

(continued)

TABLE 8.1. (*continued*)

Trial	Study subjects and outcome measures	Study arms and duration	Results	Comments	Funding source
Davidson, Norrie, et al. (2006), BOSCOT trial	*Subjects*: 106 subjects (84% female) ages 18–65 yr with BPD who received inpatient psychiatric services, were seen at emergency services, or had episode of deliberate self-harm in past 12 mo	• CBT plus TAU (*n* = 54) • TAU (*n* = 52) *Duration*: 1-yr treatment, 1-yr follow-up	Reported in Davidson, Tyrer, et al. (2006)	This article presents in detail rationale for trial, methods, and sample. Results are presented in Davidson, Tyrer, et al. (2006).	Wellcome Trust, UK
Davidson, Tyrer, et al. (2006), BOSCOT trial	*Subjects*: 106 subjects (84% female) ages 18–65 yr (see Davidson, Norrie, et al., 2006, for more details) *Outcome measures*: suicidal acts (ADSHI); inpatient psychiatric hospitalization; accident and emergency attendance; acts of self-mutilation; BDI-II; STAI; BSI; IIP-32; SFQ; YSQ; EuroQol	• CBT plus TAU (*n* = 54) • TAU (*n* = 52) *Duration*: 1-yr treatment (*m*, 27 sessions offered), plus 1 yr follow-up	CBT group had greater reduction in number of suicidal acts over 24 mo and greater improvement in psychiatric symptoms (BSI) at 12 mo and in mood (state anxiety) and cognition (YSQ) at 24 mo compared with TAU group	49% of patients attended < 15 sessions of CBT (considered by authors as inadequate and indicative of nonengagement). Average attendance was 16 sessions.	Wellcome Trust, UK
Palmer et al. (2006), BOSCOT trial	*Subjects*: 106 subjects (84% female) ages 18–65 yr *Outcome measures*: Quality-adjusted life year (measured using EuroQol Thermometer), primary and secondary health care utilization and cost	• CBT plus TAU (*n* = 54) • TAU (*n* = 52) *Duration*: 1-yr treatment (*m*, 27 sessions offered), plus 1-yr follow-up	No significant difference in quality of life improvement or in resource cost between 2 groups; CBT does not appear to be cost effective.	Used subjects from the BOSCOT trial (Davidson, Tyrer, et al., 2006); participants were difficult to engage in therapy.	Wellcome Trust, UK

Study	Subjects / Outcome measures	Design	Results	Notes	Funding
Tyrer et al. (2004)	*Subjects:* 480 patients seen in hospitals after episode of self-harm who had previous episode and were not bipolar or psychotic or psychiatric inpatients. 42% had a personality disorder (n = 67 had BPD) *Outcome measures:* proportion of self-harm episodes; costs of care	• MACT (n = 239) • TAU (n = 241) *Duration:* 1-yr study period; MACT group offered up to 7 treatment sessions	Patients with BPD had greater incidence of repetition and shorter time to 1st repeat episode; no significant difference between MACT and TAU groups for incidence of repetition and time to repeat episode, even when separated by personality status; total costs in follow-up year higher in patients with personality disorders; type of treatment had no impact on cost.	High noncompliance: 40% attended no treatment sessions; did not use intent-to-treat analysis (only used data from 430 patients with reports on parasuicide events after 1-yr study period).	Medical Research Council, UK
Huband et al. (2007)	*Subjects:* 176 subjects ages 18–65 yr with at least one DSM-IV personality disorder *Outcome measures:* Social problem solving ability (SPSI-R), social functioning (SFQ), anger (STAXI-2), impulsiveness (BIS), shame (ESS), dissociation (DES), and use of services	• Psychoeducation plus 16 problem-solving group sessions (n = 87) • Wait-list control (n = 89) *Duration:* 24 wk on average	Participants in intervention group had significantly better problem-solving skills, higher overall social functioning, lower anger expression compared with controls. No significant differences were found on use of services during intervention period or on impulsiveness (BIS), dissociation (DES), or shame.	Only 42 participants (48%) in intervention group completed entire treatment.	Programme for Forensic Mental Health R&D and the Home Office

Note. AAI, Adult Attachment Inventory; BDI-II, Beck Depression Inventory-II; BIS, Barratt Impulsiveness Scale; BOSCOT, Borderline Personality Study of Cognitive Therapy; BPDSI-IV, Borderline Personality Disorder Severity Index; BSI, Brief Symptom Inventory; CBT, cognitive-behavioral therapy; CTBE, community treatment by experts; CVT-12S, Comprehensive Validation Therapy-12 Step; DBT, dialectical behavior therapy; DDPRQ, Difficult Doctor–Patient Relationship Questionnaire; DSM, *Diagnostic and Statistical Manual of Mental Disorders*; ESS, Experience of Shame Scale; DES, Dissociative Experiences Scale; GAS, Global Assessment Scale; HAM-D, Hamilton Rating Scale for Depression; IIP-32, Inventory of Interpersonal Problems-32; IPO, Inventory of Personality Organization; MACT, manual-assisted cognitive-behavioral therapy; RCT, randomized controlled trial; RF, reflective function; SAS-II, Suicide Attempt Self-Injury Interview; SFQ = Social Functioning Questionnaire; SFT, schema-focused therapy; SPSI-R, Social Problem Solving Inventory Revised; SPT, supportive psychotherapy; STAI, State–Trait Anxiety Inventory; STAXI, State–Train Anger Expression Inventory; TAU, treatment as usual; TFP, transference-focused psychotherapy; WHOQOL, World Health Organization Quality of Life; YSQ, Young's Schema Questionnaire.

adds an eclectic mix of methods derived from other approaches. It is based on a very specific theory about BPD. Linehan hypothesizes that ED is the core pathology behind the disorder. Treatment is, therefore, specifically designed to improve emotion regulation, targeting mood intensity and mood instability.

A typical DBT session applies behavioral analysis to identify life stressors that precede incidents of self-injury and overdoses. Patients are taught to recognize their emotional states and to stand outside them so they are not flooded by their feelings. Doing so allows patients to come up with better strategies for managing stressful events.

DBT emphasizes empathic responses by therapists that provide "validation" for the inner experience of the patient. The dialectic aspect of treatment is that therapists inform patients that they acknowledge the reasons why they need to stay the same but still expect them to work hard to change.

DBT was the first psychotherapy for BPD to be tested in an RCT. The original study (Linehan et al., 1991) showed it to be superior to treatment as usual (unstructured outpatient therapy in the community). After 1 year, the sample receiving DBT was less likely to make suicide gestures or to mutilate themselves or to spend time in hospital. Although the gap between DBT and treatment as usual narrowed when a 1-year follow-up was carried out (Linehan, Heard, & Armstrong, 1993), patients treated with DBT attained a higher functional level.

One of the most interesting findings of this study was that more than 90% of patients treated with DBT stayed in therapy for a full year. This is a remarkable accomplishment in a patient population known for low treatment compliance. On the other hand, the patients in this study may not have been fully representative of the people therapists see. For one thing, they had accepted to be part of a research project. The participants also received free treatment (the cohort in the treatment-as-usual group did not). Replication studies in other centers have experienced higher rates of attrition (e.g., Verheul et al., 2003).

Nonetheless, a series of replications, in centers under Linehan's supervision as well as in clinics far from Seattle, have confirmed the efficacy of DBT (Koons et al., 2001; Verhueul et al., 2003; Bohus et al., 2004; Simpson et al., 2004). DBT has also been shown to help BPD patients with substance abuse (Linehan et al., 1999). These multiple replications give DBT an advantage over other forms of therapy that have been tested in only one or two clinical trials. However, attrition rates tend to increase the further one is from Seattle.

Although it has the strongest research support, the *specificity* of DBT as a treatment for BPD has not been demonstrated. A comparison with treatment as usual gave DBT a great advantage, because ordinary clinical management can be slipshod (or even something of a mess), particularly in comparison to well-structured programs.

To address these issues, Linehan's group conducted a second RCT (Linehan et al., 2006) in which they compared DBT with treatment by community experts (psychodynamic and client-centered therapists who were nominated by community mental health leaders as experts in the treatment of BPD patients). This time, the advantage for DBT was narrower. There were no differences in the frequency of self-injury after therapy, but DBT had a better outcome for reductions in overdoses and subsequent hospitalizations within the first year of treatment.

Even so, these findings should not be interpreted as conclusive proof that DBT is always superior to other alternatives. As is discussed later, one published report (Clarkin, Levy, Lenzenweger, & Kernberg, 2007) did not find that to be so. Also, an ongoing study is being conducted in Toronto, in which DBT is being directly compared with a management program based on American Psychiatric Association guidelines. Because data have only been analyzed for the first 4 months of treatment, it is too soon to tell what the final results will be (Links, 2007).

Several questions remain about the applicability of DBT. One concerns generalizability from clinical trials to real-world practice. We need large-scale naturalistic data to determine whether this treatment can be applied to most patients with BPD.

Another question concerns long-term effects. Linehan (1993) suggested that a complete treatment could require several years, whereas DBT has only been tested for 12 months. Most patients, although more stable after a course of treatment, continued to report high levels of dysphoria and life problems at 1-year follow-up (Linehan et al., 1993). It would also be interesting to find out how the original cohort, which received therapy 15 years ago, is doing. Unfortunately, no long-term follow-up has been carried out. Thus, we do not know whether treated samples maintain gains and continue to improve or whether they relapse.

Another problem is that DBT is resource intensive and expensive. For this reason, 15 years after its introduction, implementation has been spotty. If DBT could be shown to be cost effective in larger samples, funds might be more widely available to support it. Where DBT is available, there are often long waiting lists, not surprising for a treatment whose initial phase lasts a full year. Stanley, Brodsky, Nelson, and Dulit (2007) have shown that DBT can be streamlined into a 6-month treatment that has similar efficacy.

Finally, DBT is a complex package, and we do not know which parts are essential and which are not. Research could determine whether DBT can be dismantled (or streamlined) for greater clinical impact. Linehan (1993) noted that group psychoeducation is not effective on its own. But it is possible that a simpler version of the package might be just as effective.

We also cannot tell whether certain aspects of DBT are idiosyncratic to its creator. One question (raised in Chapter 9) is whether therapists need to carry a pager and return phone calls. It is also not clear whether Linehan's adherence to philosophical dialectics and Zen Buddhism explains anything about the efficacy of her method.

In spite of all these caveats, every therapist treating BPD owes a great deal to Marsha Linehan. Whether or not we practice formal DBT, most of us have learned a great deal from her method. (As I describe later in this book, I have incorporated many of Linehan's ideas into the way I treat patients.)

Linehan also deserves credit for carrying out the first RCT of any psychotherapy for BPD. As I have heard her say on several occasions, if other people have their own ideas, they should test them, just as she did. Up to a few years ago, nobody had. But as we have seen, that situation has changed, and there are now several "kids on the block."

OTHER FORMS OF COGNITIVE THERAPY

Linehan developed DBT when experience told her that standard cognitive therapy was not effective for BPD. However, not everyone in the CBT world agreed with that conclusion. In its more traditional forms, cognitive therapy has been subjected to clinical trials in BPD.

The founder of CBT, Aaron Beck, emphasizes the correction of maladaptive cognitions, a somewhat different focus from Linehan's emotion regulation. But his group has published only one clinical report, an open and uncontrolled trial in a small sample (G. K. Brown, Newman, Charlesworth, Crits-Christoph, & Beck, 2004).

In the United Kingdom, Peter Tyrer and colleagues tested manual-assisted cognitive–behavioral therapy (MACT) in large samples of patients who engage in recurrent deliberate self-harm (Tyrer et al., 2004). The results showed that CBT was superior to treatment as usual but less effective in patients with BPD.

The Scottish psychologist Kate Davidson, working in collaboration with Tyrer's group, conducted an RCT in which standard CBT was compared with treatment as usual in a population of BPD patients (Davidson et al., 2006). The average length of treatment was 16 sessions. Yet even after a relatively brief course, CBT had a superior outcome. A report by Weinberg, Gunderson, Hennen, and Cutter (2006) showed that MACT reduced self-harm behavior in BPD more rapidly than treatment as usual. Gratz and Gunderson (2006) described results from a pilot study in which brief group therapy for emotional regulation was effective.

These reports raise an even more important question: whether BPD can be treated briefly. Treatment lasting only a few months for such a chronic condition might seem to be counterintuitive. However, if it can give patients a jump-start and get them on the road to recovery, brief therapy could produce a large return on a small investment. The approach might not be sufficient for the most severe cases but could work for patients who are less impaired.

Schema-focused therapy (SFT) is a variant of CBT developed by Jeffrey Young (1999), a method that might be described as a hybrid of CBT and psychodynamic therapy. SFT targets some of the broader problems seen in personality disorders, focusing on the modification of maladaptive schema deriving from adverse experiences in childhood.

The first RCT, conducted in the Netherlands (Giesen-Bloo et al., 2006), compared schema therapy with transference-focused psychotherapy (see later) over a period of 3 years. The report found a similar outcome for both approaches: Although there was a slight advantage for SFT, the difference was not dramatic and would have to be replicated. The main problem with SFT is that therapy lasting as long as 3 years would probably have limited clinical application.

The Systems Training for Emotional Predictability and Problem-Solving (STEPPS) program, developed by Nancee Blum and Don Black at the University of Iowa (Blum, Pfohl, John, Monahan, & Black, 2002), is a cognitive program of psychoeducation for patients with BPD in a group format. It is not intended as a treatment to stand alone but as an adjunct to treatment as usual. A clinical trial has been conducted, and the results suggest that STEPPS adds to the efficacy of clinical management (Blum et al., 2008). A clinical trial of a similar psychoeducational program documented symptomatic improvement in a large sample of patients with personality disorder, 40% of whom had BPD (Huband, McMurran, Evans, & Duggan, 2007).

All the evidence just reviewed suggests that less extensive cognitive interventions may achieve some of the same goals set by DBT. This is a growing field that has received an expert overview. The Cochrane Reports, conservative as always, concluded that there is "some evidence" for the value of cognitive therapy in BPD (Binks et al., 2006b).

PSYCHODYNAMIC THERAPIES

Although CBT has always had a tradition of research, psychodynamic therapies were usually rooted in clinical experience. However, as the movement toward evidence-based practice gathered momentum, there was general agreement that clinical trials of all forms of psychotherapy for BPD are necessary.

Meares, Stevenson, and Comerford (1999) conducted the first published trial of any form of psychodynamic therapy for BPD. Their method is called "conversational" (broadly based on the principles of self-psychology). The study found stable improvement in a small group of patients after 2 years of therapy. Unfortunately, there was no control group; outcome was compared only with an untreated wait-list patients (and with the overall course of the disorder). Stevenson, Meares, and D'Angelo (2005) later replicated their original findings in a comparison with untreated controls, although there was no randomization. In both studies, samples were small. Moreover, patients who stay in treatment for 2 years with minimal attrition may not be representative of the clinical populations that therapists see.

Another problem in psychotherapy research concerns whether all patients in any given study are getting (more or less) the same treatment. For this purpose, manuals have been developed to guide the conduct of therapy. (Manualization has a useful side effect in that it provides a predictable structure.)

Bateman and Fonagy (1999) conducted one of the most influential clinical trials of psychodynamic therapy for BPD. This was a randomized controlled trial of a manualized therapy developed specifically for BPD, called mentalization-based therapy (MBT).

The main theory behind MBT is that BPD is the result of failed attachments in childhood. MBT is not classically psychodynamic (Bateman & Fonagy, 2006) because it does not focus to the same extent on childhood experience (or on transference). Rather, patients with BPD are seen as being unable to "mentalize" (i.e., to stand outside their feelings and accurately observe emotions in self and others). The therapy aims to teach them to do just that. Because these ideas are similar to concepts developed by Linehan, MBT might be described as a hybrid of dynamic and cognitive therapy. In that light, the data on MBT do not support more traditional forms of long-term dynamic psychotherapy.

In the Bateman and Fonagy study, MBT was administered in a day treatment program over 18 months. Patients showed significantly greater improvement in symptoms than those assigned to treatment as usual in the community. However, it was not clear to what extent these results were affected by a day hospital setting (in which the milieu itself could have led to improvement). MBT is, therefore, being tested in another RCT, comparing it with treatment as usual in an outpatient setting (with findings that have not yet been published).

We also do not know whether MBT could be streamlined or shortened. It is not established that a full 18-month treatment, with all the expense it entails, is necessary.

It will be interesting to see whether MBT will have the same impact on the clinical community as has been the case for DBT. One obstacle is that the term *mentalization* is not easy to grasp, even though it corresponds to the self-observation skills that have long been promoted by both cognitive and psychodynamic therapies.

Transference-focused psychotherapy (TFP) is a psychodynamic method that is much closer to classic psychoanalysis. Based on theories developed by Otto Kernberg (1976) at Cornell University, TFP aims to correct distortions in the patient's perception of significant others and of the therapist. Although the method has been manualized (Clarkin, Levy, Lenzenweger, & Kernberg, 2004; Levy et al., 2006), the name may be misleading. The use of the term *transference* might seem to suggest that TFP therapists provide interpretations, telling patients they are misperceiving the therapist because of the influence of early relationships. However, transference interpretations have been found in other research to be counterproductive in patients with personality disorders (W. E. Piper, Azim, Joyce, & McCallum, 1991). What TFP actually seems to do is to correct misperceptions in the context of a here-and-now interaction with a therapist, without necessarily making reference to the past.

A clinical trial to test the efficacy of TFP has been published (Clarkin, Levy, Lenzenweger, & Kernberg, 2007). In a direct comparison between TFP and DBT, both methods showed roughly equal efficacy. The study actually reported a slightly better result for TFP, but that difference could easily be accounted for by allegiance effects. Moreover, the sample size in this study was not very large. Thus, these small differences should not be considered of great importance, as already noted in relation to the comparison of SFT with TFP (Giesen-Bloo et al., 2006).

In summary, evidence indicates that psychodynamically oriented therapy offers another option for treating BPD. However, such treatment needs to be well structured and include a cognitive component. Open-ended dynamic therapy, focusing on childhood experiences and/or classic transference interpretations, is not indicated for BPD. Only a minority of patients are interested in that type of treatment, and a majority will "vote with their feet" by leaving therapy (Gunderson et al., 1989).

GROUP THERAPY AND PSYCHOEDUCATION

Group therapy can be used as either as a primary method of treatment or as an adjunct to other forms of treatment. However, data on its use in BPD are limited. Only one controlled trial of long-term group therapy exists, which compared it with individual therapy, observing similar results (Munroe-Blum & Marziali, 1995). There is also one study of short-term group therapy (Weinberg et al., 2006).

In DBT, psychoeducation is given in a group format, explaining the diagnosis, reviewing some of the research, describing how treatment can help, and then teaching techniques for emotion regulation (Linehan, 1993). Similar approaches have been used by Blum et al. (2002) and by Huband et al. (2007).

Families also need to understand the nature of BPD. Whereas the families of patients were once blamed for causing the disorder, therapists have come to realize that parents are not necessarily guilty. As described in Chapter 4, only some BPD patients come from severely dysfunctional families. Many parents are well intentioned but burdened by their children's psychopathology. Families should be useful allies, not enemies, in treatment.

Gunderson et al. (2003) has developed a program for psycho-education of family members but has not published data on its efficacy. However, a clinical trial by Hoffman, Fruzzetti, and Buteau (2007) suggested that this method can be helpful. The basic concept is to teach parents to avoid making bad situations worse, by responding in a nonjudgmental way to some of the behaviors seen in BPD.

COMMON FACTORS IN THE THERAPY OF BPD

If therapies based on different theories, and using very different techniques, can produce the same results, might they have something in common?

A large body of research has shown that common factors (also called "nonspecific factors") in therapy are the best predictors of results in all forms of psychotherapy (Lambert & Ogles, 2004). When different forms of psychotherapy are compared head to head, one almost always finds what has been called a "dodo bird verdict" (i.e., that "all have won and all shall have prizes"; Luborsky, Singer, & Luborsky, 1975; Wampold, 2001).

The most important common factor in psychotherapy is the quality of the alliance between therapist and patient. Therapy is a relationship, and the therapeutic alliance measures how well patient and therapist are working together. One can often predict how treatment will turn out by administering standard scales after a few sessions (Luborsky, 1988). Other potent common factors are empathy and a problem-solving approach to current problems (Orlinsky, Rønnestad, & Willutzki, 2004).

The quality of the alliance depends in part on the patient. This is why, by and large, people who are less sick and motivated for change get more out of therapy. However, the evidence for common factors also points to the importance of therapist skill, independent of theory or technique (Wampold, 2001).

Although common factors predict the efficacy of many forms of psychotherapy, some may be more unique to BPD. Drawing on the research reviewed earlier in this chapter, I emphasize structure, validation, and self-observation.

Structure is an essential element for patients who have chaotic lives and a deficient psychic structure. It is, therefore, no accident that structured treatments tend to achieve better results in research comparisons, whereas unstructured approaches are less successful.

Validation is an essential element of any therapy, but it is particularly important for BPD patients, who are sensitive to the slightest hint of invalidation (Linehan, 1993). These are patients who will not listen to anything else their therapist has to say unless their feelings are accepted.

Finally, self-observation is a skill that therapists need to teach all patients with BPD. It is the central feature of MBT and is equally crucial in DBT. Unless patients learn to know their feelings better (and not drown in them), they cannot stand aside from emotional crises or even begin to think about alternative solutions to problems.

The crucial role of these common factors in the treatment of BPD explains why all methods that make use of them have similar efficacy. Moreover, one does not need a manualized protocol to produce good results. One of the unfortunate aspects of recent research on the psychotherapy of BPD is that there are several competing methods, and the small number of head-to-head comparisons between them have been overinterpreted by therapists with allegiance to one approach. The more parsimonious conclusion is that all well-structured methods are superior to treatment as usual, but that none is clearly superior to any other. Rather, their success is rooted in procedures that maximize the effect of common factors in psychotherapy.

In the future, there should no longer be name brands of psychotherapy, each with its own acronym. This "alphabet soup" is not helpful in identifying the common features that make treatment effective. Although one might argue that competition is a stage of development in the science of therapy, we need to get beyond it. There should be only one kind of psychotherapy: the one that works. An integrated therapy for BPD would use the best ideas from everyone and put them together into one package.

WHAT THE DATA SHOW

The data reviewed in this chapter show that psychotherapy has strong support as a treatment for BPD. They also show that, although DBT has stimulated the most extensive research, it is no longer the only evidence-based psychotherapy, and other methods produce roughly similar results. Finally, results can often be seen within a year, with improvement often occurring within 6 months. All methods that have been subjected to clinical trials are highly structured or manualized.

These findings suggest that patients with BPD can be treated more briefly in the community with evidence-based practices and do not have to sit on endless waiting lists for specialized therapy. There are several evidence-based therapies supported by RCTs, but they tend to be expensive, resource intensive, and not widely available. Therapists need methods they can readily apply in their everyday work based on what research has shown to be most effective in BPD. This is the focus of the last section of this book.

CLINICAL IMPLICATIONS

- Several types of evidence-based psychotherapy have been shown to be effective in BPD.
- All successful therapies work through common factors.
- The most important mechanisms of these treatments are validation, self-observation, and problem solving in the present.
- Therapists can help patients by applying these principles and do not necessarily have to be trained in specialized methods.

CHAPTER 9

Guidelines for Management

Psychotherapy is the cornerstone of management for patients with BPD. Empirical evidence for the efficacy of these methods is strong. Moreover, when talking therapy works well, medication may no longer be necessary. It is possible that in the future, instead of using agents developed for other purposes, drugs more specific to BPD symptoms may be developed. However, until more convincing evidence comes in, currently available drugs are only adjuncts to psychological treatment.

Although psychotherapy works in BPD, one cannot assume that any type of talking therapy will do. These are patients who lack inner psychic structures and need well-structured treatments. They have to develop skills in a setting that provides validation for their feelings and help in managing them. Patients with BPD need to learn how to observe their emotions as well as those of other people. Each of the evidence-based therapies has developed techniques to help patients learn these life skills.

Two factors limit what we can accomplish in BPD. First, not every patient is ready to accept psychotherapy or attend sessions consistently. Some noncompliant patients do not stay in the mental health system. Others may present on multiple occasions in the emergency room, but do not accept regular follow-up.

Second, as follow-up studies show, some patients achieve a reasonable quality of life but do not attain full recovery. However, because many mental disorders are chronic, such outcomes need not be seen as a failure of treatment. Patients with BPD recover in stages, not all at once. That provides a reason for offering an intermittent schedule of therapy (see Chapter 11).

These limitations are real but need not be discouraging. Therapists should have realistic expectations. Not every patient fully recovers, even though many do. We need to give up on the idea of a definitive or curative treatment. Recovery requires that life satisfactions be "good enough," not ideal. The aim of therapy is care, not cure. Yet care can allow a natural (but gradual) process of recovery to unfold.

The severity and course of BPD can vary greatly. Not every patient is the same, and not every patient needs the same treatment. Some can be put on the road to recovery after only a brief intervention. Others will only improve after a longer and more strenuous course of treatment. Others may never improve much but can be maintained, albeit at a low level of functioning. There can be different approaches to management for each of these groups.

Although therapists have a choice of several effective treatments, evidence-based therapies that exist now are resource intensive, expensive, and time consuming. Clinicians are not usually in a position to refer patients to specialized centers (assuming such programs are even available). To manage patients, therapists need a method that can be used in normal practice.

In this chapter, I suggest ways to administer effective and practical interventions for BPD. I cannot claim that I have solid evidence to support every suggestion, and much of what I have to say is based on clinical experience. On the other hand, everything I recommend is at least *consistent* with current empirical evidence.

PSYCHOTHERAPY: WHAT TO DO
AND WHAT NOT TO DO

Patients with BPD have a reputation for *not* doing well in therapy. A series of reports published in the 1980s found that many, if not most, patients drop out of open-ended psychotherapy within a few months (Skodol, Buckley, & Charles, 1983; Waldinger & Gunderson, 1984; Gunderson et al., 1989). On the other hand, we now know that several forms of psychotherapy are effective. How can we explain this discrepancy? The answer is, once again, that not any therapy will do. Patients with BPD require structured treatment methods and get worse when therapy is unstructured and when it fails to be oriented to current problems.

As Adolf Stern (1938) was the first to observe, therapy that works for other patients may not be effective for those with BPD. One cannot expect results when patients are asked to free associate while the therapist offers a few interpretations at the end. Nor can one expect results from sessions in which patients describe crisis after crisis, while the therapist's only response is sympathy and "support." BPD patients need more practical and specific help.

In the past, talking therapies for BPD gained a bad reputation. Empirical investigation into the effectiveness of therapy for BPD was, in many ways, built on frustration. Many of the leading researchers in this field have been either trained analysts or psychodynamically oriented therapists. (I would have considered myself as belonging to the latter group until about 15 years ago.) Many of us entered research because we felt we did not understand the origins of BPD and did not have a consistently effective way to treat our patients.

Psychoanalysts were the first to describe borderline patients, and their kind of therapy was, for many years, considered standard. Many books were written on the psychotherapy of BPD, also describing theories about the disorder. The idea was that if you understood the inner world of patients (or their childhood experiences) well enough and knew how to make accurate interpretations, you could cure people. Hardly anyone actually *saw* such cures, but therapists wanted to believe that senior clinicians had answers. Clinical conferences about BPD were always well attended. These events usually featured "star" therapists talking about how to treat the most difficult patients.

Taking claims on faith was typical of that era; evidence-based practice had not yet taken hold. By current standards, there were almost no empirical data to determine which, if any, of these methods were effective. Meanwhile, quite a few therapists had disillusioning experiences and ended up going out of their way to avoid treating BPD. Whatever the claims of star therapists, the idea that BPD can be managed with sufficient technique and experience eventually aroused skepticism. And if one has not carried out successful therapy with this population, their chronic suicidality becomes even more frightening.

At the same time, many patients "voted with their feet" when offered open-ended exploratory therapy (i.e., by leaving early). Even patients who stayed longer were not always satisfied. Waldinger and Gunderson (1984), in a survey of the treatment of BPD in private practice, found that a majority had left therapy "against advice" after several years of regular treatment. (One might also interpret this finding as showing that therapists did not know when to quit when they were ahead.) Even worse, some patients stay in treatment indefinitely without change.

In addition to technical issues, the overall strategy of therapy in BPD has to be different. However unhappy childhood was, the past should not be the main subject of psychotherapy. These are patients who have too many current problems to benefit much from talking about their early life. Moreover, therapy that focuses too much on past traumas can make people worse by reinforcing victimization without improving coping.

Of course, therapists still need to understand life histories. Doing so is an essential part of empathy and alliance building. However, interpretations linking past and present have never been shown to be specifically effective elements of psychotherapy. Instead, research shows that successful psychotherapy maintains a consistent focus on current problems (Lambert & Ogles, 2004; Clarkin & Levy, 2004; Orlinsky et al., 2004; Beutler et al., 2004).

Moreover, BPD patients have an unfortunate tendency to blame others for their problems. Interpretation assumes that patients are repeating patterns from the past. Sometimes making the point can be useful, but it is just as likely not to work. The most serious problem with the analytic approach is that therapy that encourages people to blame their parents for problems is not helpful. Patients do not get better by "working through" the past. They need to acknowledge their life history and then put it behind them.

The fact that several methods of therapy based on several different theories have been shown to be effective points to the importance of common factors in treatment. Like other patients in psychotherapy, people with BPD need structure, validation, and a strong alliance.

On the other hand, empirical evidence consistently shows that therapies specifically designed for BPD are better than treatment as usual. There must, therefore, be specific elements that make a difference.

Interestingly, psychodynamic and cognitive approaches to BPD have a surprising degree of convergence. The psychodynamic methods (MBT and TFP) found to be effective do not focus on the analysis of childhood experiences. Both MBT and TFP incorporate a major cognitive component, teaching patients to observe their feelings and the feelings of others. This makes them more like cognitive therapy than like psychoanalysis, even if there is no direct attempt to modify mental schemas.

It is interesting to trace this evolution through the work of John Gunderson, a psychoanalyst who became one of the leading researchers on BPD. Whereas his first book on treatment (Gunderson, 1984) was largely based on dynamic theory, his second book (Gunderson, 2001) takes a practical and present-focused approach. In fact, most therapists who have worked for many years with BPD become increasingly "cognitive" over time, often without quite realizing it. (When I started to read about CBT, I compared myself with the character in a play by Molière, who was surprised to discover he had been speaking prose all his life.)

A practical approach to BPD that emphasizes improving life skills is essential for patients who do not benefit from either interpretation or "support." We need methods that target the basic trait dimensions (affective instability and impulsivity) that underlie the disorder. Therapy must promote emotion regulation and impulse control.

In many specialized programs for BPD, skills are taught in a group setting using a psychoeducational model (Linehan, 1993; Davidson et al., 2006a, 2006b; Weinberg et al., 2006). In group therapy, patients with similar problems can also feel validated and learn from each other's experiences. However, individual therapy can address problems in much the same way. In fact, a skills-oriented approach to emotional regulation and impulse control does not necessarily require a specialized program but can be applied to the sessions most therapists conduct in clinical practice.

The main aim is to teach patients to tolerate feelings, "decenter" from them, and reappraise emotional experiences. Tolerating feelings, no matter how intense, comes first. Decentering (i.e., standing outside one's emotions and observing them) works against being overwhelmed. Reappraising (i.e., thinking about emotions in a different way) leads patients to stop seeing feelings as realistic responses to events but rather as subjective experiences that can be revised on reflection.

These methods are central to DBT but have been long used in

other forms of CBT. And the basic concept of MBT (developing the capacity to "mentalize") is quite similar. Even TFP spends a lot of time correcting emotional distortions (by focusing on the way that patients respond to therapists). Thus, treatment for BPD should consider current problems to reflect a lack of life skills. The aim of psychotherapy is to improve those skills and apply them to the situations that give patients the most trouble.

Emotion regulation makes it less likely that patients will act on their feelings to produce immediate relief (e.g., by cutting and overdosing) and will develop more adaptive alternatives. Progress goes by steps (often two steps forward and one back). In a famous phrase popularized by Alcoholics Anonymous, recovery comes "one day at a time."

GETTING A LIFE

Although not all patients with BPD get better, those who do find a way to commit themselves to life. Getting a life is central to recovery (Zanarini, 2005). Therapy for BPD must be oriented to the present and the future and must avoid getting bogged down in the past.

The idea of curing patients by uncovering past traumas dies hard. Its drama is somehow appealing. However, successful therapy does not, as Freud thought, resemble an archaeological dig. Nor should it have the dramatic quality of a Hollywood movie (e.g., Hitchcock's *Spellbound* or the 1980s hit *Ordinary People*), in which the discovery of a past event produces an instant cure. Real therapy is more like watching grass grow. The process is one of slow but steady learning. Patients improve when they recognize maladaptive thoughts and behaviors and replace them with adaptive alternatives.

I am not suggesting that the past is unimportant. As we have seen, many patients with BPD have been exposed to severe adversities and traumas. Therapy needs to acknowledge and validate these experiences. However, that does not mean that a large chunk of treatment time should be spent on childhood.

The past provides a perspective, not an explanation. All the evidence-based therapies for BPD, even those based on psychoanalytic principles, help patients to put the past behind them and to foresee a future, in some cases, for the first time. This is why getting better requires *getting a life*.

Commitments to work and relationships are the primary ways to get a life. Therapy that focuses on the past fails to promote these goals. Navel gazing is not a good idea for anyone. It is particularly damaging for patients with BPD, who are all too ready to feel like victims and whose current lives need so much attention.

When patients get a life, the present becomes a source of satisfaction and past traumas fall into perspective. I have been amazed at the capacity of recovered patients for forgiveness and reconciliation, even for those who have badly hurt them. But their present life has to be less painful first.

Another issue, of particular relevance to BPD, is how we can convince patients to get a life when they are so busy flirting with death. To have a life, one has to decide to stay alive. That decision means giving up something: the comforting and strangely empowering option of suicide (Paris, 2006a).

Change of this magnitude resembles the decision of an addict to give up taking a favorite substance. Therapists working with alcoholics and drug addicts have developed interventions called "motivational interviewing" (W. R. Miller & Rolnick, 2002). This approach emphasizes that people must go through several psychological phases before they can decide whether to change their behavior, not to speak of actually doing so.

Motivational interviewing was developed for alcoholics, a clientele famously resistant to giving up their own preferred ways to deal with problems. Therapists working with this group must gradually create motivation for change and avoid unproductive confrontations. The approach is similar to what Linehan (1993) has termed "dialectical": Patients are asked to change, but the therapist acknowledges how extraordinarily difficult doing so would be.

Yet most patients with BPD eventually reach this goal. As outcome research shows, only a minority kill themselves, and most reenter the workforce. Even if not all find stable intimate relationships, most establish a circle of friends and links to the community that provide a sense of connection.

WORK AND RELATIONSHIPS

The most important part of getting a life is finding work. Moreover, work takes priority over love. Not all therapists understand this point. But if you are not somebody in your own right, you cannot successfully care for or be cared for by another person. You have to *be* someone to love someone.

The best place to start being somebody is in work. Many patients we see are unemployed, on disability, or on welfare. Our own program for BPD tells them that going back to work or school is an essential part of their recovery, and that doing so is necessary for treatment to be effective.

Perhaps because I have always been a hard worker, I find it difficult to understand why patients choose to remain chronically unemployed. People who neither work nor study have a great deal of time on their hands. They lack the human connections that the workplace offers as well as the satisfaction of performing a social role. For some, raising children is a full-time job, but once children are in school most mothers need to work. Without contributing *something* to the community, how can people feel good about themselves?

One of the buzzwords of recent decades has been that patients go into therapy to raise their "self-esteem." But self-esteem has to come from somewhere. It cannot be manufactured by validation. Self-esteem depends on being somebody and doing something. It is not a precondition of change but rather a result. Patients rarely do well in therapy when they remain permanently out of work or on welfare or if they fail to go back to school to build a future.

Some patients believe that they have no real life without an intense intimate relationship. That is one of the many misperceptions that afflict people with BPD. However, emptiness cannot be filled by love. Attachments based on that goal are either doomed or lead to great frustration. In a wise book about how people love, the psychoanalyst Ethel Person (2007, p. 105) quoted Antoine de St. Exupéry: "Love is not looking into each other's eyes, but two people looking outward in the same direction."

Attachment to a supportive partner can sometimes aid patients in their recovery. However, when that happens, an internal change has already taken place. People cannot find lasting love, or a good person, until they feel deserving of love. Over and over again, I have seen patients meet someone *after* making real progress in therapy.

On the other hand, intimacy is not for everyone. Divorce rates are high in our society, and many people end up living without a partner (Heatherington & Kelly, 2002). But is that a bad thing? Not necessarily. There is much more to life than love. Many people live full lives on their own. Not everyone is happier in an intimate relationship; many do better in their own space, seeing a few friends.

Thus, the fact that half of all recovered patients with BPD live alone is not bad news. People who have difficulty handling close relationships may do better avoiding them and choosing less intimate connections. Such choices can be wise, and therapists should not hesitate to validate them.

Problems arise in intimacy when both parties in a relationship have needs that cannot be met. It is more strategic to dilute one's demands and meet them piecemeal. For some patients, links with a larger community provide meaningful but less emotionally demanding connections. Religious communities accomplished this for people in the past and still do.

Many people with disappointing intimate relationships still want (and have) children. Quite a few of our patients with BPD are single mothers. Although not all do well in the role of a parent, the responsibility of raising a child tends to be a stabilizing force. Many patients give up suicidality when they have children who depend on them.

Parenting is a difficult task, for all of us. And not everyone enjoys being a parent. Thus, patients with BPD may make a correct decision *not* to have children. Children are not born to provide love to parents. Until maturity, children need to be naturally selfish and to demand more than they give. Parents who cannot adapt to demanding children may end up mistreating them. Sometimes this means that child protection services become involved, and that mothers can lose the right to care for their children.

Therapists sometimes idealize living in a family. There are other satisfactions in life. Treatment need not have a Hollywood ending, with the therapist receiving a slice of wedding cake. It is sufficient to help patients develop a life that provides a wider range of satisfactions.

There are many ways to get a life. None is a panacea. Work can be unstable or unfulfilling. Relationships may fail. Children may rebel or develop symptoms of their own. People with strong emotional needs can have trouble maintaining connections to the larger community. But an imperfect life is better than no life at all. I encourage patients not to put all their eggs in one basket. You would not put all your money into a single investment. In the same way, you need more than a job, more than an intimate relationship, and more than one friend.

In summary, treatment of BPD should, as soon as possible, set a goal of getting the patient back into the workforce or to return to school. Whatever else patients are feeling and suffering, they cannot put life in the deep freeze while working out problems in therapy.

Psychotherapy is a process of learning. The classroom is the therapist's office, but the laboratory is the patient's life. However, one cannot do well in school without doing one's homework. Not every therapy is like CBT, which actually *prescribes* homework. Yet most psychological change takes place in the patient's everyday life, outside formal sessions. There should be a consistent message from therapist to patient that doing so is expected. That counters the frequent misapprehension that most healing takes place in the therapy hour or that therapists have magical ways to make patients feel better.

EASY CASES

Although BPD is famous for being difficult to treat, some patients do remarkably well and get better rapidly. Our own program has had fairly consistent success in treating these patients. These easy cases may not always look promising at first. In retrospect, one might see ego strengths that could have suggested recovery. Although good results are almost impossible to predict in advance, the main prognostic point is that these patients will have not been consistently ill for years.

Case 1

Brenda was 24 years old and had recently graduated from university. She had been in therapy for 4 years and, in spite of some improvement, continued to have mood swings, unstable relations, and drug abuse. The therapist, who was probably worn out and discouraged, eventually referred her to an inpatient unit in an expensive and well-known private and psychoanalytically oriented hospital. (Brenda's father was a wealthy businessman.) This experience, lasting several months, only made her worse (Brenda acted out sexually and took drugs within the hospital premises). A complex cocktail of medications (escalitopram, oxcarbamazepine, alprazolam, molindone, and risperidone) entirely failed to help her.

Brenda's symptoms began in adolescence with bulimia, cutting, and polysubstance abuse. She was still cutting her arms when stressed and had twice tried to hang herself. Yet Brenda was a pretty woman who had many relationships with men. All of these intimate attachments, however, were marked by conflict and profound insecurity.

Brenda was referred to our 12-week program of individual and group therapy, where she made a remarkable recovery. Our cognitive emphasis was of more practical use to her than psychodynamic treatment. By 6 weeks she had stopped taking any of her medications. There was one further incident of cutting (Brenda had been angry at her domineering father), but Brenda learned better ways of coping. At the end of treatment, Brenda had a job. She chose not to seek further psychotherapy. At one-year follow-up, Brenda was in school, not in therapy, and not taking medication.

Case 2

Cathy was a university graduate who spent 2 months in the hospital after threatening suicide (following a rejection by a boyfriend). Cathy was drinking intermittently, having one-night stands, and suffering from panic attacks, insomnia, and severe mood swings. Cathy was out of work and becoming more socially isolated.

In a 12-week program Cathy made rapid strides. Although she continued to need medications for chronic insomnia, she clearly benefited from psychotherapy. Part of the treatment was dynamic, focusing on her problematic relationship with an inconsistent and rejecting father (and with boyfriends who resembled him). The other part of therapy was cognitive, in which Cathy learned to handle conflict more effectively, leading to reconciliation with other family members and friends. By the end of the treatment, Cathy had made plans to go back to school for professional education.

These cases demonstrate how much progress some patients can make in a short time. It may not be an accident that both were university graduates with strong career goals. Although they were temporarily grounded by symptoms, both women were able to pick up where they left off. Work and study provided them with a stable sense of self-esteem that did not depend on other people. Both of these patients wisely decided to take a break from intimacy. However, as the next case demonstrates, one does not have to be a university graduate or a professional to do well in therapy.

Case 3

Fiona was a 32-year-old divorced woman. She was living with her two sons and had recently lost a job as a manager.

Fiona had a highly traumatic history. Her stepfather sexually and physically abused her from ages 7 to 16. Fiona was very angry at her mother for ignoring the problem and for letting it happen in the first place. She felt that her mother sacrificed the interests of her children (a sister was similarly abused) to retain a relationship with an unreliable alcoholic man. At 16, Fiona put an end to the abuse by showing her injuries to a teacher at school, after which she was placed in a foster home. As a young adult, Fiona was heavily involved with drugs and had a series of relationships with abusive and criminal men. On the other hand, she always found a job and was able to raise her children.

Acknowledgment and validation of both life adversities and strengths was helpful for Fiona. She also learned to control her anger (usually associated with jealousy toward a boyfriend). At the end of her therapy, Fiona felt well enough to stop taking the antidepressant she had been prescribed a year previously. She also got a new apartment and found a good job as a flight attendant.

MIDDLING CASES

Most of the patients we see are neither unusually easy or hard. Our group has treated these "middling cases" in 12 weeks with some degree of success. However, one should not expect full remission or dramatic recovery.

The next two cases resemble the BPD patients that therapists commonly treat. Both presented with problematic behaviors and relationships that presented obstacles to effective therapy. They improved after treatment but were by no means fully recovered.

Case 4

Barbara was a 21-year-old woman who presented with symptoms of cutting and rages associated with jealousy. She had never been hospitalized and was not on medication. Barbara was living with a boyfriend, raising a child, working part time, and going to college. Barbara came from a middle-class family but felt emotionally neglected and became a rebellious adolescent. One of the main topics in therapy was her relationship with her boyfriend, a gangster to whom she was greatly attracted. While pregnant, she discovered this man also had previous children by another relationship but kept his visits to his previous family a secret. His activities required him to disappear for days at a time. In spite of earnings from drug sales, this man could not even be counted on to pay the rent.

Barbara benefited from therapy, was no longer cutting, and had better control of her anger. The relationship with the boyfriend did not change, but Barbara felt she could not even consider giving it up. She would have felt defeated if she broke up the family she had created. At 1-year follow-up, she was attending college and still lived with the boyfriend, whom she described as being in the process of "going straight."

Case 5

Oriana was a 28-year-old woman living with her husband and two children. She had been attending college, but dropped out and was not currently working. Oriana felt her husband was supportive, but she had difficulty revealing aspects of her past about which she felt ashamed. Other problems included her heavy cannabis abuse and sexual infidelities.

Oriana had first seen a therapist at age 14. Oriana would burn herself on the arms and hands, behavior that recently started again after she confessed to her husband that she had previously worked as a prostitute.

Oriana was raised in a very unstable family. Her father, who had been in the film industry, has been married three times, with a child from each marriage. From age 6, when her parents divorced, Oriana was raised by a mother who had spent time in a psychiatric hospital. She had vivid memories of being a witness to orgies lasting late into the night.

Oriana did well in a 12-week course of group and individual therapy. However, because her substance abuse was not controlled, she was referred to a specialized clinic for that problem. But Oriana found it impossible to give up cannabis entirely. For many years she had used it to deal with dysphoria and found that it worked for her. On the bright side, she was able to care reasonably well for her children.

When patients are willing to change even the most deeply ingrained patterns of behavior, they can move forward more rapidly, as illustrated by the following example.

Case 6

Leila was a 25-year-old nursing student. Over the previous 2 years, she had been in the hospital (or the emergency room) 15 times for suicide attempts. Leila had a history of being involved with men who were substance abusers. Leila lived alone, and her 5-year-old daughter was in the custody of her mother, who was also the main person in Leila's life. She only had a few friends and had one man who served as a "sex buddy." Lcila had tried to go back to school but could not handle its demands. She decided she should work as an orderly until she felt more stable.

But Leila decided that she was accomplishing little in life and that she was unwilling to remain a chronic patient, with the practical result of not being able to look after her child. She made a decision to stop all suicidal behavior and kept to it. One year later, she was working as a hospital orderly and spending much more time with her daughter. She had postponed indefinitely the idea of looking for an intimate relationship with a man.

In summary, middling cases can show real improvement but continue to have difficulties. Experienced therapists will be happy with such results. The clinical literature can sometimes be misleadingly optimistic. It tells stories about heartwarming recoveries that therapists cannot replicate in their own practices. These highly selective narratives end up being more discouraging than encouraging. Once we give up on fantasies of total cure, working with patients with BPD is much more satisfying.

HARD CASES

Not every patient with BPD recovers. There are hard cases, patients who do not do well with any therapist. Some flit in and out of the system without using up a lot of resources. But quite a few patients become "psychiatrized." By this, I mean that their life comes to revolve around the mental health system. They have few outside relationships but relate to physicians, nurses, and therapists in a "borderline" manner (i.e., with angry dependency and suicidal threats).

The main reason patients with BPD become psychiatrized is that the system is structured to reinforce their symptoms. When patients threaten to kill themselves, they may be rejected by significant others, but there is always a place for them in the emergency room (or, however briefly, on a ward). Hospitals and clinics become places where patients can behave outrageously yet expect to be understood. Therapists do not feel they have the option of saying, "I cannot help you under these circumstances." Too often, the fear of suicidality trumps clinical judgment.

I now give examples of what colleagues often call "famous" cases of BPD, patients who return over and over again and who do not respond well to any form of therapy.

Case 7

Rachel was a 25-year-old nurse who had been admitted to medical school but dropped out after a suicide attempt. Over the next 2 years, Rachel spent her life on a series of hospital wards. At first she was diagnosed with schizophrenia, then with bipolar disorder, and finally with PTSD. The confusion about Rachel's diagnosis was exacerbated by the presence of prominent cognitive symptoms, with frequent voices telling her to kill herself. However, the main features of BPD (chronic suicidality, cutting, mood swings, unstable relationships) were strikingly present.

My contribution to Rachel's treatment was to get her discharged and transferred to a day hospital. Over the next few months, she made serious threats to kill herself. While we were worried about her, the team agreed not to readmit her. In the end, she did not kill herself. But her quality of life went steeply downward. Over the next 10 years, Rachel attended psychiatric clinics and worked sporadically. She had no real relationships other than her contact with mental health professionals. If anything kept her going, it was support from her parents.

Rachel was an unusually difficult patient. In addition to her suicide threats, which often brought her to the emergency room, she often became abusive and violent. Finally, after assaulting a staff member, she was barred from the hospital.

Rachel is now 40 years old. I recently saw her in consultation for a colleague to whom she was referred after being raped by a man she picked up in a bar. Although I cannot say that any treatment helped Rachel, I am satisfied to have stopped interventions that were making her worse.

Case 8

Mary was a 42-year-old woman who had been a patient at the hospital clinic for 20 years. She has had numerous admissions for overdoses as well as emergency room visits. Her disorder was so chronic that she lost most of her social connections and was living in a residence for the mentally ill. Even there, overdoses led to a threat of expulsion.

Mary was homosexual and had many unstable relationships with women. She also was a long-term abuser of alcohol and cocaine. Although Mary attended Alcoholics Anonymous for some time, she continued to drink while claiming it was no longer a problem. However, Mary had been picked up by the police on numerous occasions for disorderly conduct.

Mary was prescribed haldoperidol, citalopram, lamotrigine, and clonazepam. None of these drugs helped her. Several of her previous therapists became burned out by her difficulties.

Mary's parents were alcoholic, and her mother left home when she was 11. After being expelled from high school, Mary had a very irregular and tumultuous life, which became worse after the breakup of a long-term relationship when she was 25.

Mary made little progress in our program. She returned to long-term outpatient care and went on to have several other admissions to hospital.

Case 9

Norma was a 29-year-old woman who had never held a job. Since the age of 18, her life had centered around her many (25) hospital admissions and frequent (weekly) emergency room visits. Norma's mood was unstable, and she had an explosive temper. Overdoses were carried out in the face of frustration, and Norma also cut herself from time to time. She heard voices in her head telling her to die but was not sure if they were real.

Norma developed a reputation for being an emergency room problem because of her threats of violence. On one occasion she pushed an experienced emergency psychiatrist against a wall and was barred from ever attending that hospital again.

Case 10

Tania was a 37-year-old woman who has been in psychiatric treatment since the age of 20. Although Tania came from a family of professors, she was currently living alone on welfare, and her social life was limited to a few friends and family.

Tania had seen many therapists in the past. Her concerned parents had made an effort to link her to well-known clinicians in the community. All of them had eventually given up in frustration. Currently, Tania was attending a psychiatric clinic where she saw a psychiatrist who evaluated her and prescribed paroxetine, desipramine, clonazepam, and valproate. But she was still hoping to find the "right" therapist.

Tania was an intelligent woman who had come close to finishing her university degree. Unlike patients with BPD who dramatize their symptoms, Tania had learned over the years to present herself as healthier than she was in order to be accepted by therapists. She could never be counted on to provide an accurate picture of her problems. On one occasion when I evaluated her, Tania described social isolation and little else. Yet she had been quite recently admitted to a ward where she spent 6 months and where her suicidality as well as violent regressed behavior made enormous difficulties for the staff.

BRIEF INTERVENTIONS AND EXTENDED CARE

The received wisdom about BPD used to be that treatment should almost always be long term. Intuitively, it seems logical to assume that patients with long-term problems need extended courses of therapy. Although this point of view originated in psychoanalysis, cognitive therapists share it. Linehan (1993) proposed a treatment lasting for years, as did Beck, Freeman, Davis, and associates (2004).

The outcome research reviewed in Chapter 6 points in a different direction. Many cases of BPD remit symptomatically within a few years, and quite a few do well in the long run. Moreover, some of the clinical trials discussed in Chapter 8 (e.g., Davidson, Norrie, et al., 2006; Stanley et al., 2007) suggest that good results can sometimes be obtained in a few months.

However, response to treatment can be quite variable. Easy cases do well, whereas hard cases do not. By and large, the most chronic and dysfunctional patients with BPD are less likely to find their way into prospective follow-up studies or clinical trials. They are too impulsive and are often occupied with emergency room visits.

Different treatment options should be considered for easy and hard cases. Younger patients who have not had the disorder for long as well as patients who have had periods of good functioning may respond to briefer interventions. Brief treatment has been shown to be effective in clinical trials (Davidson, Norrie, et al., 2006; Stanley et al., 2007) and can be sufficient for many patients as long as follow-up is available.

However, short-term programs are not likely to be successful for hard cases. These are patients who are heavily psychiatrized and who have not functioned for many years. They are chronically unemployed, and their main relationships are with mental health professionals. For these patients, interventions that work for easy and middling cases become just one of a long series of failed therapies. Although disappointing, our difficulty in helping these patients through simpler interventions is not surprising. Mental disorders, like physical illnesses, produce a wide range of functional outcomes. Some patients have episodic problems that remit. Others never get well.

But hard cases still need help. They do not benefit from the polypharmacy and repeated hospital admissions that are often the mainstay of their treatment. Like other chronic patients, they can benefit from programs focusing on rehabilitation.

With this principle in mind, our clinical group opened a second program designed for the most severe cases of BPD. The time scale was longer (6-month modules, renewable, up to a maximum of 2 years), but the basic elements were similar (group and individual therapy while weaning high-dose medications). Although we have not conducted clinical trials, pre–post analyses showed that most were "contained" by the program, in that they no longer sought help at the emergency room at the same frequency. We have also been able to discharge some of these patients to the community.

Case 11

Paula was a 30-year-old woman who had previously worked as a quality controller. Her two children, ages 4 and 7, were in the care of her sister because she felt unable to raise them and because they had witnessed violent quarrels at home between Paula and her lover.

Paula held a "world record" of emergency room visits at our hospital: 300 in 12 months. When I asked her why she came so often, she stated she felt better there than at home. She had also carried out 10 overdoses in 6 years, for which she was admitted twice. Paula was cutting herself repetitively on the wrist for tension relief. She also went to bars and had many one-night stands.

Paula was referred to a long-term specialized program for BPD offering group and individual therapy, focusing on life skills. One year later, while Paula remained dysphoric, she was stable and emergency room visits had become rare.

Some hard cases may need lifelong follow-up. However, if we can reduce morbidity through psychosocial rehabilitation, we could do much the same for this population as has long been offered to patients with chronic psychoses and mood disorders. Such an approach is worthy of clinical investigation.

CLINICAL IMPLICATIONS

- Methods of therapy used for other groups of patients may not be effective in BPD.
- Management requires helping patients to get a life. Usually work or school comes first, and improvement in relationships follows later.
- This approach is most likely to be effective in patients who have not centered their life on the mental health system.
- Even in the most difficult patients, improving life skills can be a central goal.

CHAPTER 10

Therapeutic Interventions

*T*here is no one right way to conduct psychotherapy for BPD patients. As we have seen, clinical trials show that methods based on very different theories can be effective. On the other hand, the data also show that treatment as usual is not usually good enough.

Does that mean that every patient has to be sent to specialized clinics to receive an evidence-based program of therapy? I would say "no." First, these forms of treatment are expensive and difficult to access (and they are entirely unavailable in many communities). Second, not every patient accepts referrals to a specialized program. BPD is fairly common in practice, so therapists need to find a way to treat these cases themselves.

My recommendation is that clinicians reading this book should build on what they are already doing for patients with BPD but focus more on structured interventions supported by research findings. The most important principle is to take a systematic approach to core problems. Instead of generalized support or an exploration of childhood events, we need to teach patients skills to manage emotional dysregulation and impulsivity. Although each of the evidence-based methods (DBT, MBT, SFP, and TFP) looks different and is based on a different theory, they all teach patients to observe feelings and behavior. If they didn't, none of these therapies would ever have demonstrated success in clinical trials.

I am unhappy about the current crop of competing methods of treatment for BPD, each with its own acronym. I look forward to the day when there will be one therapy, a generic approach that adapts the best ideas from all methods, combining them into one package.

THE GENERAL AND THE SPECIFIC

The treatment of BPD should be, as much as possible, evidence based. However, even when research shows that a method of therapy is effective, one cannot conclude that every specific procedure described in its manual is, by itself, a useful intervention. Clinical trials only show whether the package as a whole works. "Dismantling" studies, in which therapies are taken apart piece by piece to determine which element is crucial, are very rare and have never been conducted on treatments for BPD.

That is why it is difficult to provide an evidence-based framework for the nitty-gritty of treatment (i.e., how therapists actually talk to patients). This chapter can only illustrate some broad principles, with examples drawn from my own experience.

Over the first 25 years of my career, I treated a large number of patients in practice with either long-term or intermittent therapy. In line with my training, I applied a psychodynamic perspective. However, with time, I became convinced that open-ended treatment can lead to major pitfalls (see Chapter 11). I also became convinced that excessive concentration on past events produces regression and that interpretations relating past to present are not that helpful. Gradually, my approach to therapy became more cognitive and more oriented to current life issues.

With a group of psychologists and psychiatrists, I opened a specialized program for BPD in 2001. As noted in Chapter 9, it provides 12 weeks of group and individual therapy, a structure that is most suitable for acutely ill patients. Using such a brief period of intervention seemed radical at the time, but data later came in to support it (see Chapter 8).

In describing how I work with patients I will draw on experiences in this program. These patients remain fresh in my mind, and the interventions I describe represent my current views on how to manage BPD. However, I would like to emphasize that the clinical examples presented here are only illustrations. I am not suggesting that my way of working with BPD is superior to the established evidence-based methods described in Chapter 8. At best I offer it as a practical alternative for acutely ill patients, who have not hardened into chronicity.

Moreover, this book must offer disclaimers concerning the use of clinical data. The last thing I want to do is to write still another book presenting one clinician's approach as gospel. I do not propose that our treatment package be generally adopted, nor do I claim that the interventions we have found useful are right for every patient or every therapist. (While pre–post analyses suggest that our methods work, without a control group such data can only provide quality assurance.)

There is another reason why clinical experience must be regarded with caution. The goals of treatment can be achieved in different ways. If the methods that have been subjected to clinical trials were readily available, I would be happy to refer patients to them. But this book is about how to apply the principles of evidence-based methods to ordinary clinical practice.

Finally, one cannot ignore the personal element in psychotherapy. Over the many years I have taught psychotherapy (and clinical evaluation), I have observed that each student has a unique way of communicating effectively with people, concordant with his or her personality. Even if some are better than others, excellent therapists are far from identical. Some like to talk a lot and are lively and effusive by temperament. Others talk less but are quietly receptive.

HOW TO TALK TO A PATIENT WITH BPD

Exact words are not that important, but there are right and wrong ways to conduct therapy. To get started, you need to communicate in a way that makes patients feel comfortable.

One thing that most clinicians experienced in treating BPD have learned is that they need to maintain a higher level of activity. Prolonged silences are not useful for patients who are suspicious about what you think of them and who feel at sea without guidance. A portentous style focusing on interpretations is off-putting and unhelpful for people who need to be reassured that you are in touch with their feelings.

Instead, therapy for BPD is in some ways like a conversation. We do best by talking to patients in a natural and unpretentious way.

The more experience you have, the easier that becomes; your style of communication need not diverge totally from a social interaction. It is the content of the conversation that is different. Needless to say, therapists do not talk about themselves, and patients talk about things they have never revealed to anyone. When we are more natural, patients know we are not faking. That is what Carl Rogers (1942) called "genuineness," a characteristic of particular importance to patients with BPD, who are sensitive to interpersonal "power plays" that can put them in a subservient position.

To be genuine and to facilitate collaboration, Linehan (1993) has suggested being "irreverent" in therapy. Humor helps establish a sense of connection and also builds a neutral space around intense emotions. Surprisingly, using humor has been controversial in the clinical literature (Sultanoff, 2003). Most therapists find it useful but worry about laughing at rather than laughing with people. Of course, if you have no sense of humor, you cannot use that skill in treatment (therapists with such a deficiency might find patients with BPD too "heavy").

Psychotherapy is full of metaphors; that is how people talk most of the time. By and large, it is better to build on your patient's metaphors than to introduce your own. Doing so can be creative and enjoyable for patient and therapist; again, the process is like "jazz."

Finally, the words you use should be as simple as possible. If you cannot explain a concept simply to a patient, you probably do not understand it yourself.

BUILDING AN ALLIANCE

One of the first things every therapist learns is how to build an alliance. If treatment is going to last for only a few months, the process needs to move rapidly. Yet alliance building need not take long: If the first meeting goes well, therapy is usually off to a good start. In fact, research data show that after only three sessions measures of the alliance are good predictors of outcome (Luborsky, 1988). However, research (Gaston, Goldfried, Greenberg, & Horvath, 1995) also shows that patients perceive the connection more accurately than therapists. (In that sense, "the customer is always right.")

Difficulties in the alliance have been seen in different ways by the various evidence-based therapies for BPD. However, whether problems are defined as "therapy-interfering behaviors" (Linehan, 1993), transference (Clarkin et al., 2007), or failures of mentalization (Bateman & Fonagy, 2006), they need to addressed, or therapy will never get started.

The most important elements in alliance building are empathy, optimism, and a practical focus on current issues (Orlinsky, Ronnestad, & Willutski, 2004). An active and natural approach should bring most patients into an alliance quickly. However, some patients with BPD have a very fragile sense of trust, so that maintaining the alliance is difficult (Frank, 1992). A few can be too suspicious or too volatile to enter psychotherapy at all. Fortunately, that kind of problem is exceptional. Most patients with BPD are willing at least to try therapy (even if they do not always stay in it). The key to building an alliance is whether the patient feels understood.

The usual term to describe the process of understanding feelings is *empathy*, but we need to think about what we mean by this much-used word. It does not necessarily imply a mindless "I feel your pain" or a knee-jerk "You were right to be so angry." You can put yourself in another person's shoes without sharing their worldview.

We are, again, in debt to Marsha Linehan for introducing the term *validation*. In her book (Linehan, 1993, pp. 222–223), she states, "The essence of validation is this: the therapist communicates to the patient that her responses make sense and are understandable within her current life context or situation." In other words, validating need not mean agreeing with feelings or behaviors but understanding them in an interpersonal context. Doing so avoids dismissing the patient's reactions and leaves the door open for reframing and reappraisal.

Case 1

A 25-year-old woman described with great shame a period of her life when she was a sex worker. The therapist indicated he understood her feelings but placed her behavior in context. This was a time when the patient was living in a strange city and her only social contacts were with people involved with clubbing, substance abuse, and stripping. Although she need not have been involved in prostitution, her choices were understandable at a moment in her life when she lacked all direction. The therapist also noted that she had left that world as soon as she got a steady job.

Therapists sometimes do not understand feelings right away, and they can also get things wrong. Failure to empathize can produce strong reactions in patients who are unusually sensitive to being mis-understood (or, in the language of DBT, readily "invalidated"). The trick is to avoid being in any way insistent about one's own position and to shift gears rapidly when necessary, a flexibility that is appreci-ated by most patients.

Case 2

A 25-year-old woman was in treatment for mood instability, an-gry outbursts, suicidal threats, cutting, and unstable relation-ships. One of the issues raised in therapy concerned devaluation of other people whenever they fell below her standard of perfec-tion. The therapist suggested that this kind of idealism was likely to lead to chronic disappointment. In the next session, the pa-tient handed the therapist a long letter explaining why he had misunderstood her. She felt that the comments in the previous session had made her feel like a "freak" rather than as the ideal-ist she saw herself as. She wondered whether she could work in this therapy or whether she should be transferred to someone else.

The therapist said that he was sorry he had hurt the patient's feelings, and asked her to be sure to let him know whenever fur-ther problems came up. Sessions continued after this, marked by several more misunderstandings, but some progress was made in reducing symptoms. At the end of the program, the therapist was surprised when the patient asked whether it was possible to see him for follow-up.

TARGETING THE CORE DIMENSIONS OF BPD

Much of the work of therapy in personality disorders could be de-scribed as "working with traits" (Paris, 1997b; i.e., modifying behav-iors rooted in personality to make them work *for* patients rather than *against* them). For example, even if patients with BPD are highly emotional, that trait can be engaging and useful when toned down. Similarly, even if patients with BPD are impulsive, they can learn to make better decisions by taking more time before acting.

As for managing emotional dysregulation, there can be little doubt that Marsha Linehan "wrote the book." The first skill DBT teaches patients (Linehan, 1993) is to identify and label affect: Pa-tients may act out without actually knowing what they are feeling. What follows depends on a series of measures to modify affective instability, such as mindfulness (experiencing emotions without trying to change them) and distress tolerance techniques.

Whether in group or individual therapy, patients will bring in examples of dysregulated emotions brought on by recent events. The therapist validates the patient's responses but suggests better ways of managing them. Patients have to learn how to avoid being overwhelmed by emotion as well as to develop alternative ways of managing situations that provoked intense responses.

Case 3

A 30-year-old patient described an inability to control her emotions when fighting with her boyfriend. Initially angry, she would break things, throw things, and sometimes hit him. After these incidents, she would retreat to her room, lock the door, and feel despair, crying uncontrollably. These incidents would often end in cutting. Both the group and individual therapists responded by suggesting to this patient that she needed to identify her emotions at an earlier point and then stand back from them and reappraise her reactions. Once she could distance herself from her feelings, she would be less likely to be overwhelmed by them.

Managing impulsivity runs on a parallel track. Using "behavioral analysis" (Linehan, 1993), we can trace impulsive acts (such as injuring oneself or overdosing) to the way patients react to life events. However, impulsivity is not necessarily a direct consequence of affective instability (see Chapter 3). Many impulsive actions in BPD (e.g., the decision to join a group in abusing cocaine or to begin an intimate relationship with an unsuitable partner) reflect long-term dysfunctional patterns of behavior that develop over time, influenced by how patients see themselves and reinforced by their peer groups.

Our approach emphasizes teaching patients how to slow down and reappraise situations before acting. Most people, even those with BPD, can use these skills in some situations, but not in those that get them into difficulty.

Case 4

A 35-year-old woman described an incident in which, after her boyfriend had gone to a party without her, she took an overdose of 10 Tylenols with alcohol, ending the evening with her stomach being washed out in the emergency room. Although the patient had been angry, the action was not carried out in an emotionally dysregulated state but was part of a long-term pattern, using suicidality to control an interpersonal environment. In fact, when the boyfriend came home, he acted contrite and actually took responsibility for what had happened.

The therapist asked the patient to take full ownership of the incident. It was also pointed out that these kinds of actions, even if effective in the short run, are counterproductive in the long run. First, the boyfriend, as previous experience had shown, would inevitably be angry later, in another context. Second, taking overdoses to solve problems could hardly be good for the patient's sense of competence. Finally, it was suggested that when situations like this come up in the future, it would be better to delay any action until the patient understood her feelings, reappraised them, and considered alternative solutions.

The domain of cognitive dysfunction can produce dramatic symptoms, which sometimes need treatment with neuroleptics (see Chapter 8). However, managing these problems does not always require specific interventions. Hallucinations, paranoid feelings, and depersonalization in BPD are usually responses to stressors. They tend to disappear when emotional regulation and impulsivity come under control.

Case 5

A 23-year-old graduate student being treated for cutting herself and disturbed relationships described auditory hallucinations that came on whenever she felt extremely upset. The voices, either male or female, commented on her behavior and suggested that she should die. Once the patient formed a therapeutic alliance, these symptoms disappeared entirely. However, after she graduated and went to see a different therapist in her home city, they returned, only to drop away again once she was comfortable with a new treatment.

Finally, let us examine how therapy addresses problems in the domain of interpersonal relations. Much of the work with BPD involves exploring conflicts and pathological choices in intimacy. The task of the therapist can be easier when a relatively supportive partner is in the picture, even if relationships are subject to stress and conflict. The work of therapy is more complicated when the patient is involved with a highly pathological partner. Many of our patients have problematic relationships with people who are physically abusive, substance abusing, or frankly criminal. It is usually of little use to challenge these attachments directly as long as they perform a set of functions for the patient.

Case 6

Norah was a 35-year-old woman was in treatment for cutting and overdosing. For the last several years, she had lived with a man who was wealthy and emotionally supportive. (He even combed the Internet for information about BPD to find a better way to help her.) However, Norah experienced her partner as controlling, not supportive. She found his concern suffocating and often threatened to leave him, while flirting with other men she met on the job (and making sure she was found out). When her boyfriend was preoccupied with his own issues, she would often fly into rages.

The therapist noted the patient's frustration but pointed out that she would never find the perfect partner. In fact, most of her previous boyfriends were drug addicts. Moreover, a partner could not be expected to understand her fully. It was her task to develop enough life satisfactions to be less dependent on whether she was cared for.

Case 7

Barbara, a 21-year-old woman (described in Chapter 9), was in treatment for a series of drug overdoses. She was living with a gangster who imported drugs into the country and often disappeared for weeks at a time.

The therapist discussed with Barbara how exciting this relationship had been from the beginning (sexual power and the romance she associated with his world) and why she still found this man highly attractive. At the same time, he noted that she was now putting herself in the position of accepting things that made her furious. If there was no other way to deal with her feelings or to get her boyfriend to attend to her, she was likely to take another overdose of pills. It would be important to have other sources of satisfaction, such as carrying out her plan to return to university and develop a career. Once that was accomplished, Barbara would be in a better position to decide what to do about her relationship.

WORK AND RELATIONSHIPS

To help patients "get a life," our program follows the principle that people need to establish a social role through work or study before undertaking intimacy. These social roles are needed to avoid regression and to provide raw material for therapeutic work.

We actively encourage all patients to start either working or studying and not to delay doing so until they feel better. We tell patients from the beginning that doing so is an essential part of the recovery process.

Case 8

A 30-year-old woman was in treatment for a series of suicidal attempts. She was living with a man who was reasonably supportive but often traveled out of town for business. In his absence, she would become involved with drug abuse and carry out promiscuous love affairs.

The therapist pointed out that it was understandable that she experienced a sense of emptiness every time she felt abandoned by the boyfriend. After all, she had little else in life to make her feel competent and satisfied. He encouraged her to find employment, and when she eventually did, there was a reduction in her impulsive behaviors.

Sometimes patients are reluctant to get a life because they would rather remain in the protected environment of the mental health system.

Case 9

Rita was a 35-year-old single woman who had left a stable government job 3 years previously and spent the intervening time on medical disability while attending various therapy programs for addiction, eating disorder, and personality disorder. Rita did not really want to return to her original job and also felt that she could not look for another job until her problems were resolved (e.g., she still had bulimia despite lengthy specialized treatment). She also thought she was too old to start over again in life.

The therapist told Rita she was at a turning point. She could decide to be a permanent patient, in which case her life would continue much as it had for the last several years. Alternatively, she could take the risk of reentering the world and seriously trying for something better.

Patients who have a job or are studying are in a better position to give priority to other life goals, such as entering a serious relationship. Many patients we see are between relationships, as often happens when treatment begins after a breakup. In these cases, we advise patients not to start a new intimate attachment until their life is more consolidated.

Case 10

A 22-year-old woman was in treatment for cutting and substance abuse. She described a long series of intense relationships with men with whom she was entirely obsessed. Her entire life depended on whether her boyfriends paid enough attention to her. One by one, they left her because they could not cope with her needs and demands.

The therapist recommended to this patient that she not get involved with anyone else for the time being. He pointed out that she needed to feel more stable inside before she could handle a relationship. She followed this advice, finishing school and then traveling for a few months, after which she took up a career. It took her another full year before she felt ready to try intimacy again.

Some of the people we see do have long-term intimate attachments. In that case, work focuses on helping them to handle inevitable conflicts in a more constructive way, by maintaining better boundaries and by modulating emotional responses. It can also be useful to practice these skills in one's family of origin. One of the most frequent issues that comes up in working on relationships is black-and-white thinking (often called "splitting"). Patients with BPD can see other people, themselves, or interpersonal situations as either all good or all bad. This cognitive distortion needs to be corrected in therapy. Patients need to practice seeing the world in shades of gray.

Case 11

A 25-year-old woman was in treatment for cutting and affective instability. She expressed concern about an upcoming Christmas visit to her mother. In the past, these visits had ended in serious quarrels, after which they would not speak to each other for months. In the patient's mind, this relationship, like others in her life, should be characterized by total honesty and "communication about feelings." Anything less was seen as hypocrisy, even if it led to a disastrous holiday.

The therapist pointed out that she was seeing this situation as black and white and missing shades of gray. Even if the visit did not lead to the breakthrough she hoped for, which had never happened before and never would, it could be counted a success if conflict was kept under sufficient control for her to feel that she had "had a Christmas" and that her relationship with her mother, however disappointing, was manageable.

Again, helping patients get a life goes hand in hand with managing emotional dysregulation and impulsivity. You cannot learn much from therapy without using your life as a laboratory. One can make frank (or even mildly confrontative) comments about a patient's life problems without being judgmental or intrusive. As Linehan (1993) points out, every intervention has a dual (or "dialectical") quality. We validate the patient's feelings but challenge them to change. By doing this, therapists transmit a message of hope: Life need not be like this, and even if it is never perfect, it can be much better.

GROUP AND INDIVIDUAL THERAPY

Group therapy had its heyday several decades ago and then fell into decline. Although groups remain an important tool, the models on which it was once based are out of date. The original concept was an intensive group process focusing on interpersonal problems (Yalom & Leszcz, 2005). Today, groups are used more for psychoeducation and support.

The empirical literature on group therapy for BPD is slim, but there is some evidence for using a group setting for short-term cognitive therapy (Davidson, Norrie, et al., 2006; Weinberg et al., 2006). Our program for BPD, like DBT and other cognitively oriented methods, uses a combination of group and individual therapy. This is an approach that requires a team, preferably in an institutional setting. Although the same principles could be applied in standard practice restricted to individual therapy, we have found some advantages to the combination.

Groups are a good setting for learning skills, and that is what we do, while taking into account some of the classic process issues that arise in any group therapy. We do not use homework, but patients are asked to present examples drawn from recent events involving emotions and interpersonal problems that they had trouble handling. Then the therapist uses the opportunity to teach ways of coping that are applicable to the problems faced by all group members.

Individual therapy provides an opportunity to discuss personal issues that would not come in a group. (One patient astounded me by revealing an incestuous relationship with her father, a fact that she remembered well but had not disclosed in extensive previous therapy.) However, by and large, most of what we do individually is a reinforcement of our group approach.

Our program uses weekly group therapy to teach these skills, and the approach is further reinforced in individual sessions. All the therapists in our group have a different training: some psychodynamic, some cognitive, and some eclectic. For this reason, we watched each other on video when we started the program. We were rather surprised to find out how similar we are. (Probably experienced therapists end up doing much the same things over time.) However, to make sure that both group and individual interventions are moving on the same track, we meet once weekly and review how we are working with each patient.

I call all the patients who participate in our program a year after ending treatment to find out how they are doing. Most describe having benefited from the program, but they attribute their improvement to different components. Some tell me that they are still using the skills taught in the group on a daily basis, and that individual therapy was more or less unnecessary for them. Others tell me that they found the group to be overly structured, and that talking to a therapist individually was much more helpful.

Case 12

Tania was a 24-year-old woman living with her parents and working part time as a masseuse. Her problems include mood instability, angry outbursts, suicidal threats, cutting, unstable relationships, and heavily use of drugs.

In therapy, Tania attended both group and individual therapy regularly. What was most helpful about the group for Tania was learning how to manage emotions and control impulsivity. By the end of the program, she made firm plans to move out on her own and go back to school. She also had much better control of her anger and was appropriately assertive.

In a 1-year follow-up, Tania was able to describe the cognitive principles she had learned and describe how she was still using them. Tania had experienced more difficulty with individual therapy, in which she perceived herself devalued by criticism. This was actually a typical pattern for her in all her relationships. This issue was discussed in team meetings, and Tania herself could not help noticing that other group members were doing well with the same therapist. After some tactful clarifications, Tania began to work in both forms of therapy.

CLINICAL IMPLICATIONS

- There is no one way to talk to patients with BPD, but therapists can build an alliance rapidly by being both validating and practical. It helps to be natural, humorous, and forthright.
- Most of the work of psychotherapy involves modifying problematic traits and patterns: emotional dysregulation, impulsivity, and conflictual interpersonal relationships.
- Patients should be encouraged to "get a life" while in treatment and not wait till they feel better. Problems in recent life events are an opportunity to learn new skills and alternative behaviors.

CHAPTER 11

Problems in Therapy

No book about treating BPD can avoid addressing the special problems that arise in psychotherapy. Every clinician who works with these patients has to deal with behavioral patterns that disrupt the structure of treatment. These problems need to be thought about and planned for.

This is another chapter on nitty-gritty clinical issues that cannot be firmly based on research data. However, if any one principle can be drawn from empirical studies, it is that all proven therapies for BPD are well structured. The best results come when rules are explicit and consequences are predictable. BPD patients lack these structures—in both their inner world and their outer life. Treatment, therefore, goes better when therapists set limits and stick to them.

Sometimes rules are more honored in the breach than in the observance. It is tempting to believe that BPD patients need more love and care than other patients. It can be particularly difficult to stick to one's guns when the patient is threatening suicide. The problem is how to maintain structure even when the therapist feels "under the gun."

Therapists also need a rational basis to set rules. In this chapter, I suggest strategies for managing structural problems, criticize practices that tend to be either ineffective or counterproductive, and subject some recommended interventions to critical scrutiny.

FREQUENCY OF SESSIONS

When I was a psychiatric resident, several of my teachers told me that seeing BPD patients two or three times a week can accomplish much more than weekly sessions. The theory behind that claim was that patients need to come more often when they have difficulty in maintaining "object constancy." These ideas were based not on empirical findings but on a belief system. In an era in which psychoanalysis was the dominant paradigm, less was rarely considered more.

There has been no systematic research about the optimal frequency of psychotherapy for any group of patients. No one knows whether patients with BPD benefit from more frequent or less frequent sessions. I suggest that when you choose between options, neither of which is evidence based, you should favor the one that uses fewer resources. (That is the principle of parsimony.) I place the burden of proof on those who argue for a higher frequency of therapy.

There are two other reasons why BPD patients can be seen often. First, some patients demand more sessions, claiming they cannot wait a whole week. (One wonders whether it is a good idea to agree with that perception when you are trying to teach patients how to wait and to be less impulsive.) Second, therapists may believe that an increased frequency can prevent patients from attempting or committing suicide. (There is no evidence whatsoever to support that idea.)

In my opinion, a higher frequency of sessions is often counterproductive. The more frequently patients come, the more dependent on therapy they become. In psychoanalysis, a high frequency of visits is prescribed with a deliberate intent to break down defenses. No one has ever shown whether such an approach makes a difference, and it may be a particularly bad idea in BPD. These are patients who do not use high-level mature defenses (Bond et al., 1994). Moreover, their intimate relationships are already overly dependent (Gunderson, 2001). It is not clear what reproducing this situation in therapy can accomplish. Patients with BPD are vulnerable to developing problems (in the same way as other attachments) when a relationship to a therapist is too intense. Patients with BPD need to get a life, not center life around therapy or a therapist.

For all these reasons, I recommend that patients with BPD be seen once a week. Most do not in any case want to come more often and, if not well insured, may not be able to afford more sessions. Therapists should not feel they are providing less than optimal treatment at that frequency.

Case 1

Wendy was a 23-year-old PhD student who many found to be bright and engaging. Only her close friends knew that she had been seriously considering suicide for several years. Actually, suicidality was part of her heritage. Wendy's mother, who probably also had BPD, had a very enmeshed relationship with her daughter. At one point, the mother had had shown then 9-year-old Wendy a gun and suggested they die together.

Wendy's success in school allowed her to separate from her mother, and she left home soon after starting a serious relationship with a man. However, when the boyfriend left her, Wendy sought therapy.

The treatment began on a regular weekly basis, but, given how alarmed the therapist felt about Wendy's suicidality, was soon increased to twice a week and then to three times a week. Wendy made constant suicidal threats, although she only overdosed once during the treatment. Increasing the frequency of sessions did not reduce suicidality, but it encouraged Wendy to feel that her life depended on her therapist, and that he would do almost anything to stop her from dying. Eventually, in Wendy's mind the attachment became erotic. She began to suggest the possibility that they should have a relationship outside therapy. These complications greatly interfered with treatment and took time to work out.

ATTENDANCE

The life of a therapist brings both satisfaction and frustration. However, few things are more aggravating than arriving on time for a therapy session and discovering that the patient has not bothered to show up. (This is a particular issue first thing in the morning, especially if the therapist has had to fight traffic on the way.)

I am not, of course, referring to situations in which patients are too ill to attend. I am talking about times when patients forget to come, fail to wake up in time, or offer weak excuses for their absence. My experience is that, however much I like a patient, when I am "stood up," I wonder what to do with my anger.

If therapy is insured, the therapist may not even get paid for lost time. But when a fee is paid for every session, many therapists charge patients whether they show up or not. In that case, the therapist makes no financial sacrifice. (Lateness is less of a problem, unless patients are so late that they end up missing half their session.)

Therapists have traditionally considered absences to be examples of acting out. In a psychodynamic framework, the response might be an interpretation, although you have to wait until the next session before making it.

Cognitive–behavioral therapists also consider absences to be problems to be addressed and repaired. DBT describes them as a form of "therapy-interfering behavior" and has developed its own policy on absences: If you do not attend for a few weeks, you may be discharged from the program. But DBT can afford to leave some slack because the initial phase of treatment lasts for 12 months. In a briefer intervention, like our 12-week program, absences are more disruptive. We set up a "three strikes" rule, informing patients that missing at least three sessions (either individual or group) will be understood by the team as a decision to withdraw from the program.

Some therapies apply rules that tolerate absences. In my community, a psychologist ran a group for BPD in which patients could come and go as they pleased over several years. His approach has some similarity to intermittent therapy. The groups went on even if some of their members fail to show up. (The therapist had an institutional salary.)

There are no easy answers to the problem of attendance. My own view is that if patients do not show up on a consistent basis, they are not ready for psychotherapy. In such cases, I tend to discharge them and leave the door open for reentry. This approach is in line with the intermittent model presented later in the chapter.

TELEPHONE CALLS

Many therapists offer patients with BPD telephone contact in a crisis. Most people are reassured by this offer of availability and never call. But what if your patient calls you with a suicidal threat? You cannot conduct a psychotherapy session on the telephone. If the only advice you can give is to tell the patient to go to a hospital, the call was not really necessary. If you provide an extra emergency session, you are setting up a reinforcement pattern that can repeat itself in the future.

One option is to keep calls short and to structure them. That is the practice in DBT, which makes more use of the telephone than any other method of therapy. Linehan (1993) recommends coaching patients on the phone to reinforce techniques the patient has learned in therapy. These telephone contacts should last no more than 10 min.

Patients in DBT are actually *encouraged* to call. Every DBT therapist either carries a pager with an answering machine or is available by cell phone, home phone, or e-mail. The idea is that being allowed to make contact for coaching helps patients to avoid cutting or overdosing. However, if they do call, they usually get a machine and are expected to wait until called back (typically on the same day). Perhaps that wait reinforces the message that reflection is better than action. (This system also protects therapists from being awakened in the middle of the night.) Moreover, if patients have already cut themselves or have taken an overdose, they are told *not* to call and are barred from extrasession contact for a period of time, a negative reinforcement.

MBT, which was developed in a day hospital setting (Bateman & Fonagy, 2004), does not have a strict policy on phone contact. It may need one when adapted for use in outpatient settings.) In TFP (Yeomans, Clarkin, & Kernberg, 2002), patients are only allowed to phone to change a session or to report on serious accidents or illnesses.

In my own work, I do not give out my phone number. When patients demand contact, I tell them that waiting for the next session is part of the treatment.

Mental health work is demanding. We all need time for ourselves and for our families. Not every therapist is willing to have personal time intruded on by a telephone call. I most certainly am not. Also, I am completely useless when awoken during the night. (Fortunately, I am now too old to be required to cover the emergency room.) Finally, after-hours calls are one of the main reasons why therapists dislike managing BPD. If the only way to treat a patient is to accept carrying a pager at home, many therapists will decide they would rather treat someone else.

I am also concerned with the message that telephone availability gives. People with BPD need to be taught how to reflect and be patient. Getting in touch with the therapist when in distress, as opposed to contacting other people, can work against that goal, and it has not been shown that this is an essential element of any treatment, including DBT.

In the era of the cell phone, patients with BPD can use communication technology in a new way that fits their impulsivity. Many expect immediate responses from significant others. I have treated people who hardly ever let their cell phone out of their hands and feel indignant about messages that are not quickly returned.

Silk and Yager (2003) have suggested using the "cooler" medium of e-mail to bridge gaps between sessions, but that might create another set of problems. My in-box is full enough without having to answer messages from patients, and I do not see how an e-mail can be helpful or why it should be necessary.

Case 2

Cora had received extensive therapy from four senior psychiatrists in my community. She had not benefited from any of these treatments, having been in and out of hospital for years. Cora often went into crises and panics, and all her previous therapists had allowed her to call when she felt a need. But Cora called frequently, which was probably one of the reasons why every therapist who saw her ended up burning out. (Her last therapist refused to see Cora again after she showed up in his hospital room while he was recovering from surgery.)

My compromise in taking on Cora's care was to propose that she be allowed to call me only once a week and to keep the contact brief. (I would not do this today, but I was still a young therapist at the time.) Early on in the course of treatment, Cora called me a second time in the same week, immediately saying when I picked up the phone, "Dr. Paris, I'm going to kill myself." My response was "Cora, we'll talk about that on Tuesday." After that limit-setting intervention, Cora did not call again. She also never killed herself. Long-term follow-up found that she eventually recovered entirely from BPD.

When my team opened a specialty clinic for patients with BPD, we had long discussions about whether to offer telephone contact. We did not actually believe that being available by phone would prevent anyone from dying by suicide. Our real worry was that patients would present themselves in the emergency room and complain about us.

We concluded that accepting calls between sessions works against the goals of treatment. We were offering therapy designed to teach patients how to control impulsivity and how not to act on emotions. Waiting for the next session should be part of learning how to delay responses to distress. Over the 7 years we have run the program, 3% of our patients went to the emergency room or took overdoses, sometime during the course of treatment. In most cases, they stayed overnight and returned to the program. Most of the people we treated, in spite of having had consistent patterns of suicidal actions, accepted the team's nonreinforcement of suicidality.

In summary, I do not believe that telephone contact is necessary in the treatment of BPD. It gives the wrong message to patients about their competence and capacity. Like extra sessions, telephone calls can be used counterproductively to promote regression and dependency. The burden of proof lies with those who believe that that kind of extra contact is necessary.

THERAPIST–PATIENT BOUNDARIES

Patients with BPD are famous for not respecting or for crossing boundaries. They sometimes ask personal questions. When you are sick or in a bad mood, it is almost guaranteed that the patient who will notice will be the one with BPD.

But these examples are relatively trivial, and we have all heard about patients who have sex with therapists. I have also seen relatively benign (but still problematic) violations: patients and therapists going shopping together or taking long walks together or therapists allowing patients to know details of the therapist's life. Interestingly, these scenarios rarely come up with patients who have a diagnosis other than BPD. Most people are just not interested in having a personal relationship with their therapists. They are only mildly curious about our lives and focus on the business they came for. Serious problems with boundaries are most likely to arise in patients with BPD (Gutheil, 1985, 1989; Gutheil & Brodsky, 2008).

One must be vigilant about boundary violations (Gutheil & Gabbard, 1993) because major problems usually start on a slippery slope, with small violations gradually turning into large ones (Gabbard, 1996; Gutheil & Brodsky, 2008). And therapists may be more likely to slip down that slope when patients are threatening suicide. Yet there is actually no reason to change the frame of psychotherapy, even to accommodate suicidality (see Chapter 12). Therapists can be warm, friendly, and genuine with patients while giving them no encouragement to think that the relationship will be anything but professional.

Case 3

I was asked to consult on a case being treated by a former student of mine. Doris was an intelligent and attractive young woman of 25 who was seeing her therapist twice a week. After a few weeks, it was obvious that this relationship was very important to Doris, who overtly stated that her feelings for the therapist were the only reason she had not yet committed suicide. Doris began to offer small gifts to the therapist, which he accepted out of fear of hurting her. Another boundary issue was that the therapist would often run overtime in his sessions with Doris, who was fully aware that he was allowing this to happen.

Doris was knowledgeable about therapy and admitted that her feelings might well be called "transference." But then, she mused, is there really any difference between transference and the emotions that lead people to fall in love?

I recommended telling Doris that, although patients and therapists do have real feelings about each other, it is necessary to protect psychotherapy by maintaining boundaries. Over the course of time, she allowed an alliance to be rebuilt.

Boundary problems in BPD are less likely to arise in well-structured therapies than in high-frequency psychodynamic therapies in which patients are encouraged to develop dependency on the therapist. The problem with that approach is that patients start wanting the therapist to be the mother or the father they never had. Unfortunately, some therapists believe that reparenting of some kind should be carried out. (That idea is most associated with psychoanalysis, but "limited reparenting" is an explicit component of schema-focused therapy.)

The reality is that no matter now much love and care you expend on patients, childhood is over. People have only one chance to have parents, and if they miss it, compensation can only come through adult satisfactions. Every therapy has to be informed by the principle that life is not fair. Your life depends not on the cards you are dealt but on how you play your hand. Some people waste assets, whereas others find ways to do well in life without them.

My conclusion is that boundary problems in treating BPD are a complication of well-meaning but poorly thought-out regressive methods. When you concentrate on helping patients to get a life, they are less likely to run into this kind of trouble.

SHARING THE BPD DIAGNOSIS WITH PATIENTS

When I trained in psychiatry, we rarely discussed diagnoses with patients. In part, this was because we did not believe our categories were valid (this was, after all, the pre-DSM-III era). We were also taught that placing patients in a category failed to acknowledge their uniqueness. If patients asked for a diagnosis, one standard reply suggested by my teachers was "I don't think about you that way."

Case 4

Frances was a 24-year-old medical student who had been in therapy for a year. In addition to repeated suicidal attempts, Frances had prominent cognitive symptoms. She sometimes heard voices when on call at the hospital, and although she knew these experiences were not real, she found these symptoms disruptive and had been prescribed neuroleptics to control them. One day she said to me, "Dr. Paris, I want you tell me my diagnosis and don't give me any bull." Frances would most certainly not have accepted being put off with an evasive answer. So I told her, "You have borderline personality disorder." Her response was, "Oh, thank God, I was so worried I had schizophrenia."

Attitudes toward diagnosis have greatly changed. Given that some treatments are diagnosis specific, it makes a difference which category you fit into. Patients can read about their condition on the Internet and can sometimes quote DSM-IV-TR criteria for BPD, pointing out which ones they do and do not have. Also, if patients have been given an incorrect diagnosis of bipolar disorder, and if you want to stop lithium or valproate, you have to convince them that the BPD diagnosis is the right one.

In DBT, discussing the diagnosis is the first step in a structured psychoeducational program. Linehan (1993) begins every therapy by explaining BPD criteria to patients. In the last 10 years, I have followed much the same procedure. My initial contact with patients is generally a consultation to another professional who wants to know whether the patient has BPD and, if so, whether they can receive treatment for it. I first explain to every one I see what a personality disorder means (problems that are pervasive and go back many years). I then go over the BPD criteria (as discussed in Chapter 1, I use DIB-R in preference to DSM-IV) and explain which ones are present and which ones are absent. I invite the patient to correct me if I have misunderstood anything.

Some patients feel stigmatized by the diagnosis of BPD (Aviram, Brodsky & Stanley, 2006). They will hear "personality disorder" as meaning "you have a bad personality." Other patients will have been stigmatized by professionals who have used the diagnosis to say,

"You are a patient I don't feel like helping." Or patients may hold on to other diagnoses defensively. Some want to be diagnosed with PTSD to justify their stance as a victim. And others want to be bipolar: If they suffer from a chemical balance (not their fault), all they have to do to get better is to find the right mix of medications.

All the same, my experience has been that patients can be grateful for the diagnosis of BPD. One woman told me, "Oh my God, and I thought I was just a depressed person who didn't get better on drugs like everyone else." Another patient said to me, "When I read about BPD on the Internet this was first time I felt that anyone had been able to describe what I am going through." For this reason, the diagnosis of BPD can be validating.

INVOLVING THE FAMILY

I was trained in the 1960s, when psychiatrists played a prominent role in the development of family therapy. (I have worked for many years at the Institute of Community and Family Psychiatry, which opened in 1969.) But the models used at that time assumed that it was the parents who made their children sick. Fortunately, we have come a long way since then.

John Gunderson tells a similar story. His early writings were based on the assumption that BPD was the result of poor parenting. However, in the last 10 years he has changed his mind and has been leading psychoeducational programs for parents of patients with BPD treated at McLean Hospital (Gunderson, 2001).

We have come to realize that parents are not to blame for BPD, and that having a child with this disorder is a terrible burden. Recently, the National Association for the Mentally Ill recognized BPD as one of their priorities.

Perry Hoffman, a social worker from New York, founded the National Educational Alliance for Borderline Personality Disorder (NEA-BPD). This organization, supported by federal funds, has set up meetings all over the United States attended by professionals, family members, and patients. (There have also been two NEA-BPD conferences in Canada and one in the United Kingdom.) The organization has also sponsored a manual on BPD for families (Gunderson & Hoffman, 2005).

NEA-BPD meetings are both emotional and inspirational. Only half the time is given to researchers (who present encouraging outcome findings or describe new forms of psychotherapy). The rest of the day is allotted to parents, who bear witness to the experience of having a child with BPD, and to patients themselves, who describe what it feels like to have the disorder and what it feels like to be consistently misunderstood by mental health professionals.

NEA-BPD has also alerted the mental health community to additional missions it needs to carry out. One is to educate families and the public about this disorder. Doing so is particularly important at a time when so many psychiatrists refuse to recognize the problem (and call it "bipolar"). Thus, another mission is to reach out to settings in the community where BPD patients are likely to go unrecognized.

Our responsibility to families also affects the way we conduct therapy. I recommend that parents or spouses be routinely invited to meet with the therapist at the beginning of any treatment. This procedure serves two purposes. First, it provides information about family dynamics, which may or may not correspond to what the patient has reported. Second, it involves families in the responsibility of treatment that can be stressful and harrowing. In Chapter 12, I discuss how families can be involved when BPD patients are chronically suicidal.

Case 5

Leila was a 19-year-old student living with her parents. Her psychiatric history included admissions for anorexia–bulimia and for multiple suicide attempts during adolescence. One of these hospital admissions lasted 6 months, leading to the loss of an entire school year. Leila was a chronic cutter, had intense mood instability, and suffered from rages and an almost constant feeling of derealization. She had a number of promiscuous sexual contacts with both males and females but had not been able to establish a stable relationship. Nonetheless, she was doing well in college, where she was majoring in psychology.

I met with the family early in the treatment and discussed their concerns about Leila, particularly her suicide attempts. I noted that hospital admissions had not been helpful in the past, and that they were disruptive to her studies and her social life. The parents agreed with the therapeutic plan, which was to engage Leila in therapy, and to inform her that hospitalization would not be prescribed. If Leila went to the emergency room, as she sometimes did, she might be held overnight, but the plan would be for her to continue her psychotherapy.

Case 6

Norah was a 35-year-old office worker (described in Chapter 10) who came for consultation accompanied by her husband, John. Norah, who had an 8-year-old son by a previous marriage, suffered from angry outbursts, cutting, overdoses, conflicts at work and at home, feelings of chronic depression, emptiness, depersonalization, paranoid feelings, and hearing her own voice speaking thoughts.

Norah's second marriage was marked by severe conflict, associated with John's extreme jealousy, in which he monitored her every move. When I interviewed John, he discussed Norah with me as if he were a colleague; he had retired early, had time on his hands, and had read widely on BPD.

Individual therapy with Norah was helpful in encouraging her to assert herself more and define a separate space. However, John was unwilling to take up my suggestion to follow up with couple therapy, because he defined the problem entirely in terms of the difficulty of being married to a person with BPD.

SPLIT TREATMENTS

As a psychiatrist, I have long been concerned about defining a unique role for my profession in delivering mental health care. A few colleagues still devote their time entirely to psychotherapy. However, psychiatrists with that kind of practice are making little use of their training and can easily be replaced by psychologists or social workers, who provide the same service at a reduced cost. Although the more common practice pattern in my discipline today is a focus on writing prescriptions, primary care physicians might replace psychiatrists in that role.

One of the reasons for my interest in BPD is that treating it allows me to be a complete clinician. If patients need psychotherapy, I have the training. If patients need medication, I am also qualified.

Unfortunately, that kind of practice is no longer sustainable. The limiting factor is human resources. I work in Canada, where psychotherapy from a psychiatrist is free. However, few of us do that kind of work for more than a few hours a week. Even if my colleagues were more interested in BPD (not many are), there would never be enough of them to handle the clinical need.

Most patients with BPD see therapists who do not prescribe. Thus, split treatments have become the norm. Sometimes the physician who prescribes is a psychiatrist. Sometimes it is a family doctor or internist.

One of my students explained to me how split treatment works at a community mental health center in Vermont. A group of therapists see their patients on the same day, while the consultant psychiatrist makes rounds, knocking on each door and interrupting sessions for about 10 min to review symptoms. This "med-check" is used to determine whether to change (or renew) any drugs the patients are taking.

The problem with this system is that it encourages constant changes of medication, often every time the patient feels worse. And almost every patient with BPD ends up receiving medication, for good reasons or bad. It is not always medical doctors who drive that kind of practice. Psychologists often insist on prescriptions, without which they do not feel "covered."

Case 7

Tara was a 30-year-old woman with a psychiatric history going back to age 15, marked by multiple overdoses. She was in therapy with a psychologist who was alarmed by her chronic suicidality. He referred her to a psychiatrist who, over a period of 12 months, prescribed her citalopram, olanzapine, valproate, and clonazepam. Tara gained 40 pounds and was extremely embarrassed about her appearance. However, she was reluctant to go off any of this medication, because both the psychologist and the psychiatrist assured her that it was necessary.

In the present mental health system, split treatments are inevitable. However, treatment is likely to be easier if all professionals work in the same team. It may be no accident that all evidence-based therapies for BPD have been developed for clinics that draw on a wide range of skills, and not in solo practice settings where therapists are isolated.

LENGTH OF THERAPY

One of the most common misunderstandings about BPD is that therapy needs to be long term and continuous. There are no data to support that idea. Even if BPD is a chronic disorder, it can usually be managed in stages. Many patients do well with a brief but focused intervention. Others benefit from therapy on an intermittent schedule. Even hard cases do not necessarily need lifetime treatment.

Brief therapy (i.e., treatment lasting less than 6 months) is the form of psychotherapy that has been thoroughly researched. The data show that for most of the problems that therapists see, symptomatic improvement occurs fairly rapidly, and gains attained in a few months are usually maintained (Lambert & Ogles, 2004). Brief therapy is also prescribed for practical reasons: It costs less and is often insured. It has become what might be called the "default condition" for psychotherapy.

However, although brief therapy is effective for mood and anxiety disorders, aren't there cases for which longer treatment is required? Patients with personality disorders have, by definition, had pervasive problems for years. It is natural to wonder how problems of such severity can be managed in a short time. Moreover, with BPD, these difficulties can be life threatening. It is not surprising that clinicians tend to believe that these patients need continuous long-term therapy.

Nonetheless, no one has ever shown that therapy of greater length is necessary in BPD. Although most evidence-based treatments (DBT, MBT, TFP, schema therapy) were designed as long-term treatments, the studies that have supported them do not prove that greater length is necessary (by conducting comparisons of treatment lasting for 6 months with treatment lasting for 2 years or more). Instead, RCTs have compared these therapies either with other methods or with relatively inert follow-up methods over the same length of time. Yet many of the gains seen in these therapies occur in the first few months (Koons et al., 2001). More recent evidence has shown that treatment for BPD lasting about 6 months can be effective, whether using DBT (Stanley et al., 2007), CBT (Davidson, Norrie, et al., 2006), or psychoeducation (Weinberg et al., 2006). Therefore, I question the rationales for extended periods of psychotherapy. Such ideas are based on theory, not data.

One argument that is sometimes put forward to justify years of treatment is that therapy provides a protected environment for learning, where mistakes are understood rather than punished. However, treatment is more like an educational program leading to a degree than a single course, and, like some students, our patients are not always interested in "graduating." That is why protection can become a trap. Patients remain in treatment, waiting for a magical moment of illumination. Therapy goes on for years, becoming an end in itself, without improving the patient's quality of life.

I am not describing a "Woody Allen" caricature of psychotherapy. (In any case, comedy is funny only when it tells the truth.) There is something intrinsic about extended psychotherapy that makes it potentially interminable. Although psychoanalysis is most famous for keeping patients in treatment, one also sees patients going to cognitive therapists for years. Some people find it safer to go on talking than to start living. In his old age, Freud (1937/1962) acknowledged the problem, even if he did not really understand it.

INTERMITTENT THERAPY

Brief but highly structured interventions for BPD can lead to significant patient improvement within a few months. What we do not know is whether these changes stick. Probably they sometimes do and sometimes do not. How we can identify those who may need further therapy?

Our clinic encourages patients to return after 6 months if they feel the need. This is a reasonable time to see how well they can do on their own. If they need further therapy at that time, we arrange it.

More generally, I recommend intermittent therapy as the best model for patients with BPD (McGlashan, 1993; Paris, 2007). The long-term outcome of BPD—slow but sure recovery in most cases—points to the value of this form of treatment.

Alexander and French (1946) were the first to write about intermittent therapy. These authors were concerned about the addictive properties of frequent and lengthy psychotherapy. Applying this approach to BPD, Silver (1983) suggested that each time a patient comes for treatment, "a piece of work" is accomplished. Then, when symptoms stabilize, therapy is deliberately interrupted, and patients are asked to see how well they can apply in the real world what they have learned in the consulting room. After a break, patients can return for another series of sessions. The procedure is designed to avoid stagnation and excessive dependence on the therapist.

McGlashan (1993) also proposed that the treatment of BPD should be intermittent. He noted that therapists can actually capitalize on the impulsivity of BPD by applying an intermittent schedule. A patient who has "had enough" would be allowed (and encouraged) to leave but with the security of being able to return.

Patients with BPD do not always like continuous therapy. As already discussed, in a naturalistic survey (Waldinger & Gunderson, 1984), the majority of patients ended up leaving against advice. By and large, therapists perceived these patients as having broken off treatment prematurely, even though they had been coming for several years. However, we do not know whether they fared any worse than if they had left by mutual agreement.

Unfortunately, there is hardly any published literature on intermittent therapy. Some authors (Cummings & Sayama, 1995; Ursano, Sonnenberg, & Lazar, 2004) have described the model and provide clinical illustrations. However, no clinical trials have ever been conducted. We also lack documentation of how often intermittent therapy is carried out in practice, although it may be prescribed frequently.

Some patients naturally go through therapy intermittently. Clinicians who work with university students, a population who take time off for exams and summer vacations, will be familiar with this approach.

An intermittent model is consistent with the view that patients with BPD have the capacity to heal themselves. If we actively discourage patients from interrupting therapy, we are giving the wrong message, hardly a vote of confidence. However, there are also patients who want to remain in continuous treatment even when their lives have improved. In that scenario, one can interrupt therapy without being perceived by the patient as abandoning.

Case 8

Cassie was a university student who first came for therapy at age 21. Her main symptoms (cutting and overdosing) resolved within 6 months, after which she left treatment after falling in love with a man. The therapist encouraged her to come back if she ran into further difficulties. A year later Cassie returned after breaking up with the boyfriend. This time she responded to her loss with sadness but not with impulsive actions. The second round of therapy lasted 2 months. Five years later, at age 25, Cassie returned. At this point, she was married and had two young children. Cassie spent another 2 months in therapy talking about her relationship to her alcoholic mother. The mother had abandoned her to foster care as a child. Although Cassie wanted to involve her mother in her new family life, she had difficulty maintaining boundaries. This phase of therapy lasted for another 2 months, and Cassie felt secure knowing that she retained access to her therapist. In fact, she dropped in for a series of occasional one-session consultations over the next 10 years.

TERMINATION ISSUES

There is rarely a clear termination point for therapy, particularly in BPD. Some patients drop out early. Others want to stay forever. The question is, When is "good enough" good enough?

The intermittent model that I am recommending attempts to cover these bases. In our program for BPD, we usually encourage patients not to continue treatment right away but suggest they take a 6-month break, in which they can consolidate what they have learned. I regularly follow up with these patients and have been impressed at how many patients make further progress after leaving formal therapy. Of course, this is not true for everyone, and there are always a few who go "back to square one." But not everyone is ready for therapy at any given point. My experience is that patients come up at different developmental points and can make progress in different areas at different times.

A main concern for the therapist of BPD patients has always been sensitivity to abandonment and loss. How can we discharge people who seem to depend on us so much?

But therapy can go wrong by encouraging dependency. The model of re-creating a parent–child relationship (i.e., transference) has been a major source of error. No one has ever shown that this is a necessary part of psychotherapy, and treatment of that kind has a particular danger for patients subject to regressions.

Moreover, if we want patients to get a life, we have to believe they are capable of doing so. When we respond with our own anxiety to the patient's (understandable) worry about terminating therapy, we are giving the wrong message.

I tell patients that a BPD diagnosis does not mean they have to remain ill. On the contrary, I inform them that research shows that most are likely to recover with time, and that treatment can speed things up.

Another message I send to patients is that therapy is not intended to solve all problems quickly or definitely. Rather, it is designed to "give a leg up" on the way to gradual recovery over time.

With these principles in mind, our program does not routinely refer patients to therapists at the end of treatment. Those who were already seeing therapists can choose to return. For those who insist on regular follow-up, we make referrals. However, in most cases, we advise patients to continue working on problems on their own. We also let them know that if they want to discuss further therapy after 6 months, they can do so. By leaving the door open in this way, termination becomes easier. But the crucial aspect of our approach is to give the message that we see patients as having the capacity to get better as opposed to being dependent on support from mental health professionals.

Case 9

Melanie was a 30-year-old woman who presented with chronic suicidality. She went into treatment with a prominent psychoanalyst, who she saw two to three times a week for the next 30 years. She usually spent hours in the hospital building where he worked, chatting up the secretarial staff. The analyst, talking about this case to his students, stated, "This treatment will end when one of us dies first." Melanie never did commit suicide, although it was impossible to know whether that outcome was related to therapy.

After her analyst died (first), she saw another psychiatrist, who monitored her less closely and put her on an SSRI. One year later, Melanie was doing better than she had for some time, enjoying work as a volunteer in the same hospital where she had received treatment for many years.

Another problem in treatment that continues indefinitely without progress is that it can burn out therapists. Sometimes that scenario leads to true abandonment.

Case 10

Kate was a 32-year-old woman who had been chronically suicidal for many years. She was in an 8-year live-in situation with a man but was too depressed to remain close to him, and the relationship was no longer sexual. Her position at work had become increasingly tenuous, because she felt unable to give anything to others.

Kate, whose father was a wealthy businessman, entered psychoanalysis three times a week. After 2 years, she gave up her job and did not seek further employment. The analyst, who was concentrating on interpreting the past and the transference, did not raise objections to this plan. But 2 years later, the boyfriend finally left her, despairing of any improvement. At this time, Kate made three serious suicide attempts by overdose that required hospitalization, followed by a day hospital admission. She was also treated in our 12-week program, which produced a temporary improvement. However, after another year had passed with no change, the analyst admitted Kate to the hospital and informed her on the ward that he could not see her again. After this incident, Kate was accepted into our long-term BPD program.

Case 11

Anne was a 23-year-old university student who had been seen by five different therapists since the age of 16. Her therapist during graduate school was the one on whom she was most dependent. He allowed her to phone him anytime she wished and showed a strong paternal interest in her welfare. However, Anne continued to make suicide attempts, leading to obvious therapist fatigue. The last straw occurred when the therapist went into hospital for a major operation and found Anne among his visitors. Shortly afterward, he informed her that she did not need further treatment.

I was the next therapist to see Anne, and although her BPD did not remit, she managed to finish school. Some years later I learned (to my surprise, I must admit) that she had fully recovered, was a professional, and was married and living with her two children in another city.

Therapists often worry about managing termination in psychotherapy. However, the assumption that endings are always traumatic or almost have to be when the patient has BPD is unnecessarily regressive. It is not particularly helpful to tell people they are having trouble leaving because no one loved them as a child. Again, that gives the message that we expect the patient to remain sick.

Instead, termination of therapy can be a vote of confidence. Even if patients express anxiety about stopping, the therapist can remind them of the times in their life they have functioned well and of the progress they have made. The message is that the patient is expected to continue doing well. Needless to say, we must remain available if problems arise. Sometimes the "retread" may only consist of one session. The key is that patients are encouraged to get a life, not to live in expectation of their next therapy session.

CLINICAL IMPLICATIONS

- Patients with BPD present special problems in therapy that can be handled by adhering to structures and rules.
- Therapy for BPD runs the risk of excessive frequency and length. This problem can be avoided by an intermittent schedule.
- Termination of therapy in BPD need not represent a full stop, but a transition to a new phase where patients work on their own with occasional consultation.

CHAPTER 12

Suicidality and Hospitalization

*L*ife-and-death issues make working with BPD challenging. Suicidality, a central feature of this disorder, is frightening. But what do therapists mean when they say a patient is "suicidal"? This term can refer to many things: thinking about suicide, cutting one's wrist, taking overdoses, or making life-threatening attempts. Each of these scenarios is different and requires a different response.

SUICIDAL THOUGHTS

Suicidal thoughts are frequent in BPD. Some patients think about dying every day. Life is so painful that suicide has to be an option. These ideas reflect a very high level of distress and dysphoria. Yet because they offer a way to escape pain, suicidal thoughts are comforting to patients with BPD.

However, we need not respond to suicidal ideas in BPD with alarm. First, thoughts have very little value as predictors of suicide. Moreover, some patients have thought about suicide since they were adolescents. That is what it is like to have BPD. Chronic suicidal ideation "goes with the territory."

The absence of a consistent relationship between thoughts and suicidal actions applies to anyone who feels depressed. Many people who feel sad for an extended period will think about ending their lives. In fact, suicidal ideas are extremely common. About 5% of the general population experience transient suicidal ideas in any one year, and prevalence over a lifetime is as high as 15% (Kessler, Berglund, Borges, Nock, & Wang, 2005). These numbers run in close parallel with the lifetime community prevalence of major depressive episodes, which is at least 10% (Kessler, Chiu, et al., 2005).

One cannot make predictions of rare events like suicide completion from such a high base rate. Nor can attempts be easily predicted. When so many more people think about suicide than actually attempt it, attempts at prediction inevitably result in a large number of false positives. If a therapist cannot predict whether a patient will make a suicidal attempt, he or she is best advised not to panic. Instead, the therapist can focus energies on understanding *why* the patient feels suicidal.

It is impossible not to be concerned when patients talk about suicidal thoughts. After all, therapists care about the people they see. But *excessive* anxiety about suicidal thoughts reflects the way therapists have been trained. Standard clinical training teaches us to ask patients about suicidal ideas with the purpose of determining intent. The assumption has been that if intent seems serious, one should intervene (admit the patient to a hospital).

It may come as a surprise to some readers to learn that the assessment of suicidal risk is not a scientific procedure. Even the most serious types of ideation do not predict completed suicide. Although patients who make near-lethal attempts (and who know in advance that they are likely to die) have been found to be more likely to commit suicide (G. K. Brown, Steer, Henriques, & Beck, 2004), the relationship is not of great clinical value. Harriss and Hawton (2005) used the Suicidal Intent Scale (SIS) developed by Aaron Beck to predict completion in a large sample of attempters. Although SIS scores had a statistical relationship to completed suicide, their positive predictive value was only 4%.

In summary, there is no evidence that suicidal thoughts indicate anything useful about risk. Suicide prevention through clinical assessment is largely a myth, even if it makes therapists feel more empowered (Paris, 2006a, 2006b).

The problem is even more complicated in patients with BPD, who think about suicide and threaten it frequently. Standard guidelines found in textbooks (e.g., Bongar, 1991) are intended to manage the acute risk associated with mood disorders, not the chronic suicidality of BPD.

Level of intent is difficult to measure when suicidality is used as a way of communicating (i.e., patients reporting how bad they feel). It is very rare for patients with BPD to threaten a mild gesture just to make that point. Many of the patients I have treated have been expert at describing blood-curdling scenarios. They are not shy about frightening me. If therapists respond to every one of these hair-raising threats by intervention, then every patient with BPD will have to be hospitalized.

Case 1

Susan was a 23-year-old college student who had been thinking about suicide since early adolescence. She came for therapy in a crisis after a broken love affair. For the next year, she talked about suicide in every session, often telling the therapist that she would be dead before he saw her again. She often described vividly a scene she imagined, which may have come from her reading of gothic novels: her body, pale but still beautiful, lying on the morgue table.

In the course of therapy, Susan eventually made one suicide attempt, but it only consisted of a small overdose, after which she called the therapist, came to his office, and took ipecac to make herself throw up the pills.

This is not say that patients who think about suicide never make attempts or never kill themselves. Sometimes they do. But we cannot predict such events or prevent them from happening. We might as well as get on with our job.

Like any other therapist, I worry about my patients. But I focus my efforts on finding out *why* people are thinking about killing themselves. Suicidal ideation is a marker for distress. The job of the therapist is to understand that distress.

SELF-INJURY

Repetitive injury to self and wrist cutting are characteristic features of BPD, but they are *not* suicidal behaviors. Self-injury has an entirely different pattern and purpose (Winchel & Stanley, 1991; Gerson & Stanley, 2005). The pattern involves superficial cuts on the wrists and arms, actions not associated with serious danger. Once in a while, one sees dangerous slashes, but most cutting is skin deep. Although the most common site is on the wrists, some patients will cut their arms and legs in relatively nonvisible places (to avoid commentary from others). When patients cut, they feel little pain (Russ, Campbell, Kakuma, Harrison, & Zanine, 1999), and some are in a dissociated state (Leibenluft, Gardner, & Cowdry, 1987).

The purpose of cutting is to relieve negative emotions (Linehan, 1993; M. Z. Brown, Comtois, & Linehan, 2002; Stanley, Gameroff, Michalsen, & Mann, 2001). You only have to ask your patients and they will tell you so. They feel better after they cut and on a bad day may actually look forward to getting home and doing it.

The mechanism is that injury to self provides short-term regulation of intense dysphoric affects by substituting physical for mental suffering. In other words, you forget about your painful emotions when you distract yourself by cutting.

The relationship of cutting to dysphoria has an upside. When patients feel better, they give up the behavior. As noted in Chapter 8, several types of therapy lead to marked reductions in self-injury, and it is often the first behavior to get under control.

Cutting is also susceptible to social contagion (Taiminen, Kallio-Soukainen, Nokso-Koivisto, Kaljonen, & Helenius, 1998). As is the case for other impulsive symptoms (bulimia, substance abuse), cutting can be learned by imitation. This pattern of behavior has existed in other cultures and in earlier historical periods (Favazza, 1996) but is restricted to religious rituals. Some patients might have never considered doing such a thing until they heard about it from a friend, read about it, saw it discussed on TV, or were admitted to a mental health unit where other people were doing the same thing.

Zanarini, Frankenburg, Ridolfi, et al. (2006) reported that, among a large sample of BPD patients with self-injury, 32.8% began before age 12, 30.2% began as adolescents, and 37% began as adults; those with a childhood onset had a more chronic course.

Case 2

Frances was a 25-year-old woman with problems that dated back 10 years. Her relationships were chaotic and unstable, and she consistently became involved with men who exploited her. Nonetheless, she managed to keep these problems out of her work and was a successful university student.

At 15, Frances became friendly with a girl who had similar problems, after which they both began to cut themselves repetitively. She found relief in self-injury: Each time she felt angry and upset, a few cuts would calm her down greatly. After several months, Frances became concerned about the visibility of her problem, particularly when she wore short sleeves. She, therefore, found a spot on her upper arm that she could burn regularly with a cigarette, making her problem nonvisible to others.

SUICIDE ATTEMPTS

Suicide attempts provide more of a reason for therapists to worry. Research shows that 10 to 15% of all suicide attempters eventually commit suicide, and that the higher the overall number of attempts, the greater is the lifetime risk of completion (Maris et al., 2000). Similarly previous attempts are associated with completion in BPD (Paris et al., 1988).

Nonetheless, it is impossible to predict death by suicide from any attempt or series of attempts in any particular patient. Two large-scale studies of people admitted to hospitals for suicidal actions attempted to predict completion with algorithims based on standard risk factors described in the literature (Pokorny, 1983; Goldstein, Black, Nasrallah, & Winokur, 1991). This procedure was unable to identify *any* individuals who ended up taking their life. The reason is, again, that there were too many false positives: people who had the risk factors but who never killed themselves.

The problem of prediction is even more complex in BPD. Most patients make more than one suicide attempt. However, a frequent event (attempts) cannot be used to predict an infrequent event (suicide completion). In spite of the overall statistical relationship between attempts and completions found in patients with mental disorders, it is almost impossible to make accurate predictions (Paris, 2006b).

As reviewed in Chapter 6, completions tend to occur late in the course of illness, mainly among patients who fail to recover from BPD. However, because research in this area is sparse, the published literature tends to focus on the prediction of continued suicidal behaviors. In a prospective study over a 2-year period, Yen et al. (2004) reported that AI was the diagnostic criterion that best predicted continuation.

The severity and purpose of suicidal behaviors in BPD vary greatly. Suicide attempts can sometimes be gestures in the sense that they have a communicative function and do not involve life-threatening actions. Such incidents may involve taking a small number of pills (sometimes with other people present). They go with the territory of BPD and should not be too worrisome. Mild attempts of this kind usually occur after life events involving interpersonal conflict (Yen et al., 2005).

However, patients can also take serious overdoses that require hospital treatment. Some make near-lethal attempts. Soloff, Fabio, Kelly, Malone, and Mann (2005) compared patients with high- and low-lethality attempts and found that high-lethality acts were associated with low socioeconomic, comorbid ASPD, and extensive treatment histories. Making a clinical judgment about risk is difficult because these scenarios are not always that separate.

Another complication is that patients lack knowledge as to which drugs are actually dangerous. I have seen people die after taking 15 barbiturates, and I have seen people take a whole bottle of aspirin not expecting to die. (Patients do not know that a drug sold without a prescription can still be dangerous.)

Even when they are objectively life threatening, many overdoses are ambivalent in motivation. The patient is playing a game of Russian roulette, in which she may or may not be saved. (Will I make a telephone call in time to be rescued, or will I pass out first?)

Suicide attempts are part and parcel of the course and treatment of BPD. Needless to say, such actions should be discouraged, because they rarely accomplish anything except in the short term. However, they cannot always be prevented. When attempts do occur, therapists should not panic. I cannot begin to count the number of patients I have seen with 10 or 20 overdoses who have nonetheless gone on living.

Case 3

Brigitte was a 20-year-old single, unemployed mother. After losing custody of her 2-year-old daughter to child protection services, she took two overdoses and was treated in a day hospital program. Brigitte had been living with a man who was a cocaine addict, with whom she had recently broken up.

Brigitte began to have problems at 14 with cutting and overdosing and had lived in various group homes. She became a polysubstance abuser and was involved intermittently in prostitution. Brigitte would take an overdose of pills about once every 2 months. The precipitants might vary—problems with boyfriends, quarrels with family—but taking pills, leading to multiple emergency visits, became the universal solvent for many difficulties.

Case 4

Elaine was a 25-year-old unemployed woman living alone. She had a 5-year-old son by a previous relationship; the boy now lived with his father. Elaine was cutting regularly, and an overdose led to a hospital admission. A second admission occurred after Elaine jumped from her mother's balcony. This happened at midnight after a major quarrel. Elaine landed five floors below, breaking two vertebra in her neck, but was fortunately not paralyzed.

Elaine later stated that God must have wanted her to survive given the seriousness of her suicide attempt. She has also found strong and loving support from her parents after this event. She made no further suicide attempts and took a job as a clerk. Her increased stability allowed her to obtain joint custody of her daughter, and she now felt comfortable as a parent.

SUICIDE COMPLETION

Nearly 10% of patients with BPD eventually commit suicide. (I am inclined to go with this figure, drawn from naturalistic studies, rather than the lower numbers found in prospectively followed cohorts.)

Yet it is difficult to identify who is at high risk. There is also little evidence that suicide can be prevented through clinical intervention, not just in BPD but in *any* mental disorder. The best data on suicide prevention derive from the effects of reducing access to means (i.e., gun control, barriers on bridges, nontoxic natural gas, less dangerous medications). Some drug treatments (lithium for mania, clozapine for schizophrenia) may lower suicide rates (Paris, 2006b).

Unfortunately, none of these interventions is known to have any effect on suicide in BPD. Patients with BPD are most likely to commit suicide when they fail to recover. The patients who improve have no need to kill themselves. However, people for whom therapy after therapy has failed may despair. And most are not even in treatment when they die.

There may also be cases in the community whom we never see and who commit suicide without ever seeking treatment. In a psychological autopsy study of young adult suicides, 30% of cases met criteria for BPD, but less than a third were in treatment, fewer than half had seen a therapist during the previous year, and a third had never been evaluated (Lesage et al., 1994). However, that is a different population from what we see clinically (more males than females).

In a study using the psychological autopsy method (McGirr et al., 2007), our research group compared patients with BPD who completed suicide with patients who attempted only. The completers were 80% male. Not surprisingly, the factors best differentiating completers were the presence of antisocial personality and substance abuse.

Case 5

Helen had first been admitted to the hospital at age 12 for anorexia and bulimia. Her second admission, at age 17, occurred after she took an overdose. Over the succeeding years, Helen was in and out of the hospital with overdoses, wrist slashes, and episodes of burning herself. She had very stormy relationships with therapists. Helen would either dismiss them for lack of understanding or be herself dismissed. On the last occasion, treatment ended when she threw a desk clock at a psychiatrist, who refused to see her again.

Helen had similarly stormy intimate relationships with men. Although Helen had hoped to become a professional musician, she did not make the cut. At age 33, she entered law school as a mature student. Helen worked for a year after graduation and was offered a job in a law firm. But Helen felt unloved and felt that professional success would not compensate for her emptiness and isolation. At age 37, Helen took a fatal overdose.

Case 6

George had a long history of cutting, overdoses, and polysubstance abuse. When drunk, he could be violent and had spent several nights in jail. He never stayed in treatment for long.

George's problems had begun in early adolescence with conduct disorder and depression. He had never finished high school and had never held a steady job. Although he had many relationships with women, they never lasted for long, largely because of his instability and jealousy. At age 30, George died from an overdose.

CHRONIC SUICIDALITY

Suicidality in BPD can become a way of life. The pattern can persist over years, leading to what has been called a "suicidal career" (Maris, 1981).

Chronic suicidality is a fascinating problem about which I have written a book (Paris, 2006a). Patients with BPD have chronic suicidal ideations and chronic suicidal threats, and 85% of patients make attempts (Soloff et al., 2000). (It would be interesting to find out why 15% *never* make an attempt.) The more frequent the attempts, the more severe is the course of illness (Soloff et al., 2000). However, suicidality in BPD varies in intensity over time. Many patients function reasonably well between crises; symptoms tend to wax and wane, depending on life events.

The clinical literature offers some insight into these phenomena. Schwartz, Flinn, and Slawson (1974) described patients who have a "suicidal character." Suicidality becomes a part of personality structure and is not just a symptom of a temporary condition such as depression. Fine and Sansone (1990) expanded on this point by noting that when chronic suicidality performs a function for patients, it cannot easily be removed. Paradoxically, patients may need to be suicidal in order to go on living. An open exit door gives them just enough autonomy to tolerate the way they feel.

Chronic suicidality is a way of coping with painful emotions. The inner experience of the patient involves isolation and despair. Patients have a sense of emptiness about self as well as a feeling that life is meaningless. But there is always a way to escape, and the option of suicide offers a sense of control and empowerment. My book (Paris, 2006a) used a title that borrowed a phrase from John Keats's "Ode to a Nightingale": BPD patients are "half in love with death."

Yet suicidality tends to decline as life improves. As we have seen, long-term follow-up studies of BPD show that most patients recover with time and give up this option. When they achieve a degree of mastery in their lives, they no longer need to be masters of death.

Case 7

Moira was a 28-year-old pharmacist who had been thinking about suicide since the age of 15. Although she held a university degree, her personal life was, to say the least, unstable. She had been involved with a series of criminal men, in one case hiding a boyfriend from the police for several months. Moira talked in therapy about suicide in almost every session. Moreover, Moira knew exactly how to kill herself effectively.

It took about a year of treatment for Moira to retreat from this suicidal stance. Making use of therapy, she developed a more benign view of people and became involved in her religious community. The satisfaction of belonging allowed Moira to think less about dying.

MANAGING SUICIDALITY

Chronic suicidality takes a toll on therapists. Thirty years ago, Maltsberger and Buie (1974) wrote a clinical report describing some of the scenarios that can develop. When the therapist withdraws emotionally in the face of an onslaught of suicidal threats, the patient's sense of abandonment only grows stronger. To manage these problems, we have to learn how to tolerate suicidal threats or, to put it colloquially, to "hang in there."

In two seminal studies, Maltsberger (1994a, 1994b) argued that the treatment of chronically suicidal patients requires taking calculated risks. If you spend all your time trying to prevent suicide, you end up not being able to work with your patients. Treatment is destroyed by an endless cycle of repeated hospitalizations and crises. For this reason, therapists working with BPD need to think less about preventing completion and more about managing the problems that make patients feel suicidal in the first place.

When we treat BPD, we may see patients who have been suicidal for years. You are not going to change that pattern by putting people in a hospital. Links and Kolla (2005), who are more sympathetic to hospital admission, present the counterargument that patients with BPD can have a level of suicidality described as "acute on chronic." The idea is that even chronically suicidal patients have crises in which risk is elevated. Unfortunately, it is not clear what this concept means. Chronically suicidal patients spend a lot of time feeling acutely suicidal. "Acute on chronic" is a scenario that occurs all too frequently, and there is no evidence that we must intervene differently in these situations.

Therapists who treat patients with BPD must have a thick skin and sangfroid. Paradoxically, therapists who can tolerate suicidal ideation may be helping patients with BPD to stay alive. These are people who *need* to be suicidal, and we cannot take the option away from them too rapidly. The message has to be "You can kill yourself if you really want to, but I want to keep working with you to help you to find a way to live."

HOSPITALIZATION

With a few exceptions, patients with BPD should *not* be hospitalized, because there is no evidence that admission to a ward has any value. In fact, hospital stays can be counterproductive and harmful.

That was not the position taken by the American Psychiatric Association guidelines (Oldham et al., 2001), which recommended hospitalization whenever patients are "suicidal." These guidelines, criticized when they were first published (Sanderson, Swenson, & Bohus, 2002; Tyrer, 2002), should now be revised to correspond to the scientific evidence. (However, the fact that they were published by a professional association means that those of us who disagree may be wise to document our rationale for practicing differently.)

Most experts on BPD agree with my position on hospitalization. However, there are important nuances. Linehan (1993) accepts that overnight holds are likely to happen but advises patients to avoid going to the emergency room (unless, of course, they need medical attention after an overdose or self-injury). Gunderson (2001) proposed a paradoxical intervention in which the therapist agrees to hospitalize a patient for suicidality when they ask for admission, while stating that doing so would not be helpful and hoping that the patient will then elect to decline the offer. Kernberg (1987) avoids hospitalization for suicidality, although he used to believe (before managed care) that therapy can go "deeper" in an inpatient setting).

Dawson and McMillan (1993) argue against hospitalization under almost any circumstances, mainly out of fear of "malignant regressions," in which patients become more suicidal on a ward. Most therapists have had the experience of patients finding ways to cut themselves, even when on "suicidal precautions." Even worse, some patients refuse to be discharged by threatening suicide if they are sent home. Although this scenario is strongly discouraged by a managed-care system, it can occur in public hospital settings. (The following example comes from Canada, where psychiatrists can keep patients almost indefinitely if they choose to.)

Case 8

Yael was a 35-year-old woman admitted to the hospital after an overdose. Yael had been a troubled adolescent whose life stabilized when she married young. For many years, she was busy with her children and seemed to have put problems behind her. However, at this stage of her life, as her husband spent more time at work and her children needed her less, Yael felt rejected by her family. Possibly for this reason, she was not anxious to go home. The longer she spent on the ward, the more she talked about suicide and stated she would jump under a subway train if she were sent out. Yael was often put on suicidal precautions and was frequently discussed by the nurses.

The psychiatrist assigned to Yael's case took an interest in her, prescribing a wide range of drugs, and assigning trainee therapists to spend much time with her. He often told the team that they were saving a life. But Yael did not improve. In the end, she spent 2 years on the ward. Discharge occurred at the insistence of the nursing staff, who told the psychiatrist that they were burned out and unwilling to spend more time with this patient. Yael was sent home but did not in the end commit suicide.

The paradox is that you cannot help suicidal people without allowing them the option to die. Most of the time, patients will choose to live. But until they get better, they need to keep the exit door open.

Moreover, suicides do occur, but we do not know how to prevent them. Suicide, however traumatic, is a normal part of therapy practice. If you have never had one, you are probably not treating sick patients.

Some therapists may not be willing to practice in this way. They are afraid of losing their patients. They are particularly afraid of litigation. Let us, therefore, examine these issues in more detail.

First, consider why frequent and repetitive hospitalizations are bad for patients with BPD. This is a practice that makes therapy almost impossible. You cannot help people learn to cope with life or get a life if they are living on a psychiatric ward. The more time they spend in the hospital, the more likely it is that they will lose social networks and skills.

Trying to manage patients who are moving in and out of hospital wards is like jogging through a hurricane. I have heard it said that managed care was the best thing for patients with BPD because it discourages hospitalization, particularly longer admissions.

Second, patients can get worse in hospital because wards reinforce pathology. What happens is that the environment reinforces the very behaviors that one would like to extinguish. This is a point that is obvious to behaviorally trained clinicians. Marsha Linehan once suggested (at a conference) that the best ward for BPD should be as unpleasant as possible. In her DBT program, only overnight holds are tolerated.

A patient who wrote about her experiences in the journal *Psychiatric Services* (Williams, 1998) made the following comment:

> Do not hospitalize a person with borderline personality disorder for more than 48 hours. My self-destructive episodes—one leading right into another—came out only after my first and subsequent hospital admissions, after I learned the system was usually obligated to respond.

Third, hospitalization would be useful only if, as is the case for many severe mental disorders, it provided an opportunity to administer effective treatments inside the hospital that cannot be provided in outpatient settings. What would that treatment be in BPD? We have long since stopped offering patients intensive inpatient psychotherapy. Medications for BPD have not been shown to yield specific effects and in any case do not require a hospital setting for their administration. (This stands in contrast to the situation in schizophrenia, in which patients can be brought out of psychosis in a few days, or in melancholic depression, in which electroconvulsive therapy can produce a dramatic recovery.)

Fourth, there is no evidence that hospitalization actually prevents patients from committing suicide. Some patients make attempts while in the hospital, and many are as chronically suicidal on discharge as they were on admission.

I allow for two exceptions to these rules. The first concerns micropsychotic episodes, which can require treatment with drugs in a hospital setting. The second exception concerns near-lethal suicide attempts. In those circumstances, a brief admission can be used to reevaluate the treatment plan.

When patients are threatening suicide and therapy is out of control, there is an evidence-based alternative to hospital admission. Day hospital programs have been used for patients with BPD for many years and have an evidence base behind them (Bateman & Fonagy, 1999; W. E. Piper, Rosie, & Joyce, 1996). My experience has been that these programs are most effective when time limited, so that patients are less likely to regress. However, the most important element in day treatment is structure and predictability. Patients have a schedule to follow, with no time to slash their wrists.

The problem with day programs is lack of accessibility. They usually have a waiting list and you cannot get a patient in rapidly, either from the emergency room or from a therapist's office. That is another reason why patients with BPD can end up being admitted to hospital.

MANAGING CHRONIC SUICIDALITY

Several decades ago, Schwartz et al. (1974) wrote:

> The management of the person for whom suicidality has become a way of life requires a willingness to take risks and an acceptance of the fact that one cannot prevent all suicides. Those are two qualities which not all therapists have. Once one has concluded that the only way to strive toward the ultimate reduction of lethality is to accept the risk of suicide in the interim, one next needs to determine to what degree the patient and the other people important in the patient's life are ready to accept those risks and to share the responsibility for treatment.

This position implies a philosophical acceptance of risk and a strong sense of therapeutic limits. Kernberg (1987) stated he might tell a patient "that he would feel sad but not responsible if the patient killed himself," that he would avoid unusual measures to prevent completion. He lets them know that in the long run he cannot take responsibility for their survival. This rationale is similar to that offered by Rachlin (1980), who suggested that attempts to save lives in suicidal patients deprive patients of their quality of life. Hendin (1981) described scenarios in which therapists feel they must do *everything* to stop suicide as "coercive bondage" (i.e., the patient comes to control the behavior of the therapist).

The strategy of accepting risk may be paradoxical, but it avoids many pitfalls. It must, of course, be explained carefully to the patient. It also requires involving the patient's family, as noted by both Gunderson (2001) and Kernberg (1987).

WILL I BE SUED?

When I present my suggestions for the management of chronically suicidal patients to colleagues, I can always expect to be asked the question, "But what if I am sued?" (or, to put the matter more delicately, "What are the medicolegal implications of your approach?"). Even clinicians who are aware of the limited value of hospitalization can feel compelled to admit patients who threaten suicide if they believe they would face litigation if the patient carries out the threat.

However, courts generally understand that, in the practice of any therapist, suicides will occur. Surveys have shown that suicide occurs at least once in the careers of 50% of psychiatrists and 20% of psychologists (Chemtob, Hamada, Bauer, Kinney, & Torigoe, 1988a, 1988b).

However, the basis of litigation is not the fact of suicide itself but a failure by the therapist to meet standards of practice. Although suicide accounts for 20% of lawsuits against mental health professionals (Kelley, 1996), only a very small fraction of completions lead to litigation and only 20% of lawsuits will be upheld (Packman & Harris, 1998).

Juries do not hold therapists responsible unless they are convinced that treatment was *negligent* (i.e., that the therapist failed to provide reasonable care [in relation to standards set by their community of clinicians]). Moreover, because malpractice requires proof that any failure of care is the actual *cause* of a suicidal outcome, therapists can only be held liable if it seems likely that the suicide would not have occurred if care had been better (Gutheil, 1992).

If you treat suicidal people, some of them are going to die. So how can you reduce the risk? The work of noted forensic psychiatrist Thomas Gutheil (2004) has helped clarify these issues. The most important risk factor for malpractice is the failure to document the treatment plan and to write down the result of every assessment. Therapists can protect themselves by keeping careful notes that state the rationale for avoiding hospitalization. (In short, document, document, document!)

One procedure that should be standard for chronically suicidal patients is a consultation from a trusted colleague. Whatever you do with a patient, you are always protected if a colleague agrees with you and says so in writing. It is surprising that consultations are not routine, but they should be, no matter how experienced the therapist.

Finally, lawsuits after suicide can occur if the family was never consulted. If you take on a chronically suicidal patient, you need to meet with the family at the beginning of treatment to explain the problem and what you plan to do about it. You can explain that suicide cannot always be prevented and that hospitalization will probably not be useful.

Moreover, if you do not contact the patient's family, you lose a crucial ally. Family members, who have often had to endure a patient's suicidality without having anyone to help them, will feel supported by being brought into an alliance and will have less reason to feel angry and excluded. The situation sometimes becomes even worse if a patient does commit suicide and if therapists fail to return phone calls and fail to meet with family members to comfort them.

In summary, you do not have to practice defensively to manage a chronically suicidal patient. You have to document, consult, and bring the family into the treatment plan.

CLINICAL IMPLICATIONS

- Clinical assessment for suicidal risk is mostly a myth. If you cannot predict completion, it makes more sense to focus on the reasons for suicidality.
- Hospitalizing chronically suicidal patients is counterproductive and usually makes therapy impossible.
- Managing suicidality cannot be guided by fear of lawsuits.

CHAPTER 13

Research Directions

We know much more about BPD than we did 10 years ago. But there is much more that we do not know. Much additional research will be needed to answer the questions raised in this book and to help clinicians to carry out a more systematic and evidence-based practice.

DIAGNOSIS AND BOUNDARIES

The problem of defining the BPD diagnosis has yet to be solved. Unfortunately, research on the validity of DSM criteria for all mental disorders has been slow. At this point, the data are insufficient to make a major impact on DSM-V.

We can envisage a number of solutions to the problem. We might, as suggested in this book, define BPD in a more valid way by narrowing the diagnostic criteria. Alternatively, once we understand more about it, BPD could end up with a different name based on knowledge about its cause. Or, if BPD is a syndrome that emerges from multiple etiological pathways, it might be chopped up into a group of diagnoses. But however we classify the disorder, therapists will be faced with the same clinical problems.

In our present state of knowledge, radically reformulating BPD would be premature. Calling it something else or folding it into another category will not solve the problem. Rediagnosis will not make difficult patients go away. Thus far, most proposed reformulations have done a disservice to patients. Calling BPD a form of depression has led to prescriptions of antidepressants, with only marginal results. Calling BPD bipolar disorder, the currently fashionable option, has led to prescriptions of mood stabilizers and antipsychotics, again with only marginal results. Calling BPD a form of PTSD has led to bad therapy, regressing patients by focusing on their past instead of their present and future.

I consider proposals to dimensionalize BPD to be premature. Taking the category out of DSM by diagnosing personality disorder in general (and then describing trait profiles) would do little to clarify clinical problems. Although trait dimensions add useful information, they cannot replace a diagnosis. I do not see how self-report questionnaires developed in normal populations will ever properly describe patients who overdose and cut themselves. BPD is not like the other categories listed on Axis II. It is not even best thought of as a personality disorder. In view of its range of symptoms, BPD could be a separate category on Axis I.

On the other hand, there could be a real benefit to rewriting the criteria so as to require the presence of psychopathology in all domains affected by BPD. The more specific we can make the diagnosis, the more specific therapy will be. To consider an example of a disorder we know more about, DSM defines schizophrenia as requiring the presence of multiple characteristic symptoms (and specifies duration as well as effects on functioning). BPD also needs required criteria. It should not be diagnosed unless patients have symptoms in at least three of four domains (AI, impulsivity, cognition, and relationships). The "Chinese menu" list currently in use should become history.

No matter what happens, change is bound to be slow. I lived through the DSM-III revolution, which opened a new era in mental health research and practice. This was an exciting time when we all had to rethink our approach to diagnosis. Since then, however, conservatism has set in. At first, caution seemed justified: People complained about a system that changed every 7 years or so. That is why DSM-IV was almost identical to DSM-III. However, the current method of classification has been in place, with only minor revision, for almost three decades. It has taken on a life of its own.

To sustain the changes I suggest (or any alternative that has been proposed), supporting data are needed. Systematic studies examining different criteria sets have to be carried out to show how well each alternative predicts outcome and treatment response. Until then, the burden of proof lies with those who ask for radical change.

Biological research could also have a major effect on classification. One can speak of "cutting nature at its joints," but just where are they? One way to find out is by uncovering genes and neurobiological correlates of pathology that can help define the boundary between one disorder and another.

Most medical specialties take it for granted that while history and physical examination of patients will always be useful, precise diagnosis depends on blood tests and x-ray films. But psychiatry was different, and still is. We do not have any genetic marker, blood test, or imaging technique that can tell us whether a patient has schizophrenia, bipolar disorder, or any other condition.

Given the current boom in neuroscience research, this situation could change. However, it would be a mistake to expect breakthroughs soon; the time scale is more likely to be decades than years. In the meantime, we have to struggle along with current methods of measuring symptoms and traits.

Finally, it is worth asking why the diagnosis of BPD has been the focus of so much controversy when equally serious problems accompany most other major mental disorders. This is just another example of the stigma associated with borderline pathology, which affects both patients and the therapists who want to help them.

ETIOLOGY

We do not know what causes BPD. The answer is, almost certainly, many things, not one. I have proposed a model in this book that is consistent with what we know, but more research is needed to support it.

Several problems have held back progress. First and foremost, the idea that one diagnosis has one cause has been difficult for people to give up. Evidently, the mind prefers simplicity to complexity. Yet we know that many diseases have complex causes. You do not suffer a heart attack for one reason only; the pathways depend on genetic risk as well as lifestyle effects such as diet and smoking.

Second, until BPD is more precisely defined, progress in etiological research is bound to be slow. Because the diagnosis describes a heterogeneous group of patients, it is no wonder that findings have been inconsistent.

Third, there has been some tendency to throw whatever is current in the mental health field in the direction of the BPD problem. This problem has bedeviled biological research but has also affected psychosocial research, which can be just as faddish.

Although progress in science sometimes comes from serendipity and dumb luck, most progress comes out of hard slogging. We have to test hypotheses about BPD, and they must not be simplistic. The most useful line of research would seek to combine biological and psychosocial measures to assess gene–environment interactions.

That principle applies to all mental disorders, not just BPD. When studying biological factors, one needs to consider how the environment affects gene expression. We might think of many genes (15 or 20, if not more) interacting with each other, and each being turned on or off by the environment.

For this reason, it is no longer sufficient to study environmental risks for BPD without considering biological vulnerability. When studying psychosocial factors, one needs to control for heritability (as in twin studies) or directly measure genetic input. We are just beginning to see genetically informed studies of environmental affects on psychopathology. There are bound to be more in the future.

TREATMENT

I disagree with much of the therapy currently being offered to patients with BPD. Many are being mistreated. Even when the diagnosis is recognized, patients with BPD are given large doses of multiple drugs that they do not need and that help them very little. They are hospitalized when they threaten suicide, preventing effective therapy from being carried out. Some are given ideologically driven forms of psychotherapy that make them worse. Most patients are managed simply with treatment as usual, without making use of systematic or evidence-based interventions.

Research has made considerable progress in testing effective psychotherapies for BPD. Unfortunately, these therapies are not easy to apply in practice, and the lessons they teach have not been widely absorbed.

Drug treatment for BPD is much less impressive than most people think. I can only agree with the conclusions of the Cochrane

Collaboration (Binks et al., 2006a) that the literature provides little evidence for any pharmacological intervention in this patient population. Unfortunately, because hope is stronger than facts, patients continue to receive polypharmacy.

The only antidote to bad treatment is clinical research. I look forward to two directions in particular: (1) the development of new drugs that are specific to BPD traits, and (2) the unification of psychotherapy for BPD into one standard method and the end of all "name brands."

My concern about the future is that people with BPD will continue either to be ignored or to be treated in simplistic ways. However, those of us who have chosen to devote our lives to these fascinating patients are optimistic. No matter how hopeless treatment can seem, most patients eventually recover. No matter how difficult the path of scientific discovery will be, we will get there in the end.

References

Achenbach, T. M., & McConaughy, S. H. (1997). *Empirically based assessment of child and adolescent psychopathology: Practical applications* (2nd ed.). Thousand Oaks, CA: Sage.

Addis, M. E., Cardemil, E. V., Duncan, B. L., & Miller, S. D. (2006). Does manualization improve therapy outcomes? In J. C. Norcross, L. E. Beutler, & R. F. Levant (Eds.), *Evidence-based practices in mental health: Debate and dialogue on the fundamental questions* (pp. 131–160). Washington, DC: American Psychological Association.

Adler, G. (1985). *Borderline psychopathology and its treatment.* New York: Jason Aronson.

Akiskal, H. S. (2002). The bipolar spectrum: The shaping of a new paradigm in psychiatry. *Current Psychiatry Reports, 4,* 1–3.

Akiskal, H. S., Chen, S. E., & Davis, G. C. (1985). Borderline: An adjective in search of a noun. *Journal of Clinical Psychiatry, 46,* 41–48.

Alexander, F., & French, T. (1946). *Psychoanalytic therapy.* New York: Ronald Press.

American Psychiatric Association. (1980). *Diagnostic and statistical manual of mental disorders* (3rd ed.). Washington, DC: Author.

American Psychiatric Association. (1987). *Diagnostic and statistical manual of mental disorders* (3rd ed., rev.). Washington, DC: Author.

American Psychiatric Association. (1994). *Diagnostic and statistical manual of mental disorders* (4th ed., text rev.). Washington, DC: Author.

American Psychiatric Association. (2000). *Diagnostic and statistical manual of mental disorders* (4th ed., text rev). Washington, DC: Author.

Angst, J., & Gamma, A. (2002). A new bipolar spectrum concept: A brief review. *Bipolar Disorders, 4,* 11–14.

Arnold, S. E. (1999). Neurodevelopmental abnormalities in schizophrenia: Insights from neuropathology. *Development and Psychopathology, 11,* 439–456.

Aviram, R. B., Brodsky, B. S., & Stanley, B. (2006). Borderline personality disorder, stigma, and treatment implications. *Harvard Review of Psychiatry, 14,* 249–256.

Aviram, R. B., Hellerstein, D. J., Gerson, J., & Stanley, B. (2004). Adapting supportive psychotherapy for individuals with borderline personality disorder who self-injure or attempt suicide. *Journal of Psychiatric Practice, 10,* 145–155.

Bateman, A., & Fonagy, P. (1999). Effectiveness of partial hospitalization in the treatment of borderline personality disorder: A randomized controlled trial. *American Journal of Psychiatry, 156,* 1563–1569.

Bateman, A., & Fonagy, P. (2001). Treatment of borderline personality disorder with psychoanalytically oriented partial hospitalization: An 18-month follow-up. *American Journal of Psychiatry, 158,* 36–42.

Bateman, A., & Fonagy, P. (2004). *Psychotherapy for borderline personality disorder: Mentalization based treatment.* Oxford, UK: Oxford University Press.

Bateman, A., & Fonagy, P. (2006). *Mentalization based treatment: A practical guide.* New York: Wiley.

Baum, K. M., & Walker, E. F. (1995). Childhood behavioral precursors of adult symptom dimensions in schizophrenia. *Schizophrenia Research, 16,* 111–120.

Beblo, T., Driessen, M., Mertens, M., Wingenfeld, K., Piefke, M., Rullkoetter, N., et al. (2006). Functional MRI correlates of the recall of unresolved life events in borderline personality disorder. *Psychological Medicine, 36,* 845–856.

Beck, A. T., Freeman, A., Davis, D. D., & Associates. (2002). *Cognitive therapy of personality disorders* (2nd ed.). New York: Guilford Press.

Becker, D. F., Grilo, C. M., Edell, W. S., & McGlashan, T. H. (2002). Diagnostic efficiency of borderline personality disorder criteria in hospitalized adolescents: Comparison with hospitalized adults. *American Journal of Psychiatry, 159,* 2042–2047.

Bemporad, J. R., Smith, H. F., Hanson, G., & Cicchetti, D. (1982). Borderline syndromes in childhood: Criteria for diagnosis. *American Journal of Psychiatry, 139,* 596–601.

Bernstein, D. P., Cohen, P., Skodol, A., Bezirganian, S., & Brook, J. S. (1993). Prevalence and stability of the DSM-III personality disorders in a community-based survey of adolescents. *American Journal of Psychiatry, 150,* 1237–1243.

Beutler, L. E., Malik, M., Alimohamed, S., Harwood, M., Talchi, H., Noble, S., et al. (2004). Therapist variables. In M. J. Lambert (Ed.), *Bergin and Garfield's handbook of psychotherapy and behavior change* (5th ed., pp. 227–306). New York: Wiley.

Biederman, J. (2006). The evolving face of pediatric mania. *Biological Psychiatry, 60,* 901–902.

Binks, C. A., Fenton, M., McCarthy, L., Lee, T., Adams, C. E., & Duggan, C. (2006a). Pharmacological interventions for people with borderline personality disorder. *Cochrane Database of Systematic Reviews,* Issue 1, CD005653.

Binks, C. A., Fenton, M., McCarthy, L., Lee, T., Adams, C. E., & Duggan, C. (2006b). Psychological therapies for people with borderline personality disorder. *Cochrane Database of Systematic Reviews,* Issue 1, CD005652.

Black, D. W., Baumgard, C. H., & Bell, S. E. (1995). A 16–45-year follow-up of 71 men with antisocial personality disorder. *Comprehensive Psychiatry, 36,* 130–140.

Bland, R. C., Dyck, R. J., Newman, S. C., & Orn, H. (1998). Attempted suicide in Edmonton. In A. A. Leenaars, S. Wenckstern, I. Sakinofsky, R. J. Dyck, M. J.

Kral, & R. C. Bland (Eds.), *Suicide in Canada* (pp. 136–150). Toronto: University of Toronto Press.

Block, M. J., Westen, D., Ludolph, P., Wixom, J., & Jackson, A. (1991). Distinguishing female borderline adolescents from normal and other disturbed female adolescents. *Psychiatry, 54,* 89–103.

Blum, H. P. (1974). The borderline childhood of the wolf man. *Journal of the American Psychoanalytic Association, 22,* 721–742.

Blum, N., Pfohl, B., St. John, D., Monahan, P., & Black, D. W. (2002). STEPPS: A cognitive-behavioral systems-based group treatment for outpatients with borderline personality disorder: A preliminary report. *Comprehensive Psychiatry, 43,* 301–310.

Blum, N., St. John, D., Pfohl, B., Stuart, S., McCormick, B., Allen, S. A., & Black, D. W. Systems Training for Emotional Predictability and Problem Solving (STEPPS) for outpatients with borderline personality disorder: A randomized controlled trial and 1-year follow-up. *American Journal of Psychiatry, 165,* April 2008.

Bogenschutz, M. P., & Nurnberg, G. H. (2004). Olanzapine versus placebo in the treatment of borderline personality disorder. *Journal of Clinical Psychiatry, 65,* 104–109.

Bohus, M., Haaf, B., Simms, T., Limberger, M. F., Schmahl, C., Unckel, D., et al. (2004). Effectiveness of inpatient dialectical behavioral therapy for borderline personality disorder: A controlled trial. *Behaviour Research and Therapy, 42,* 487–499.

Bohus, M., Schmahl, C., & Lieb, K. (2004). New developments in the neurobiology of borderline personality disorder. *Current Psychiatry Reports, 6,* 43–50.

Bond, M., Paris, J., & Zweig-Frank, H. (1994). The Defense Style Questionnaire in borderline personality disorder. *Journal of Personality Disorders, 8,* 28–31.

Bongar, B. M. (1991). *The suicidal patient: Clinical and legal standards of care.* Washington, DC: American Psychological Association.

Bradley, R., & Westen, D. (2005). The psychodynamics of borderline personality disorder: A view from developmental psychopathology. *Development and Psychopathology, 17,* 927–957.

Brambilla, P., Soloff, P. H., Sala, M., Nicoletti, M. A., Keshavan, M. S., & Soares, J. C. (2004). Anatomical MRI study of borderline personality disorder patients. *Psychiatry Research, 131,* 125–133.

Brent, D. A. (2001). Assessment and treatment of the youthful suicidal patient. *Annals of the New York Academy of Sciences, 932,* 106–128.

Brodsky, B. S., Groves, S. A., Oquendo, M. A., Mann, J. J., & Stanley, B. (2006). Interpersonal precipitants and suicide attempts in borderline personality disorder. *Suicide and Life-Threatening Behavior, 36,* 313–322.

Brown, G. K., Newman, C. F., Charlesworth, S. E., Crits-Christoph, P., & Beck, A. (2004). An open clinical trial of cognitive therapy for borderline personality disorder. *Journal of Personality Disorders, 18,* 257–271.

Brown, G. K., Steer, R. A., Henriques, G. R., & Beck, A. T. (2005). The internal struggle between the wish to die and the wish to live: A risk factor for suicide. *American Journal of Psychiatry, 162,* 1977–1979.

Brown, M. Z., Comtois, K. A., & Linehan, M. M. (2002). Reasons for suicide attempts and nonsuicidal self-injury in women with borderline personality disorder. *Journal of Abnormal Psychology, 111,* 198–202.

Browne, A., & Finkelhor, D. (1986). Impact of child sexual abuse: A review of the literature. *Psychological Bulletin, 99,* 66–77.

Caspi, A., McClay, J., Moffitt, T. E., Mill, J., Martin, J., Craig, I. W., et al. (2002). Role of genotype in the cycle of violence in maltreated children. *Science, 297,* 851–854.

Caspi, A., Moffitt, T. E., Newman, D. L., & Silva, P. A. (1996). Behavioral observations at age three predict adult psychiatric disorders: Longitudinal evidence from a birth cohort. *Archives of General Psychiatry, 53,* 1033–1039.

Caspi, A., Sugden, K., Moffitt, T. E., Taylor, A., Craig, I. W., Harrington, H., et al. (2003). Influence of life stress on depression: Moderation by a polymorphism in the 5-HTT gene. *Science, 301,* 386–389.

Cassidy, J., & Shaver, P. R. (Eds.). (1999). *Handbook of attachment: Theory, research and clinical aspects.* New York: Guilford Press.

Chambers, R. A., Taylor, J. R., & Potenza, M. N., (2003). Developmental neurocircuitry of motivation in adolescence: A critical period of addiction vulnerability. *American Journal of Psychiatry, 160,* 1041–1052.

Chemtob, C. M., Hamada, R. S., Bauer, G. B., Kinney, B., & Torigoe, R. Y. (1988a). Patient suicide: Frequency and impact on psychiatrists. *American Journal of Psychiatry, 145,* 224–228.

Chemtob, C. M., Hamada, R. S., Bauer, G. B., Kinney, B., & Torigoe, R. Y. (1988b). Patient suicide: Frequency and impact on psychologists. *Professional Psychology: Research and Practice, 19,* 416–420.

Chen, L. S., Eaton, W. W., Gallo, J. J., Nestadt, G., & Crum, R. M. (2000). Empirical examination of current depression categories in a population-based study: Symptoms, course, and risk factors. *American Journal of Psychiatry, 157,* 573–580.

Chess, S., & Thomas, A. (1984). *Origins and evolution of behavior disorders: From infancy to adult life.* New York: Brunner/Mazel.

Cicchetti, D., & Rogosch, F. A. (2002). A developmental psychopathology perspective on adolescence. *Journal of Consulting and Clinical Psychology, 70,* 6–20.

Cicchetti, D., & Toth, S. (1998). The development of depression in childhood and adolescence. *American Psychologist, 53,* 221–241.

Clark, L. A. (1993). *Schedule for non-adaptive and adaptive personality.* Minneapolis: University of Minnesota Press.

Clark, L. A., Livesley, W. J., & Morey, L. (1997). Personality disorder assessment: The challenge of construct validity. *Journal of Personality Disorders, 11,* 205–231.

Clarkin, J. F., & Levy, K. L. (2004). The influence of client variables on psychotherapy. In M. J. Lambert (Ed.), *Bergin and Garfield's handbook of psychotherapy and behavior change* (5th ed., pp. 227–308). New York: Wiley.

Clarkin, J. F., Levy, K. N., Lenzenweger, M. F., & Kernberg, O. F. (2004). The Personality Disorders Institute/Borderline Personality Disorder Research Foundation randomized control trial for borderline personality disorder: Rationale, methods, and patient characteristics. *Journal of Personality Disorders, 18,* 52–72.

Clarkin, J. F., Levy, K. N., Lenzenweger, M. F., & Kernberg, O. F. (2007). Evaluating three treatments for borderline personality disorder: A multiwave study. *American Journal of Psychiatry, 164,* 1–8.

Clarkin, J. F., Widiger, T. A., Frances, A., Hurt, S. W., & Gilmore, M. (1983). Propotypic typology and the borderline personality disorder. *Journal of Abnormal Psychology, 92,* 263–275.

Clifton, A., & Pilkonis, P. (2007). Evidence for a single latent class of *Diagnostic and statistical manual of mental disorders* borderline personality pathology. *Comprehensive Psychiatry, 48,* 70–78.

Cloninger, R. C. (1987). A systematic method for clinical description and classification of personality variants. *Archives of General Psychiatry, 44,* 573–588.

Coccaro, E. F., & Kavoussi, R. J. (1997). Fluoxetine and impulsive aggressive behavior in personality-disordered subjects. *Archives of General Psychiatry, 54,* 1081–1088.

Coccaro, E. F., Siever, L. J., Klar, H. M., Maurer, G., Cochrane, K., Cooper, T. B., et al. (1989). Serotonergic studies in patients with affective and personality disorders. *Archives of General Psychiatry, 46,* 587–599.

Cohen, D. J., Paul, R., & Volkmar, F. (1987). Issues in the classification of pervasive developmental disorders and associated conditions. In D. J. Cohen & A. M. Donnelean (Eds.), *Handbook of autism and pervasive developmental disorders* (pp. 20–39). New York: Wiley.

Cohen, P., Crawford, T. N., Johnson, J. G., & Kasen, S. (2005). The children in the community study of developmental course of personality disorder. *Journal of Personality Disorders, 19,* 466–486.

Coid, J., Yang, M., Tyrer, P., Roberts, A., & Ullrich, S. (2006). Prevalence and correlates of personality disorder in Great Britain. *British Journal of Psychiatry, 188,* 423–431.

Conte, J. R., Wolf, S., & Smith, T. (1989). What sexual offenders tell us about prevention strategies. *Child Abuse and Neglect, 13,* 293–301.

Costa, P. T., & Widiger, T. A. (Eds.). (2001). *Personality disorders and the five factor model of personality* (2nd ed.). Washington, DC: American Psychological Association.

Cowdry, R. W., & Gardner, D. L. (1988). Pharmacotherapy of borderline personality disorder: Alprazolam, carbamazepine, trifluoperazine, and tranylcypromine. *Archives of General Psychiatry, 45,* 111–119.

Crawford, T. N., Cohen, P., & Brook, J. S. (2001a). Dramatic-erratic personality disorder symptoms: I. Continuity from early adolescence to adulthood. *Journal of Personality Disorders, 15,* 319–335.

Crawford, T. N., Cohen, P., & Brook, J. S. (2001b). Dramatic-erratic personality disorder symptoms: II. Developmental pathways from early adolescence to adulthood. *Journal of Personality Disorders, 15,* 336–350.

Crawford, T. N., Cohen, P., Johnson, J. G., Kasen, S., First, M. B., Gordon, K., et al. (2005). Self-reported personality disorder in the children in the community sample: Convergent and prospective validity in late adolescence and adulthood. *Journal of Personality Disorders, 19,* 30–52.

Crick, N. R., & Zahn-Waxler, C. (2003). The development of psychopathology in females and males: Current progress and future challenges. *Development and Psychopathology, 15,* 719–742.

Cummings, N. A., & Sayama, M. (1995). *Focused psychotherapy: A casebook of brief, intermittent psychotherapy throughout the life cycle.* Philadelphia: Brunner/Mazel.

Davidson, K., Norrie, J., Tyrer, P., Gumley, A., Tata, P., Murray, H., et al. (2006). The effectiveness of cognitive behavior therapy for borderline personality disorder: Results from the borderline personality disorder study of cognitive therapy (BOSCOT) trial. *Journal of Personality Disorders, 20,* 450–465.

Davidson, K., Tyrer, P., Gumley, A., Tata, P., Norrie, J., Palmer, S., et al. (2006). A randomized controlled trial of cognitive behavior therapy for borderline personality disorder: Rationale for trial, method, and description of sample. *Journal of Personality Disorders, 20,* 431–449.

Dawson, D., & McMillan, H. L. (1993). *Relationship management of the borderline patient: From understanding to treatment.* New York: Brunner/Mazel.

de Bruijn, E. R., Grootens, K. P., Verkes, R. J., Buchholz, V., Hummelen, J. W., & Hulstijn, W. (2006). Neural correlates of impulsive responding in borderline personality disorder: ERP evidence for reduced action monitoring. *Journal of Psychiatric Research, 40,* 428–437.

De la Fuente, J. M., Bobes, J., Vizuete, C., & Mendlewicz, J. (2001). Sleep-EEG in borderline patients without concomitant major depression: A comparison with major depressives and normal control subjects. *Psychiatry Research, 105,* 87–95.

De Lima, M. S., & Hotopf, M. (2003). A comparison of active drugs for the treatment of dysthymia. *Cochrane Database of Systematic Reviews,* Issue 3, CD00404.

Depue, R. A., & Lenzenweger, M. (2001). A neurobehavioral dimensional model. In W. J. Livesley (Ed.), *Handbook of personality disorders: Theory, research, and treatment* (pp. 136–176). New York: Guilford Press.

Distel, M. A., Trull, T. J., Derom, C. A., Thiery, E. W., Grimmer, M. A., Martin, G., et al. (in press). Heritability of borderline personality disorder features is similar across three countries. *Psychological Medicine.*

Donegan, N. H., Sanislow, C. A., Blumberg, H. P., Fulbright, R. K., Lacadie, C., Skudlarski, P., et al. (2003). Amygdala hyperreactivity in borderline personality disorder: Implications for emotional dysregulation. *Biological Psychiatry, 54,* 1284–1293.

Driessen, M., Herrmann, J., Stahl, K., Zwaan, M., Meier, S., Hill, A., et al. (2000). Magnetic resonance imaging volumes of the hippocampus and the amygdala in women with borderline personality disorder and early traumatization. *Archives of General Psychiatry, 57,* 1115–1122.

Dunner, D. I., & Tay, K. L. (1993). Diagnostic reliability of the history of hypomania in bipolar II patients and patients with major depression. *Comprehensive Psychiatry, 34,* 303–307.

Ebner-Priemer, U. W., Kuo, J., Kleindienst, N., Welch, S. S., Reisch, T., Reinhard, I., et al. (2007). State affective instability in borderline personality disorder assessed by ambulatory monitoring. *Psychological Medicine, 37,* 961–970.

Engel, G. L. (1980). The clinical application of the biopsychosocial model. *American Journal of Psychiatry, 137,* 535–544.

Farabaugh, A., Mischoulon, D., Fava, M., Guyker, W., & Alpert, J. (2004). The overlap between personality disorders and major depressive disorder. *Annals of Clinical Psychiatry, 16,* 217–224.

Favazza, A. R. (1996). *Bodies under siege: Self-mutilation and body modification in culture and psychiatry* (2nd ed.). Baltimore, MD: Johns Hopkins University Press.

Feldman, R. B., Zelkowitz, P., Weiss, M., Heyman, M., Vogel, J., & Paris, J. (1995). A comparison of the families of borderline personality disorder mothers and the families of other personality disorder mothers. *Comprehensive Psychiatry, 36,* 157–163.

Fergusson, D. M., Lynskey, M. T., & Horwood, J. (1996). Childhood sexual abuse and psychiatric disorder in young adulthood: II. Psychiatric outcomes of childhood sexual abuse. *Journal of the American Academy of Child and Adolescent Psychiatry, 34,* 1365–1374.

Fergusson, D. M., & Mullen, P. E. (1999). *Childhood sexual abuse: An evidence based perspective.* Thousand Oaks, CA: Sage.

Fertuck, E. A., Lenzenweger, M. F., Clarkin, J. F., Hoermann, S., & Stanley, B. (2006). Executive neurocognition, memory systems, and borderline personality disorder. *Clinical Psychology Review, 26,* 346–375.

Fine, M. A., & Sansone, R. A. (1990). Dilemmas in the management of suicidal behavior in individuals with borderline personality disorder. *American Journal of Psychotherapy, 44,* 160–171.

First, M. B. (2005). Clinical utility: A prerequisite for the adoption of a dimensional approach in DSM. *Journal of Abnormal Psychology, 114,* 560–564.

Fonagy, P., & Bateman, A. W. (2006). Mechanisms of change in mentalization-based treatment of BPD. *Journal of Clinical Psychology, 62,* 411–430.

Fonagy, P., Target, M., & Gergely, G. (2000). Attachment and borderline personality disorder: A theory and some evidence. *Psychiatric Clinics of North America, 23,* 103–122.

Forman, E. M., Berk, M. S., Henriques, G. R., Brown, G. K., & Beck, A. T. (2004). History of multiple suicide attempts as a behavioral marker of severe psychopathology. *American Journal of Psychiatry, 161,* 437–443.

Fossati, A., Madeddu, F., & Maffei, C. (1999). Borderline personality disorder and childhood sexual abuse: A metanalytic study. *Journal of Personality Disorders, 13,* 268–280.

Frank, A. F. (1992). The therapeutic alliances of borderline patients. In J. F. Clarkin, E. Marziali, & H. Munroe-Blum (Eds.), *Borderline personality disorder: Clinical and empirical perspectives* (pp. 220–247). New York: Guilford Press.

Frank, J. D., & Frank, J. B. (1991). *Persuasion and healing* (3rd ed.). Baltimore, MD: Johns Hopkins University Press.

Frank, H., & Hoffman, N. (1986). Borderline empathy: An empirical investigation. *Comprehensive Psychiatry, 27,* 387–395.

Frank, H., & Paris, J. (1981). Recollections of family experience in borderline patients. *Archives of General Psychiatry, 38,* 1031–1034.

Frankenburg, F. R., & Zanarini, M. C. (2002). Divalproex sodium treatment of women with borderline personality disorder and bipolar II disorder: A double-blind placebo-controlled pilot study. *Journal of Clinical Psychiatry, 63,* 442–446.

Freud, S. (1962). Analysis terminable and interminable. In *The standard edition of the psychological works of Sigmund Freud* (Vol. 23, pp. 216–254). London: Hogarth Press. (Original work published 1937).

Furstenberg, F. F. (2000). The sociology of adolescence and youth in the 1990s: A critical commentary. *Journal of Marriage and the Family, 62*(4), 896–910.

Gabbard, G. O. (1996). Lessons to be learned from the study of sexual boundary violations. *American Journal of Psychotherapy, 50,* 311–322.

Garner, D. M., & Garfinkel, P. E. (1980). Socio-cultural factors in the development of anorexia nervosa. *Psychological Medicine, 10,* 647–656.

Garnet, K. E., Levy, K. N., Mattanah, J. F., Edell, W. S., & McGlashan, T. H. (1994). Borderline personality disorder in adolescents: Ubiquitous or specific? *American Journal of Psychiatry, 151,* 1380–1382.

Gaston, L., Goldfried, M. R., Greenberg, L. S., & Horvath, A. O. (1995). The therapeutic alliance in psychodynamic, cognitive-behavioral, and experiential therapies. *Journal of Psychotherapy Integration, 5,* 1–26.

Gerson, J., & Stanley, B. (2002). Suicidal and self-injurious behavior in personality disorder: Controversies and treatment directions. *Current Psychiatry Reports, 4,* 30–38.

Ghaemi, S. N., Ko, J. Y., & Goodwin, F. K. (2002). "Cade's disease" and beyond: Misdiagnosis, antidepressant use, and a proposed definition for bipolar spectrum disorder. *Canadian Journal of Psychiatry, 47,* 125–134.

Giesen-Bloo, J., van Dyck, R., Spinhoven, P., van Tilburg, W., Dirksen, C., van

Asselt, T., et al. (2006). Outpatient psychotherapy for borderline personality disorder: Randomized trial of schema-focused therapy versus transference-focused psychotherapy. *Archives of General Psychiatry, 63*, 649–658.

Goldapple, K., Segal, Z., Garson, C., Lau, M., Bieling, P., & Kennedy, S. (2004). Modulation of cortical-limbic pathways in major depression: Treatment-specific effects of cognitive behavior therapy. *Archives of General Psychiatry, 61*, 34–41.

Goldman, S. J., D'Angelo, E. J., & DeMaso, D. R. (1993). Psychopathology in the families of children and adolescents with borderline personality disorder. *American Journal of Psychiatry, 150*, 1832–1835.

Goldman, S. J., D'Angelo, E. J., DeMaso, D. R., & Mezzacappa, E. (1992). Physical and sexual abuse histories among children with borderline personality disorder. *American Journal of Psychiatry, 149*, 1723–1726.

Goldstein, R. B., Black, D. W., Nasrallah, A., & Winokur, G. (1991). The prediction of suicide. *Archives of General Psychiatry, 48*, 418–422.

Goodman, G., Hull, J. W., Clarkin, J. F., & Yeomans, F. E. (1999). Childhood antisocial behaviors as predictors of psychotic symptoms and DSM-III-R borderline criteria among inpatients with borderline personality disorder. *Journal of Personality Disorders, 13*, 35–46.

Gottesman, I. I. (1991). *Schizophrenia genesis.* New York: Freeman.

Gottesman, I. I., & Gould, T. D. (2003). The endophenotype concept in psychiatry: Etymology and strategic intentions. *American Journal of Psychiatry, 160*, 636–645.

Grant, B. F., Hasin, D. S., Stinson, F. S., Dawson, D. A., Chou, S. P., Ruan, W. J., et al. (2004). Prevalence, correlates, and disability of personality disorders in the United States: Results from the National Epidemiologic Survey on Alcohol and Related Conditions. *Journal of Clinical Psychiatry, 65*, 948–958.

Gratz, K. L., & Gunderson, J. G. (2006). Preliminary data on an acceptance-based emotion regulation group intervention for deliberate self-harm among women with borderline personality disorder. *Behavior Therapy, 37*, 25–35.

Gratz, K. L., Rosenthal, M. Z., Tull, M. T., Lejuez, C. W., & Gunderson, J. G. (2006). An experimental investigation of emotion dysregulation in borderline personality disorder. *Journal of Abnormal Psychology, 115*, 850–855.

Greenman, D. A., Gunderson, J. G., Cane, M., & Saltzman, P. R. (1986). A examination of the borderline diagnosis in children. *American Journal of Psychiatry, 143*, 998–1002.

Grilo, C. M., Becker, D. F., Edell, W. S., & McGlashan, T. H. (2001). Stability and change of DSM-III-R personality disorder dimensions in adolescents followed up 2 years after psychiatric hospitalization. *Comprehensive Psychiatry, 42*, 364–368.

Grilo, C. M., Sanislow, C. A., Gunderson, J. G., Pagano, M. E., Yen, S., Zanarini, M. C., et al. (2004). Two-year stability and change of schizotypal, borderline, avoidant, and obsessive-compulsive personality disorders. *Journal of Consulting and Clinical Psychology, 72*, 767–775.

Grinker, R. R., Werble, B., & Dyre, R. C. (1968). *The borderline patient.* New York: Basic Books.

Grootens, K. P., & Verkes, R. J. (2005). Emerging evidence for the use of atypical antipsychotics in borderline personality disorder. *Pharmacopsychiatry, 38*, 20–23.

Gross, R., Olfson, M., Gameroff, M., Shea, S., Feder, A., Fuentes, M., et al. (2002). Borderline personality disorder in primary care. *Archives of Internal Medicine, 162*, 53–60.

Gunderson, J. G. (1984). *Borderline personality disorder.* Washington, DC: American Psychiatric Press.

Gunderson, J. G. (2001). *Borderline personality disorder: A clinical guide.* Washington, DC: American Psychiatric Press.

Gunderson, J. G., Bender, D., Sanislow, C., Yen, S., Rettew, J. B., Dolan-Sewell, R., et al. (2003). Plausibility and possible determinants of sudden "remissions" in borderline patients. *Psychiatry, 66*, 111–119.

Gunderson, J. G., Daversa, M. T., McGlashan, T. H., Grilo, C. M., Zanarini, M. C., Shea, M. T., et al. (2006). Predictors of two-year outcome for patients with borderline personality disorder. *American Journal of Psychiatry, 163*, 822–826.

Gunderson, J. G., Frank, A. F., Ronningstam, E. F., Wahter, S., Lynch, V. J., & Wolf, P. J. (1989). Early discontinuance of borderline patients from psychotherapy. *Journal of Nervous and Mental Disease, 177*, 34–38.

Gunderson, J. G., & Hoffman, P. D. (Eds.). (2005). *Understanding and treating borderline personality disorder: A guide for professionals and families.* Washington, DC: American Psychiatric Press.

Gunderson, J. G., & Phillips, K. A. (1991). A current view of the interface between borderline personality disorder and depression. *American Journal of Psychiatry, 148*, 967–975.

Gunderson, J. G., & Singer, M. T. (1975). Defining borderline patients: An overview. *American Journal of Psychiatry, 132*, 1–9.

Gunderson, J. G., Weinberg, I., Daversa, M. T., Kueppenbender, K. D., Zanarini, M. C., Shea, M. T., et al. (2006). Descriptive and longitudinal observations on the relationship of borderline personality disorder and bipolar disorder. *American Journal of Psychiatry, 163*, 1173–1178.

Gutheil, T. A., & Brodsky, A. (2008). *Preventing boundary violations in clinical practice.* New York: Guilford Press.

Gutheil, T. G. (1985). Medicolegal pitfalls in the treatment of borderline patients. *American Journal of Psychiatry, 142*, 9–14.

Gutheil, T. G. (1989). Borderline personality disorder, boundary violations, and patient–therapist sex: Medicolegal pitfalls. *American Journal of Psychiatry, 146*, 597–602.

Gutheil, T. G. (1992). Suicide and suit: Liability after self-destruction. In D. Jacobs (Ed.), *Suicide and clinical practice* (pp. 147–167). Washington, DC: American Psychiatric Press.

Gutheil, T. G. (2004). Suicide, suicide litigation, and borderline personality disorder. *Journal of Personality Disorders, 18*, 248–256.

Gutheil, T. G., & Gabbard, G. O. (1993). The concept of boundaries in clinical practice: Theoretical and risk-management dimensions. *American Journal of Psychiatry, 150*, 188–196.

Guzder, J., Paris, J., Zelkowitz, P., & Feldman, R. (1999). Psychological risk factors for borderline pathology in school-aged children. *Journal of the American Academy of Child and Adolescent Psychiatry, 38*, 206–212.

Guzder, J., Paris, J., Zelkowitz, P., & Marchessault, K. (1996). Risk factors for borderline pathology in children. *Journal of the American Academy of Child and Adolescent Psychiatry, 35*, 26–33.

Harding, C. M., Brooks, G. W., Ashikaga, T., Strauss, J. S., & Brier, A. (1987). Vermont Longitudinal Study of persons with severe mental illness. *American Journal of Psychiatry, 143,* 727–735.

Harrington, R., Rutter, M., & Fombonne, E. (1996). Developmental pathways in depression: Multiple meanings, antecedents, and endpoints. *Development and Psychopathology, 8,* 601–616.

Harris, J. R. (1998). *The nurture assumption.* New York: Free Press.

Harriss, L., & Hawton, K. (2005). Suicidal intent in deliberate self-harm and the risk of suicide: The predictive power of the Suicide Intent Scale. *Journal of Affective Disorders, 86,* 225–233.

Hawton, K., Zahl, D., & Weatherall, R. (2003). Suicide following deliberate self-harm: Long-term follow-up of patients who presented to a general hospital. *British Journal of Psychiatry, 182,* 537–542.

Hazlett, E. A., New, A. S., Newmark, R., Haznedar, M. M., Lo, J. N., Speiser, L. J., et al. (2005). Reduced anterior and posterior cingulate gray matter in borderline personality disorder. *Biological Psychiatry, 58,* 614–623.

Heatherington, E. M., & Kelly, J. (2002). *For better or for worse: Divorce reconsidered.* New York: Norton.

Helzer, J. E., & Canino, G. J. (Eds.). (1992). *Alcoholism in North America, Europe, and Asia.* New York: Oxford University Press.

Hendin, H. (1981). Psychotherapy and suicide. *American Journal of Psychotherapy, 35,* 469–480.

Henry, C., Mitropoulou, V., New, A. S., Koenigsberg, H. W., Silverman, J., & Siever, L. J. (2001). Affective instability and impulsivity in borderline personality and bipolar II disorders: Similarities and differences. *Journal of Psychiatric Research, 35,* 307–312.

Herman, J. L. (1992). *Trauma and recovery.* New York: Basic Books.

Herman, J. L., Perry, J. C., & van der Kolk, B. A. (1989). Childhood trauma in borderline personality disorder. *American Journal of Psychiatry, 146,* 490–495.

Herman, J., & van der Kolk, B. (1987). Traumatic antecedents of borderline personality disorder. In B. van der Kolk (Ed.), *Psychological trauma* (pp. 111–126). Washington, DC: American Psychiatric Press.

Herpertz, S. C., Kunert, H. J., Schwenger, U. B., & Sass, H. (1999). Affective responsiveness in borderline personality disorder: A psychophysiological approach. *American Journal of Psychiatry, 156,* 1550–1556.

Hoch, P. H., Cattell, J. P., Strahl, M. D., & Penness, H. H. (1962). The course and outcome of pseudoneurotic schizophrenia. *American Journal of Psychiatry, 119,* 106–115.

Hoffman, P. D., Fruzzetti, A. E., & Buteau, E. (2007). Understanding and engaging families: An education, skills and support program for relatives impacted by borderline personality disorder. *Journal of Mental Health, 16,* 69–82.

Hollander, E., Allen, A., Lopez, R. P., Bienstock, C. A., Grossman, R., Siever, L. J., et al. (2001). A preliminary double-blind, placebo-controlled trial of divalproex sodium in borderline personality disorder. *Journal of Clinical Psychiatry, 62,* 199–203.

Hollander, E., Swann, A. C., Coccaro, E. F., Jiang, P., & Smith, T. B. (2005). Impact of trait impulsivity and state aggression on divalproex versus placebo response in borderline personality disorder. *American Journal of Psychiatry, 162,* 621–624.

Horwitz, A. V., & Wakefield, J. C. (2007). *The loss of sadness: How psychiatry transformed normal sorrow into depressive disorder.* New York: Oxford University Press.

Horwitz, A. V., Widom, C. S., McLaughlin, J., & White, H. R. (2001). The impact of childhood abuse and neglect on adult mental health: A prospective study. *Journal of Health and Social Behavior, 42*, 184–201.

Huband, N., McMurran, M., Evans, C., & Duggan, C. (2007). Social problem-solving plus psychoeducation for adults with personality disorder: Pragmatic randomised controlled trial. *British Journal of Psychiatry, 190*, 307–313.

Hwu, H. G., Yeh, E. K., & Change, L. Y. (1989). Prevalence of psychiatric disorders in Taiwan defined by the Chinese Diagnostic Interview Schedule. *Acta Psychiatrica Scandinavica, 79*, 136–147.

Irle, E., Langc, C., & Sachssc, U. (2005). Reduced size and abnormal asymmetry of parietal cortex in women with borderline personality disorder. *Biological Psychiatry, 57*, 173–182.

Jang, K. L., Livesley, W. J., & Vernon, P. A. (1996). The genetic basis of personality at different ages. *Journal of Personality and Individual Differences, 21*, 299–301.

Jang, K. L., Livesley, W. J., Vernon, P. A., & Jackson, D. N. (1996). Heritability of personality traits: A twin study. *Acta Psychiatrica Scandinavica, 94*, 438–444.

Johnson, J. G., Cohen, P., Brown, J., Smailes, E. M., & Bernstein, D. P. (1999). Childhood maltreatment increases risk for personality disorders during early adulthood. *Archives of General Psychiatry, 56*, 600–606.

Johnson, J. G., Cohen, P., Chen, H., Kasen, S., & Brook, J. S. (2006). Parenting behaviors associated with risk for offspring personality disorder during adulthood. *Archives of General Psychiatry, 63*, 579–587.

Johnson, J. G., First, M. B., Cohen, P., Skodol, A. E., Kasen, S., & Brook, J. S. (2005). Adverse outcomes associated with personality disorder not otherwise specified in a community sample. *American Journal of Psychiatry, 162*, 1926–1932.

Kasen, S., Cohen, P., Skodol, A. E., Johnson, J. G., & Brook, J. S. (1999). Influence of child and adolescent psychiatric disorders on young adult personality disorder. *American Journal of Psychiatry, 156*, 1529–1535.

Kaufman, J. (2006). Stress and its consequences: An evolving story. *Biological Psychiatry, 60*, 669–670.

Kavoussi, R. J., & Coccaro, E. F. (1998). Divalproex sodium for impulsive aggressive behavior in patients with personality disorder. *Journal of Clinical Psychiatry, 59*, 676–680.

Keel, P. K., Mitchell, J. E., Miller, K. B., Davis, T. L., & Crow, S. J. (1999). Long-term outcome of bulimia nervosa. *Archives of General Psychiatry, 56*, 63–69.

Kelley, J. T. (1996). *Psychiatric malpractice*. New Brunswick, NJ: Rutgers University Press.

Kendler, K. S., & Prescott, C. A. (2006). *Genes, environment and psychopathology*. New York: Guilford Press.

Kernberg, O. F. (1970). A psychoanalytic classification of character pathology. *Journal of the American Psychoanalytic Association, 18*, 800–822.

Kernberg, O. F. (1976). *Borderline conditions and pathological narcissism*. New York: Jason Aronson.

Kernberg, O. F. (1987). Diagnosis and clinical management of suicidal potential in borderline patients. In J. S. Grotstein & M. F. Solomon (Eds.), *The borderline patient: Emerging concepts in diagnosis, psychodynamics and treatment* (pp. 69–80). New York: Psychoanalytic Inquiry Book Series.

Kernberg, P. F., Weiner, A. S., & Bardenstein, K. K. (2000). *Personality Disorders in Children and Adolescents*. New York: Basic Books.

Kessler, R. C., Berglund, P., Borges, G., Nock, M., & Wang, P. S. (2005). Trends in suicide ideation, plans, gestures, and attempts in the United States, 1990–1992 to 2001–2003. *Journal of the American Medical Association, 293,* 2487–2495.

Kessler, R. C., Chiu, W. T., Demler, O., Merikangas, K. R., & Walters, E. E. (2005). Prevalence, severity, and comorbidity of 12-month DSM-IV disorders in the National Comorbidity Survey Replication. *Archives of General Psychiatry, 62,* 617–627.

Kessler, R. C., McGonagle, K. A., Zhao, S., Nelson, C. B., Hughes, M., Eshleman, S., et al. (1994). Lifetime and 12-month prevalence of DSM-III-R psychiatric disorders in the United States: Results from the National Comorbidity Survey. *Archives of General Psychiatry, 51,* 8–19.

Kjelsberg, E., Eikeseth, P. H., & Dahl, A. A. (1991). Suicide in borderline patients: Predictive factors. *Acta Psychiatrica Scandinavica, 84,* 283–287.

Klein, D. A., & Walsh, B. T. (2003). Eating disorders. *International Review of Psychiatry, 15,* 205–216.

Klonsky, E. D., Oltmanns, T. F., & Turkheimer, E. (2003). Deliberate self-harm in a nonclinical population: Prevalence and psychological correlates. *American Journal of Psychiatry, 160,* 1501–1508.

Knight, R. (1953). Borderline states. *Bulletin of the Menninger Clinic, 17,* 1–12.

Koenigsberg, H. W., Harvey, P. D., Mitropoulou, V., Schmeidler, J., New, A. S., Goodman, M., et al. (2002). Characterizing affective instability in borderline personality disorder. *American Journal of Psychiatry, 159,* 784–788.

Koons, C. R., Robins, C. J., Bishop, G. K., Morse, J. Q., Tweed, J. L., Lynch, T. R., et al. (2001). Efficacy of dialectical behavior therapy with borderline women veterans: A randomized controlled trial. *Behavior Therapy, 32,* 371–390.

Korner, A., Gerull, F., Meares, R., & Stevenson, J. (2006). Borderline personality disorder treated with the conversational model: A replication study. *Comprehensive Psychiatry, 47,* 406–411.

Kroll, J., Carey, K., & Sines, L. (1982). Are there borderlines in Britain? *Archives of General Psychiatry, 39,* 60–63.

Krueger, R. F. (1999). The structure of common mental disorders. *Archives of General Psychiatry, 56,* 921–926.

Krueger, R. F., Caspi, A., Moffitt, T. E., Silva, P. A., & McGee, R. (1996). Personality traits are differentially linked to mental disorders: A multitrait multidiagnosis study of an adolescent birth cohort. *Journal of Abnormal Psychology, 105,* 299–312.

Krueger, R. F., Skodol, A. E., Livesley, W. J., Shrout, P., & Huang, Y. (2007). Synthesizing dimensional and categorical approaches to personality disorders: Refining the research agenda for DSM-V. *International Journal of Methods in Psychiatric Research, 16,* S65–S73.

Kullgren, G. (1988). Factors associated with completed suicide in borderline personality disorder. *Journal of Nervous and Mental Diseases, 176,* 40–44.

Kumra, S., Jacobsen, L. K., Lenane, M., Zahn, T. P., Wiggs, E., Alaghband-Rad, J., et al. (1998). Multidimensionally impaired disorder: Is it a variant of very early-onset schizophrenia? *Journal of the American Academy of Child and Adolescent Psychiatry, 37,* 91–99.

Lambert, M. J., & Ogles, B. M. (2004). The efficacy and effectiveness of psychotherapy. In M. J. Lambert (Ed.), *Bergin and Garfield's handbook of psychotherapy and behavior change* (5th ed., pp. 139–193). New York: Wiley.

Lampe, K., Konrad, K., Kroener, S., Fast, K. H., Kunert, J., & Herpertz, S. (2007).

Neuropsychological and behavioural disinhibition in adult ADHD compared to borderline personality disorder. *Psychological Medicine, 37*, 1717–1729.

Leibenluft, E., Gardner, D. L., & Cowdry, R. W. (1987). The inner experience of the borderline self-mutilator. *Journal of Personality Disorders, 1*, 317–324.

Leighton, D. C., Harding, J. S., & Macklin, D. B. (1963). *The character of danger: Psychiatric symptoms in selected communities.* New York: Basic Books.

Lenzenweger, M. F., Johnson, M. D., & Willett, J. B. (2004). Individual growth curve analysis illuminates stability and change in personality disorder features: The longitudinal study of personality disorders. *Archives of General Psychiatry, 61*, 1015–1024.

Lenzenweger, M. F., Lane, M. C., Loranger, A. W., & Kessler, R. C. (2007). DSM-IV personality disorders in the National Comorbidity Survey Replication. *Biological Psychiatry, 62*, 553–556.

Lenzenweger, M. F., Loranger, A. W., Korfine, L., & Neff, C. (1997). Detecting personality disorders in a nonclinical population. Application of a 2-stage procedure for case identification. *Archives of General Psychiatry, 54*, 345–351.

Lerner, D. (1958). *The passing of traditional society.* New York: Free Press.

Lesage, A. D., Boyer, R., Grunberg, F., Morisette, R., Vanier, C., & Morrisette, R. (1994). Suicide and mental disorders: A case control study of young men. *American Journal of Psychiatry, 151*, 1063–1068.

Levy, D. A., & Nail, P. R. (1993). Contagion: A theoretical and empirical review and reconceptualization. *Genetic, Social, and General Psychology Monographs, 119*, 233–284.

Levy, K. N. (2005). The implications of attachment theory and research for understanding borderline personality disorder. *Development and Psychopathology, 17*, 959–986.

Levy, K. N., Meehan, K. B., Kelly, K. M., Reynoso, J. S., Weber, M., Clarkin, J. F., et al. (2006). Change in attachment patterns and reflective function in a randomized control trial of transference-focused psychotherapy for borderline personality disorder. *Journal of Consulting and Clinical Psychology, 74*, 1027–1040.

Lewinsohn, P. M., Rohde, P., Seeley, J. R., Klein, D. N., & Gotlib, I. H. (2000). Natural course of adolescent major depressive disorder in a community sample, predictors of recurrence in young adults. *American Journal of Psychiatry, 157*, 1584–1591.

Leyton, M., Okazawa, H., Diksic, M., Paris, J., Rosa, P., Mzengeza, S., et al. (2001). Brain regional alpha-[11C]methyl-L-tryptophan trapping in impulsive subjects with borderline personality disorder. *American Journal of Psychiatry, 158*, 775–782.

Lincoln, A. J., Bloom, D., Katz, M., & Boksenbaym, N. (1998). Neuropsychological and neurophysiological indices of auditory processing impairment in children with multiple complex developmental disorder. *Journal of the American Academy of Child and Adolescent Psychiatry, 37*, 100–112.

Linehan, M. M. (1993). *Dialectical behavior therapy for borderline personality disorder.* New York: Guilford Press.

Linehan, M. M., Armstrong, H. E,, Suarez, A., Allmon, D., & Heard, H. (1991). Cognitive behavioral treatment of chronically parasuicidal borderline patients. *Archives of General Psychiatry, 48*, 1060–1064.

Linehan, M. M., Comtois, K. A., Murray, A. M., Brown, M. Z., Gallop, R. J., Heard, H. L., et al. (2006). Two-year randomized controlled trial and follow-up of dialectical behavior therapy vs. therapy by experts for suicidal behaviors and borderline personality disorder. *Archives of General Psychiatry, 63,* 757–766.

Linehan, M. M., Dimeff, L. A., Reynolds, S. K., Comtois, K. A., Welch, S. S., Heagerty, P., et al. (2002). Dialectical behavior therapy versus comprehensive validation therapy plus 12-step for the treatment of opioid dependent women meeting criteria for borderline personality disorder. *Drug and Alcohol Dependence, 67,* 13–26.

Linehan, M. M., Heard, H. L., & Armstrong, H. E. (1993). Naturalistic follow-up of a behavioral treatment for chronically parasuicidal borderline patients. *Archives of General Psychiatry, 50,* 971–974.

Linehan, M. M., Schmidt, H., III, Dimeff, L. A., Craft, J. C., Kanter, J., & Comtois, K. A. (1999). Dialectical behavior therapy for patients with borderline personality disorder and drug-dependence. *American Journal on Addictions, 8,* 279–292.

Links, P. S. (2007, September). *Initial findings from the Canadian RCT for chronically suicidal patients with BPD.* Paper presented at the meeting of the International Society for the Study of Personality Disorders, The Hague, The Netherlands.

Links, P. S., Heslegrave, R. J., Mitton, J. E., van Reekum, R., & Patrick, J. (1995). Borderline personality disorder and substance abuse: Consequences of comorbidity. *Canadian Journal of Psychiatry, 40,* 9–14.

Links, P. S., Heslegrave, R., & van Reekum, R. (1998). Prospective follow-up study of borderline personality disorder: Prognosis, prediction of outcome, and Axis II comorbidity. *Canadian Journal of Psychiatry, 43,* 265–270.

Links, P. S., Heslegrave, R., & van Reekum, R. (1999). Impulsivity, core aspect of borderline personality disorder. *Journal of Personality Disorders, 13,* 131–139.

Links, P. S., & Kolla, N. (2005). Assessing and managing suicidal risk. In J. Oldham, A. Skodol, & D. Bender (Eds.), *Textbook of personality disorders* (pp. 449–462). Washington, DC: American Psychiatric Press.

Links, P. S., Mitton, J. E., & Steiner, M. (1990). Predicting outcome for borderline personality disorder. *Comprehensive Psychiatry, 31,* 490–498.

Links, P. S., Steiner, M., Boiago, I., & Irwin, D. (1990). Lithium therapy for borderline patients: Preliminary findings. *Journal of Personality Disorders, 4,* 173–181.

Links, P. S., Steiner, B., & Huxley, G. (1988). The occurrence of borderline personality disorder in the families of borderline patients. *Journal of Personality Disorders, 2,* 14–20.

Livesley, W. J. (2003). *The practical management of personality disorder.* New York: Guilford Press.

Livesley, W. J., Jang, K. L., & Vernon, P. A. (1998). Phenotypic and genetic structure of traits delineating personality disorder. *Archives of General Psychiatry, 55,* 941–948.

Loew, T. H., Nickel, M. K., Muehlbacher, M., Kaplan, P., Nickel, C., Kettler, C., et al. (2006). Topiramate treatment for women with borderline personality disorder: A double-blind, placebo-controlled study. *Journal of Clinical Psychopharmacology, 26,* 61–66.

Lofgren, D. P., Bemporad, J., King, J., Lindem, K., & O'Driscoll, G. (1991). A prospective follow-up of so-called borderline children. *American Journal of Psychiatry, 148,* 1541–1545.

Looper, K., & Paris, J. (2000). What are the dimensions underlying cluster B personality disorders? *Comprehensive Psychiatry, 41,* 432–437.

Loranger, A. W., Hirschfeld, R. M. A., Sartorius, N., & Regier, D. A. (1991). The WHO/ADAMHA International Pilot Study of Personality disorders: Background and purpose. *Journal of Personality Disorders, 5,* 296–306.

Loranger, A. W., Sartorius, N., Andreoli, A., Berger, P., Buchheim, P., Channabasavanna, S. M., et al. (1994). The International Personality Disorder Examination. The World Health Organization/Alcohol, Drug Abuse, and Mental Health Administration international pilot study of personality disorders. *Archives of General Psychiatry, 51,* 215–224.

Luborsky, L. (1988). *Who will benefit from psychotherapy?* New York: Basic Books.

Luborsky, L., Singer, B., & Luborsky, L. (1975). Comparative studies of psychotherapy: Is it true that "everyone has won and all shall have prizes"? *Archives of General Psychiatry, 41,* 165–180.

Ludolph, P. S., Westen, D., & Misle, B. (1990). The borderline diagnosis in adolescents, symptoms and developmental history. *American Journal of Psychiatry, 147,* 470–476.

Lyoo, I. K., Han, M. H., & Cho, D. Y. (1998). A brain MRI study in subjects with borderline personality disorder. *Journal of Affective Disorders, 50,* 235–243.

Malinovsky-Rummell, R., & Hansen, D. J. (1993). Long-term consequences of physical abuse. *Psychological Bulletin, 114,* 68–79.

Maltsberger, J. T. (1994a). Calculated risk taking in the treatment of suicidal patients: Ethical and legal problems. *Death Studies, 18,* 439–452.

Maltsberger, J. T. (1994b). Calculated risk in the treatment of intractably suicidal patients. *Psychiatry, 57,* 199–212.

Maltsberger, J. T., & Buie, D. H. (1974). Countertransference hate in the treatment of suicidal patients. *Archives of General Psychiatry, 30,* 625–633.

Maris, R. (1981). *Pathways to suicide.* Baltimore, MD: Johns Hopkins University Press.

Maris, R. W., Berman, A. L., & Silverman, M. M. (2000). *Comprehensive textbook of suicidology.* New York: Guilford Press.

Markowitz, P. J. (1995). Pharmacotherapy of impulsivity, aggression, and related disorders. In E. Hollander & D. J. Stein (Eds.), *Impulsivity and aggression* (pp. 263–286). New York: Wiley.

Martial, J., Paris, J., Leyton, M., Zweig-Frank, H., Schwartz, G., Teboul, E., et al. (1997). Neuroendocrine study of serotonergic sensitivity in female borderline personality disorder patients. *Biological Psychiatry, 42,* 737–739.

Martunnen, M., Henrikkson, M. M., Aro, H. M., Heikkinen, M. E., Isometsa, E. T., & Lonnqvist, J. K. (1995). Suicide among female adolescents: Characteristics and comparison with males in the age group 13 to 22 years. *Journal of the American Academy of Child and Adolescent Psychiatry, 34,* 1297–1307.

Masse, L. C., & Tremblay, R. E. (1996). Behavior of boys in kindergarten and the onset of substance use during adolescence. *Archives of General Psychiatry, 54,* 62–68.

Masterson, J., & Rinsley, D. (1975). The borderline syndrome: Role of the mother in the genesis and psychic structure of the borderline personality. *International Journal of Psychoanalysis, 56,* 163–177.

Mattanana, B. A., Becker, D. F., Levy, K. N., Edell, W. S., & McGlashan, T. H. (1995). Diagnostic stability in adolescents followed up 2 years after hospitalization. *American Journal of Psychiatry, 152,* 889–894.

McCrae, R. R., & Terracciano, A. (2005). Personality profiles of cultures: Aggregate personality traits. *Journal of Personality and Social Psychology, 89,* 407–425.

McGirr, A., Paris, J., Lesage, A., Renaud, J., & Turecki, G. (2007). Risk factors for suicide completion in borderline personality disorder: A case-control study of cluster B comorbidity and impulsive aggression. *Journal of Clinical Psychiatry, 68,* 721–729.

McGlashan, T. H. (1985). The prediction of outcome in borderline personality disorder. In T. H. McGlashan (Ed.), The borderline: Current empirical research (pp. 61–98). Washington, DC: American Psychiatric Press.

McGlashan, T. H. (1986). The Chestnut Lodge follow-up study: III. Long-term outcome of borderline personalities. *Archives of General Psychiatry, 43,* 2–30.

McGlashan, T. H. (1993). Implications of outcome research for the treatment of borderline personality disorder. In J. Paris (Ed.), *Borderline personality disorder: Etiology and treatment* (pp. 235–260). Washington, DC: American Psychiatric Press.

McGlashan, T. H. (2002). The borderline personality disorder practice guidelines: The good, the bad, and the realistic. *Journal of Personality Disorders, 16,* 119–121.

McGloin, J. M., & Widom, C. S. (2001). Resilience among abused and neglected children grown up. *Development and Psychopathology, 13,* 1021–1038.

McMain, S., & Pos, A. E. (2007). Advances in psychotherapy of personality disorders: A research update. *Current Psychiatry Reports, 9,* 46–52.

McNally, R. J. (2003). *Remembering trauma.* Cambridge, MA: Belknap Press/ Harvard University Press.

Meares, R., Stevenson, J., & Comerford, A. (1999). Psychotherapy with borderline patients: I. A comparison between treated and untreated cohorts. *Australian and New Zealand Journal of Psychiatry, 33*(4), 467–472.

Meijer, M., Goedhart, A. W., & Treffers, P. D. (1998). The persistence of borderline personality disorder in adolescence. *Journal of Personality Disorders, 12,* 13–22.

Merskey, H. (1997). *The analysis of hysteria* (2nd ed.). London: Royal College of Psychiatrists.

Miller, T. W., Nigg, J. T., & Faraone, S. V. (2007). Axis I and II comorbidity in adults with ADHD. *Journal of Abnormal Psychology, 116,* 519–528.

Miller, W. R., & Rollnick, S. (2002). *Motivational interviewing* (2nd ed.). New York: Guilford Press.

Millon, T. (1993). Borderline personality disorder: A psychosocial epidemic. In J. Paris (Ed.), *Borderline personality disorder: Etiology and treatment* (pp. 197–210). Washington, DC: American Psychiatric Press.

Moeller, F. G., Barratt, E. S., Dougherty, D. M., Schmitz, J. M., & Swann, A. C. (2001). Psychiatric aspects of impulsivity. *American Journal of Psychiatry, 158,* 1783–1793.

Moffitt, T. E. (1993). "Life-course persistent" and "adolescence-limited" antisocial behavior: A developmental taxonomy. *Psychological Review, 100,* 674–701.

Moncrieff, J., & Kirsch, I. (2005). Efficacy of antidepressants in adults. *British Medical Journal, 331,* 155–157.

Monroe, S. M., & Simons, A. D. (1991). Diathesis-stress theories in the context of life stress research. *Psychological Bulletin, 110,* 406–425.

Morey, L. C., & Zanarini, M. C. (2000). Borderline personality: Traits and disorder. *Journal of Abnormal Psychology, 109,* 733–737.

Morton, N. E. (2001). Complex inheritance: The 21st century. *Advances in Genetics, 42,* 535–543.

Moskowitz, D. S., Pinard, G., Zuroff, D. C., Annable, L., & Young, S. N. (2003). Tryptophan, serotonin and human social behavior. *Advances in Experimental Medicine and Biology, 527,* 215–224.

Mulder, R. T. (2004). Depression and personality disorder. *Current Psychiatry Reports, 6,* 51–57.

Munroe-Blum, H., & Marziali, E. (1995). A controlled trial of short-term group treatment for borderline personality disorder. *Journal of Personality Disorders, 9,* 190–198.

Murphy, H. B. M. (1982). *Comparative psychiatry.* New York: Springer.

Nandi, D. N., Banerjee, G., Nandi, S., & Nandi, P. (1992). Is hysteria on the wane? *British Journal of Psychiatry, 160,* 87–91.

Nash, M. R., Hulsely, T. L., Sexton, M. C., Harralson, T. L., & Lambert, W. (1993). Long-term effects of childhood sexual abuse: Perceived family environment, psychopathology, and dissociation. *Journal of Consulting and Clinical Psychology, 61,* 276–283.

Newcomer, J. W., & Haupt, D. W. (2006). The metabolic effects of antispsychotic medication. *Canadian Journal of Psychiatry, 51,* 480–491.

Newton-Howes, G., Tyrer, P., & Johnson, T. (2006). Personality disorder and the outcome of depression: Meta-analysis of published studies. *British Journal of Psychiatry, 188,* 13–20.

Ng, F., Paris, J., Zweig-Frank, H., Swartz, G., Steiger, H., & Nair, V. (2005). Paroxetine binding in relation to diagnosis and underlying traits in patients with borderline personality disorder compared with normal controls. *Psychopharmacology, 182,* 447–451.

Ni, X., Chan, K., Bulgin, N., Sicard, T., Bismil, R., McMain, S., et al. (2006). Association between serotonin transporter gene and borderline personality disorder. *Journal of Psychiatric Research, 40,* 448–453.

Ni, X., Sicard, T., Bulgin, N., Bismil, R., Chan, K., McMain, S., et al. (2007). Monoamine oxidase: A gene is associated with borderline personality disorder. *Psychiatric Genetics, 17,* 153–157.

Nickel, M. K., Muehlbacher, M., Nickel, C., Kettler, C., Pedrosa Gil, F., Bachler, E., et al. (2006). Aripiprazole in the treatment of patients with borderline personality disorder: A double-blind, placebo-controlled study. *American Journal of Psychiatry, 163,* 833–838.

Nickel, M. K., Nickel, C., Kaplan, P., Lahmann, C., Muhlbacher, M., Tritt, K., et al. (2005). Treatment of aggression with topiramate in male borderline patients: A double-blind, placebo-controlled study. *Biological Psychiatry, 57,* 495–499.

Nickel, M. K., Nickel, C., Mitterlehner, F. O., Tritt, K., Lahmann, C., Leiberich, P. K., et al. (2004). Topiramate treatment of aggression in female borderline personality disorder patients: A double-blind, placebo-controlled study. *Journal of Clinical Psychiatry, 65,* 1515–1519.

Nicolson, R., Lenane, M., Brookner, F., Gochman, P., Kumra, S., Spechler, L., et al. (2001). Children and adolescents with psychotic disorder not otherwise specified: A 2- to 8-year follow-up study. *Comprehensive Psychiatry, 42,* 319–325.

Nigg, J. T., Silk, K. R., Stavro, G., & Miller, T. (2005). Disinhibition and borderline personality disorder. *Development and Psychopathology, 17,* 1129–1149.

Nose, M., Cipriani, A., Biancosino, B., Grassi, L., & Barbui, C. (2006). Efficacy of pharmacotherapy against core traits of borderline personality disorder: Meta-analysis of randomized controlled trials. *International Clinical Psychopharmacology, 21,* 345–353.

Nurnberg, G., Raskin, M., Levine, P. E., Pollack, S., Siegel, O., & Prince, R. (1991). The comorbidity of borderline personality disorder with other DSM-III-R axis II personality disorders. *American Journal of Psychiatry, 148,* 1311–1317.

Offer, D., & Offer, J. (1975). Three developmental routes through normal male adolescence. *Adolescent Psychiatry, 4,* 121–141.

Ogata, S. N., Silk, K. R., Goodrich, S., Lohr, N. E., Westen, D., & Hill, E. M. (1990). Childhood sexual and physical abuse in adult patients with borderline personality disorder. *American Journal of Psychiatry, 147,* 1008–1013.

Oldham, J. M., Gabbard, G. O., Goin, M. K., Gunderson, J., Soloff, P., Spiegel, D., et al. (2001). Practice guideline for the treatment of borderline personality disorder. *American Journal of Psychiatry, 158*(Suppl.), 1–52.

Oldham, J. M., Skodol, A. E., Kellman, D., Hyler, S. E., Rosnick, L., & Davies, M. (1992). Diagnosis of DSM-III-R personality disorders by two structured interviews: Patterns of comorbidity. *American Journal of Psychiatry, 149,* 213–220.

O'Leary, K. M. (2000). Borderline personality disorder: Neuropsychological testing results. *Psychiatric Clinics of North America, 23,* 41–60.

O'Leary, K. M., & Cowdry, R. W. (1994). Neuropsychological testing results with patients with borderline personality disorder. In K. R. Silk (Ed.), *Biological and neurobehavioral studies of borderline personality disorder* (pp. 127–158). Washington, DC: American Psychiatric Press.

Orlinsky, D. E., Ronnestad, M. H., & Willutski, U. (2004). Fifty years of psychotherapy process-outcome research: Continuity and change. In M. J. Lambert (Ed.), *Bergin and Garfield's handbook of psychotherapy and behavior change* (5th ed., pp. 307–390). New York: Wiley.

Packman, W. L., & Harris, E. A. (1998). Legal issues and risk management in suicidal patients. In B. Bongar, A. L. Berman, R. W. Maris, M. M. Silverman, E. A. Harris, & W. L. Packman (Eds.), *Risk management with suicidal patients* (pp. 150–186). New York: Guilford Press.

Palmer, S., Davidson, K., Tyrer, P., Gumley, A., Tata, P., Norrie, J., et al. (2006). The cost-effectiveness of cognitive behavior therapy for borderline personality disorder: Results from the BOSCOT trial. *Journal of Personality Disorders, 20,* 466–481.

Paris, J. (1994). *Borderline personality disorder: A multidimensional approach.* Washington, DC: American Psychiatric Press.

Paris, J. (1996a). Antisocial personality disorder: A biopsychosocial model. *Canadian Journal of Psychiatry, 41,* 75–80.

Paris, J. (1996b). *Social factors in the personality disorders: A biopsychosocial approach to etiology and treatment.* Cambridge, UK: Cambridge University Press.

Paris, J. (1997a). Antisocial and borderline personality disorders: Two separate diagnoses or two aspects of the same psychopathology? *Comprehensive Psychiatry, 38,* 237–242.

Paris, J. (1997b). *Working with traits.* New York: Jason Aronson.

Paris, J. (1998). *Nature and nurture in psychiatry: A predisposition-stress model.* Washington, DC: American Psychiatric Press.

Paris, J. (2000a). Childhood precursors of borderline personality disorder. *Psychiatric Clinics North America, 23,* 77–88.

Paris, J. (2000b). *Myths of childhood.* Philadelphia: Brunner/Mazel.

Paris, J. (2000c). Predispositions, personality traits, and post-traumatic stress disorder. *Harvard Review of Psychiatry, 8,* 175–183.

Paris, J. (2003). *Personality disorders over time: Precursors, course, and outcome.* Washington, DC: American Psychiatric Press.

Paris, J. (2004). Borderline or bipolar?: Distinguishing borderline personality disorder from bipolar spectrum disorders. *Harvard Review of Psychiatry, 12,* 140–145.

Paris, J. (2005a). The developmental psychopathology of impulsivity and suicidality in borderline personality disorder. *Development and Psychopathology, 17,* 1095–1104.

Paris, J. (2005b). Neurobiological dimensional models of personality disorders: A review of the models of Cloninger, Depue, and Siever. *Journal of Personality Disorders, 19,* 156–170.

Paris, J. (2005c). Understanding self-mutilation in borderline personality disorder. *Harvard Review of Psychiatry, 13,* 179–185.

Paris, J. (2006a). *Half in love with death: Managing the chronically suicidal patient.* Florence, KY: Erlbaum.

Paris, J. (2006b). Predicting and preventing suicide: Do we know enough to do either? *Harvard Review of Psychiatry, 14,* 233–240.

Paris, J. (2007). Intermittent psychotherapy: An alternative for patients with personality disorders. *Journal of Psychiatric Practice, 13,* 153–158.

Paris, J. (2008). *Prescriptions for the mind: A critical view of contemporary psychiatry.* New York: Oxford University Press.

Paris, J., & Braverman, S. (1995). Successful and unsuccessful marriages in borderline patients. *Journal of the American Academy of Psychoanalysis, 23,* 153–166.

Paris, J., Brown, R., & Nowlis, D. (1987). Long-term outcome of borderline patients in a general hospital. *Comprehensive Psychiatry, 28,* 530–535.

Paris, J., & Frank, H. (1989). Perceptions of parental bonding in borderline patients. *American Journal of Psychiatry, 146,* 1498–1499.

Paris, J., Gunderson, J. G., & Weinberg, I. (2007). The interface between borderline personality disorder and bipolar spectrum disorder. *Comprehensive Psychiatry, 48,* 145–154.

Paris, J., Nowlis, D., & Brown, R. (1988). Developmental factors in the outcome of borderline personality disorder. *Comprehensive Psychiatry, 29,* 147–150.

Paris, J., Nowlis, D., & Brown, R. (1989). Predictors of suicide in borderline personality disorder. *Canadian Journal of Psychiatry, 34,* 8–9.

Paris, J., Zelkowitz, P., Guzder, J., Joseph, S., & Feldman, R. (1999). Neuropsychological factors associated with borderline pathology in children. *Journal of American Academy of Child and Adolescent Psychiatry, 38,* 770–774.

Paris, J., & Zweig-Frank, H. (2001). A 27-year follow-up of patients with borderline personality disorder. *Comprehensive Psychiatry, 42,* 482–487.

Paris, J., Zweig-Frank, H., & Guzder, J. (1993). Psychological risk factors in recovery from borderline personality disorder in female patients. *Comprehensive Psychiatry, 34,* 410–413.

Paris, J., Zweig-Frank, H., & Guzder, J. (1994a). Psychological risk factors for borderline personality disorder in female patients. *Comprehensive Psychiatry, 35,* 301–305.

Paris, J., Zweig-Frank, H., & Guzder, J. (1994b). Risk factors for borderline personality in male outpatients. *Journal of Nervous and Mental Disease, 182,* 375–380.

Paris, J., Zweig-Frank, H., & Guzder, J. (1995). Psychological factors associated with homosexuality in males with borderline personality disorder. *Journal of Personality Disorders, 9,* 56–61.

Paris, J., Zweig-Frank, H., Ng, F., Schwartz, G., Steiger, H., & Nair, V. (2004). Neurobiological correlates of diagnosis and underlying traits in patients with borderline personality disorder compared with normal controls. *Psychiatry Research, 121,* 239–252.

Parker, G. (1983). *Parental overprotection: A risk factor in psychosocial development.* New York: Grune & Stratton.

Patten, S. B. (2006). Does almost everybody suffer from a bipolar disorder? *Canadian Journal of Psychiatry, 51,* 6–8.

Patton, J. H., Stanford, M. S., & Barratt, E. S. (1995). Factor structure of the Barratt Impulsiveness Scale. *Journal of Clinical Psychology, 51,* 768–774.

Pepper, C. M., Klein, D. N., Anderson, R. L., Riso, L. P., Ouimette, P. C., & Lizardi, H. (1995). DSM-III-R axis II comorbidity in dysthymia and major depression, *American Journal of Psychiatry, 152,* 239–247.

Perry, J. C., Banon, E., & Ianni, F. (1999). Effectiveness of psychotherapy for personality disorders. *American Journal of Psychiatry, 156,* 1312–1321.

Person, E. (2007). *Dreams of love and fateful encounters: The power of romantic passion* (2nd ed.). Washington, DC: American Psychiatric Press.

Petti, T. A., & Vela, R. M. (1990). Borderline disorders of childhood: An overview. *Journal of American Academy of Child and Adolescent Psychiatry, 29,* 327–337.

Pfeffer, C. R. (2002). Suicide in mood disordered children and adolescents. *Child and Adolescent Psychiatric Clinics of North America, 11,* 639–647.

Pfohl, B., Coryell, W., Zimmerman, M., & Stangl, D. (1986). DSM-III personality disorders: Diagnostic overlap and internal consistency of individual DSM-III criteria. *Comprehensive Psychiatry, 27,* 21–34.

Philipsen, A., Feige, B., Al-Shajlawi, A., Schmahl, C., Bohus, M., Richter, H., et al. (2005). Increased delta power and discrepancies in objective and subjective sleep measurements in borderline personality disorder. *Journal of Psychiatric Research, 39,* 489–498.

Pinto, A., Grapentine, W. L., Francis, G., & Picariello, C. M. (1996). Borderline personality disorder in adolescents: Affective and cognitive features. *Journal of the American Academy of Child and Adolescent Psychiatry, 35,* 1338–1343.

Pinto, C., Dhavale, H. S., Nair, S., Patil, B., & Dewan, M. (2000). Borderline personality disorder exists in India. *Journal of Nervous and Mental Disease, 188,* 386–388.

Piper, A., & Merskey, H. (2004a). The persistence of folly: A critical examination of dissociative identity disorder: Part I. The excesses of an improbable concept. *Canadian Journal of Psychiatry, 49,* 592–600.

Piper, A., & Merskey, H. (2004b). The persistence of folly: A critical examination of dissociative identity disorder: Part II. The defence and decline of multiple personality or dissociative identity disorder. *Canadian Journal of Psychiatry, 49,* 678–683.

Piper, W. E., Azim, H. A., Joyce, A. S., & McCallum, M. (1991). Transference interpretations, therapeutic alliance, and outcome in short-term individual psychotherapy. *Archives of General Psychiatry, 48,* 946–953.

Piper, W. E., Rosie, J. S., & Joyce, A. S. (1996). *Time-limited day treatment for personality disorders: Integration of research and practice in a group program.* Washington, DC: American Psychological Association.

Plakun, E. M., Burkhardt, P. E., & Muller, J. P. (1985). 14-year follow-up of borderline and schizotypal personality disorders. *Comprehensive Psychiatry, 27,* 448–455.

Plomin, R., & Bergeman, C. (1991). Genetic influence on environmental measures. *Behavioral and Brain Sciences, 14,* 373–427.

Plomin, R., DeFries, J. C., McClearn, G. E., & Rutter, M. M. (2000). *Behavioral genetics: A primer* (3rd ed.). New York: Freeman.

Pokorny, A. D. (1983). Prediction of suicide in psychiatric patients: Report of a prospective study. *Archives of General Psychiatry, 40,* 249–257.

Pope, H. G., Jonas, J. M., & Hudson, J. I. (1983). The validity of DSM-III borderline personality disorder. *Archives of General Psychiatry, 40,* 23–30.

Prince, R., & Tseng-Laroche, F. (1900). Culture-bound syndromes and international disease classification. *Culture, Medicine, and Psychiatry, 11,* 1–49.

Putnam, E., & Silk, K. (2005). Emotional dysregulation and the development of borderline personality disorder. *Development and Psychopathology, 17,* 899–925.

Rachlin, S. (1984). Double jeopardy: Suicide and malpractice. *General Hospital Psychiatry, 6,* 302–307.

Reiss, D., Hetherington, E. M., & Plomin, R. (2000). *The relationship code.* Cambridge, MA: Harvard University Press.

Rey, J. M., Singh, M., Morris-Yates, A,, & Andrews, G. (1997). Referred adolescents as young adults: The relationship between psychosocial functioning and personality disorder. *Australian and New Zealand Journal of Psychiatry, 31,* 219–226.

Rind, B., & Tromovitch, P. (1997). A meta-analytic review of findings from national samples on psychological correlates of child sexual abuse. *Journal of Sexual Research, 34,* 237–255.

Rind, B., Tromovitch, P., & Bauserman, R. (1998). A meta-analytic examination of assumed properties of child sexual abuse using college samples. *Psychological Bulletin, 124,* 22–53.

Rinne, T., de Kloet, E. R., Wouters, L., Goekoop, J. G., DeRijk, R. H., & van den Brink, W. (2002). Hyperresponsiveness of hypothalamic–pituitary–adrenal axis to combined dexamethasone/corticotropin-releasing hormone challenge in female borderline personality disorder subjects with a history of sustained childhood abuse. *Biological Psychiatry, 52,* 1102–1112.

Rinne, T., van den Brink, W., Wouters, L., & van Dyck, R. (2002). SSRI treatment of borderline personality disorder: A randomized, placebo-controlled clinical trial for female patients with borderline personality disorder. *American Journal of Psychiatry, 159,* 2048–2054.

Rinne, T., Westenberg, H. G., den Boer, J. A., & van den Brink, W. (2000). Serotonergic blunting to meta-chlorophenylpiperazine (m-CPP) highly correlates with sustained childhood abuse in impulsive and autoaggressive female borderline patients. *Biological Psychiatry, 47*(6), 548–556.

Robins, E., & Guze, S. B. (1970). Establishment of diagnostic validity in psychiatric illness: Its application to schizophrenia. *American Journal of Psychiatry, 126,* 107–111.

Robins, L. N. (1966). *Deviant children grown up*. Baltimore, MD: Williams & Wilkins.

Robins, L. N., & Regier, D. A. (Eds.). (1991). *Psychiatric disorders in America*. New York: Free Press.

Rodgers, J. L., Rowe, D. C., & Busten, M. (1998). Social contagion, adolescent sexual behavior, and pregnancy: A nonlinear dynamic EMOSA model. *Developmental Psychology 34*: 1095–1113.

Rogers, C. (1942). *Counseling and psychotherapy: Newer concepts in practice*. Boston: Houghton Mifflin.

Runeson, B., & Beskow, J. (1991). Borderline personality disorder in young Swedish suicides. *Journal of Nervous and Mental Diseases, 179*, 153–156.

Rush, A. J. (2007). STAR*D: What have we learned? *American Journal of Psychiatry, 164*, 201–204.

Russ, M. J., Campbell, S. S., Kakuma, T., Harrison, K., & Zanine, E. (1999). EEG theta activity and pain insensitivity in self-injurious borderline patients. *Psychiatry Research, 89*, 201–214.

Russell, J., Moskowitz, D., Sookman, D., & Paris, J. (2007). Affective instability in patients with borderline personality disorder. *Journal of Abnormal Psychology, 116*, 578–588.

Rutter, M. (1987). Temperament, personality, and personality disorders. *British Journal of Psychiatry, 150*, 443–448.

Rutter, M. (1995). Clinical implications of attachment concepts: Retrospect and prospect. *Journal of Child Psychology and Psychiatry, 36*, 549–571.

Rutter, M. (2006). *Genes and behavior: Nature-nurture interplay explained*. London: Blackwell.

Rutter, M., & Madge, N. (1976). *Cycles of disadvantage: A review of research*. London: Heinemann.

Rutter, M., & Rutter, M. (1993). *Developing minds: Challenge and continuity across the life span*. New York: Basic Books.

Rutter, M., & Smith, D. J. (1995). *Psychosocial problems in young people*. Cambridge, UK: Cambridge University Press.

Salzman, C., Wolfson, A. N., Schatzberg, A., Looper, J., Henke, R., Albanese, M., et al. (1995). Effect of fluoxetine on anger in symptomatic volunteers with borderline personality disorder. *Journal of Clinical Psychopharmacology, 15*, 23–29.

Samuels, J., Eaton, W. W., Bienvenu, J., Clayton, P., Brown, H., Costa, P. T., et al. (2002). Prevalence and correlates of personality disorders in a community sample. *British Journal of Psychiatry, 180*, 536–542.

Sanderson, C., Swenson, C., & Bohus, M. (2002). A critique of the American psychiatric practice guideline for the treatment of patients with borderline personality disorder. *Journal of Personality Disorders, 16*, 122–129.

Sar, V., Akyuz, G., Kugu, N., Ozturk, E., & Ertem-Vehid H. (2006). Axis I dissociative disorder comorbidity in borderline personality disorder and reports of childhood trauma. *Journal of Clinical Psychiatry, 67*, 1583–1590.

Sato, T., & Takeichi, M. (1993). Lifetime prevalence of specific psychiatric disorders in a general medicine clinic. *General Hospital Psychiatry, 15*, 224–233.

Saulsman, M., & Page, A. C. (2004). The five-factor model and personality disorder empirical literature: A meta-analytic review. *Clinical Psychology Review, 23*, 1055–1085.

Schacter, D. L. (1996). *Searching for memory: The brain, the mind, and the past*. New York: Basic Books.

Scheel, K. R. (2000). The empirical basis of dialectical behavior therapy: Summary, critique, and implications. *Clinical Psychology: Science and Practice, 7,* 68–86.

Schmahl, C. G., Vermetten, E., Elzinga, B. M., & Bremner, D. J. (2003). Magnetic resonance imaging of hippocampal and amygdala volume in women with childhood abuse and borderline personality disorder. *Psychiatry Research, 122,* 193–198.

Schmideberg, M. (1959). The borderline patient. In S. Arieti (Ed.), *The American handbook of psychiatry* (Vol. 1, pp. 398–416). New York: Basic Books.

Schuckit, M. A., & Smith, T. L. (1996). An 8-year follow-up of 450 sons of alcoholic and control subjects. *Archives of General Psychiatry, 53,* 202–210.

Schwartz, D. A., Flinn, D. E., & Slawson, P. F. (1974). Treatment of the suicidal character. *American Journal of Psychotherapy, 28,* 194–207.

Shea, M. T., Pilkonis, P. A., Beckham, E., Collins, J. F., Elikin, E., & Sotsky, S. M. (1990). Personality disorders and treatment outcome in the NIMH Treatment of Depression Collaborative Research Program. *American Journal of Psychiatry, 147,* 711–718.

Shorter, E. (1997). *A history of psychiatry.* New York: Wiley.

Siever, L. J., Buchsbaum, M. S., New, A. S., Spiegel-Cohen, J., Wei, T., Hazlett, E. A., et al. (1999). d,l-fenfluramine response in impulsive personality disorder assessed with [^{18}F]fluorodeoxyglucose positron emission tomography. *Neuropsychopharmacology, 20,* 413–423.

Siever, L. J., & Davis, K. L. (1991). A psychobiological perspective on the personality disorders. *American Journal of Psychiatry, 148,* 1647–1658.

Siever, L. J., Torgersen, S., Gunderson, J. G., Livesley, W. J., & Kendler, K. S. (2002). The borderline diagnosis III: Identifying endophenotypes for genetic studies. *Biological Psychiatry, 51*(12), 964–968.

Silk, K. R., Lee, S., Hill, E. M., & Lohr, N. E. (1995). Borderline personality disorder and severity of sexual abuse. *American Journal of Psychiatry, 152,* 1059–1064.

Silk, K. R., & Yager, J. (2003). Suggested guidelines for e-mail communication in psychiatric practice. *Journal of Clinical Psychiatry, 64,* 799–806.

Silver, D. (1983). Psychotherapy of the characterologically difficult patient. *Canadian Journal of Psychiatry, 28,* 513–521.

Silver, D., & Cardish, R. (1991, May). *BPD outcome studies: Psychotherapy implications.* Paper presented at the American Psychiatric Association, New Orleans, LA.

Simpson, E. B., Yen, S., Costello, E., Rosen, K., Begin, A., Pistorello, J., et al. (2004). Combined dialectical behavior therapy and fluoxetine in the treatment of borderline personality disorder. *Journal of Clinical Psychiatry, 65,* 379–385.

Sisk, C. L., & Zehr, J. L. (2005). Pubertal hormones organize the adolescent brain and behavior. *Frontiers in Neuroendocrinology, 26,* 163–174.

Skodol, A. E., Bender, D. S., Pagano, M. E., Shea, M. T., Yen, S., Sanislow, C. A., et al. (2007). Positive childhood experiences: resilience and recovery from personality disorder in early adulthood. *Journal of Clinical Psychiatry, 68,* 1102–1108.

Skodol, A. E., Buckley, P., & Charles, E. (1983). Is there a characteristic pattern in the treatment history of clinic outpatients with borderline personality? *Journal of Nervous and Mental Disease, 171,* 405–410.

Skodol, A. E., Gunderson, J. G., Shea, M. T., McGlashan, T. H., Morey, L. C., Sanislow, C. A., et al. (2005). The Collaborative Longitudinal Personality

Disorders Study (CLPS): Overview and implications. *Journal of Personality Disorders, 19,* 487–504.

Soler, J., Pascual, J. C., Campins, J., Barrachina, J., Puigdemont, D., Alvarez, E., et al. (2005). Double-blind, placebo-controlled study of dialectical behavior therapy plus olanzapine for borderline personality disorder. *American Journal of Psychiatry, 162,* 1221–1224.

Soloff, P. H., Cornelius, J., George, A., Nathan, S., Perel, J. M., & Ulrich, R. F. (1993). Efficacy of phenelzine and haloperidol in borderline personality disorder. *Archives of General Psychiatry, 50,* 377–385.

Soloff, P. H., Fabio, A., Kelly, T. M., Malone, K. M., & Mann, J. J. (2005). High-lethality status in patients with borderline personality disorder. *Journal of Personality Disorders, 19,* 386–399.

Soloff, P. H., George, A., Nathan, S., Schulz, P. M., Cornelius, J. R., Herring, J., et al. (1989). Amitriptyline versus haloperidol in borderlines: Final outcomes and predictors of response. *Journal of Clinical Psychopharmacology, 9,* 238–246.

Soloff, P. H., Lynch, K. G., & Kelly, T. M. (2002). Childhood abuse as a risk factor for suicidal behavior in borderline personality disorder. *Journal of Personality Disorders, 16,* 201–214.

Soloff, P. H., Lynch, K. G., Kelly, T. M., Malone, K. M., & Mann, J. J. (2000). Characteristics of suicide attempts of patients with major depressive episode and borderline personality disorder: A comparative study. *American Journal of Psychiatry, 157,* 601–608.

Soloff, P. H., Meltzer, C. C., Becker, C., Greer, P. J., & Constantine, D. (2005). Gender differences in a fenfluramine-activated FDG PET study of borderline personality disorder. *Psychiatry Research: Neuroimaging, 138,* 183–195.

Soloff, P. H., Price, J. C., Meltzer, C. C., Fabio, A., Frank, G. K., & Kaye, W. H. (2007). 5HT2A receptor binding is increased in borderline personality disorder. *Biological Psychiatry, 62,* 580–587.

Spinhoven, P., Giesen-Bloo, J., van Dyck, R., Kooiman, K., & Arntz, A. (2007). The therapeutic alliance in schema-focused therapy and transference-focused psychotherapy for borderline personality disorder. *Journal of Consulting and Clinical Psychology, 75,* 104–115.

Spitzer, R. L., Endicott, J., & Gibbon, M. (1979). Crossing the border into borderline personality disorder. *Archives of General Psychiatry, 36,* 17–24.

Spitzer, R. L., & Williams, J. B. W. (1986). *Structured clinical Interview for DSM-III-R personality disorders.* New York: Biometric Research Department, New York State Psychiatric Institute.

Stangl, D., Pfohl, B., Zimmerman, M., Bowers, W., & Corenthal, C. (1985). A structured interview for the DSM-III personality disorders. *Archives of General Psychiatry, 42,* 591–596.

Stanley, B., Brodsky, B., Nelson, J., & Dulit, R. (2007). Brief dialectical behavior therapy for suicidality and self-injurious behaviors. *Archives of Suicide Research, 11,* 337–341.

Stanley, B., Gameroff, M. J., Michalsen, V., & Mann, J. J. (2001). Are suicide attempters who self-mutilate a unique population? *American Journal of Psychiatry, 158,* 427–432.

Stanley, B., & Wilson, S. T. (2006). Heightened subjective experience of depression in borderline personality disorder. *Journal of Personality Disorders, 20,* 307–318.

Stern, A. (1938). Psychoanalytic investigation of and therapy in the borderline group of neuroses. *Psychoanalytic Quarterly, 7,* 467–489.

Stevenson, J., & Meares, R. (1992). An outcome study of psychotherapy for patients with borderline personality disorder. *American Journal of Psychiatry, 141*, 358–362.

Stevenson, J., Meares, R., & D'Angelo, R. (2005). Five-year outcome of outpatient psychotherapy with borderline patients: Successful outcome and psychiatric practice. *Psychological Medicine, 35*(1), 79–87.

Stone, M. H. (1990). *The fate of borderline patients.* New York: Guilford Press.

Strakowski, S. M., DelBello, M. P., Zimmerman, M. E., Getz, G. E., Mills, N. P., Ret, J., et al. (2002). Ventricular and periventricular structural volumes in first- versus multiple-episode bipolar disorder. *American Journal of Psychiatry, 159*, 1841–1847.

Sultanoff, S. M. (2003). Integrating humor into psychotherapy. In C. E. Schaefer (Ed.), *Play therapy with adults* (pp. 107–143). New York: Wiley.

Swartz, M., Blazer, D., George, L., & Winfield, I. (1990). Estimating the prevalence of borderline personality disorder in the community. *Journal of Personality Disorders, 4*, 257–272.

Taiminen, T. J., Kallio-Soukainen, K., Nokso-Koivisto, H., Kaljonen, A., & Helenius, H. (1998). Contagion of deliberate self-harm among adolescent inpatients. *Journal of the American Academy of Child and Adolescent Psychiatry, 37*, 211–217.

Tebartz van Elst, L., Hesslinger, B., Thiel, T., Geiger, E., Haegele, K., Lemieux, L., et al. (2003). Frontolimbic brain abnormalities in patients with borderline personality disorder: A volumetric magnetic resonance imaging study. *Biological Psychiatry, 54*, 163–171.

Tebartz van Elst, L., Ludaescher, P., Wilke, M., Huppertz, H. J., Thiel, T., Schmahl, C., et al. (2003). A voxel-based morphometric MRI study in female patients with borderline personality disorder. *Neuroimage, 20*, 385–392.

Torgersen, S., Kringlen, E., & Cramer, V. (2001). The prevalence of personality disorders in a community sample. *Archives of General Psychiatry, 58*, 590–596.

Torgersen, S., Lygren, S., Oien, P. A., Skre, I., Onstad, S., Edvardsen, J., et al. (2000). A twin study of personality disorders. *Comprehensive Psychiatry, 41*, 416–425.

Tremblay, R. E. (2006). Prevention of youth violence: Why not start at the beginning? *Journal of Abnormal Child Psychology, 34*, 481–487.

Tremblay, R. E., Pihl, R. O., Vitaro, F., & Dobkin, P. L. (1994). Predicting early onset of male antisocial behavior from preschool behavior. *Archives of General Psychiatry, 51*, 732–739.

Tritt, K., Nickel, C., Lahmann, C., Leiberich, P. K., Rother, W. K., Loew, T. H., et al. (2005). Lamotrigine treatment of aggression in female borderline-patients: A randomized, double-blind, placebo-controlled study. *Journal of Psychopharmacology, 19*, 287–291.

Trivedi, M. H., Fava, M., Wisniewski, S. R., Thase, M. E., Quitkin, F., Warden, D., et al. (2006). Medication augmentation after the failure of SSRIs for depression. *New England Journal of Medicine, 354*, 1243–1252.

True, W. R., Rice, J., Eisen, S. A., Heath, A. C., Goldberg, J., & Lyons, M. J. (1993). A twin study of genetic and environmental contributions to liability for post traumatic stress symptoms. *Archives of General Psychiatry, 50*, 257–264.

Trull, T. J., Widiger, T. A., Lynam, D. R., & Costa, P. T. (2003). Borderline personality disorder from the perspective of general personality functioning. *Journal of Abnormal Psychology, 112*, 193–202.

Tyrer, P. (1988). *Personality disorders.* London: Wright.

Tyrer, P. (2002). Practice guideline for the treatment of borderline personality disorder: A bridge too far. *Journal of Personality Disorders, 16,* 119–121.

Tyrer, P., Tom, B., Byford, S., Schmidt, U., Jones, V., Davidson, K., et al. (2004). Differential effects of manual assisted cognitive behavior therapy in the treatment of recurrent deliberate self-harm and personality disturbance: The POPMACT study. *Journal of Personality Disorders, 18,* 102–116.

Ursano, R. J., Sonnenberg, S. M., & Lazar, S. G. (2004). *Concise guide to psychodynamic psychotherapy: Principles and techniques of brief, intermittent, and long-term psychodynamic psychotherapy* (3rd ed.). Washington, DC: American Psychiatric Press.

Vaillant, G. E. (1977). *Adaptation to life.* Cambridge, MA: Little Brown.

Vaillant, G. E. (1995). *The natural history of alcoholism revisited.* Cambridge, MA: Harvard University Press.

van der Kolk, B. A., Perry, J. C., & Herman, J. L. (1991). Childhood origins of self destructive behavior. *American Journal of Psychiatry, 148,* 1665–1671.

Verheul, R., van den Bosch, L. M. C., Maarten, W. J., de Ridder, M. A. J., Stijnen, T., & van den Brink, W. (2003). Dialectical behaviour therapy for women with borderline personality disorder: 12-month, randomised clinical trial in The Netherlands. *British Journal of Psychiatry, 182,* 135–140.

Völlm, B., Richardson, P., Stirling, J., Elliott, R., Dolan, M., Chaudhry, I., et al. (2001). Evidence of abnormal amygdala functioning in borderline personality disorder: A functional MRI study. *Biological Psychiatry, 50,* 292–298.

Völlm, B., Richardson, P., Stirling, J., Elliott, R., Dolan, M., Chaudhry, I., et al. (2004). Neurobiological substrates of antisocial and borderline personality disorder: Preliminary results of a functional fMRI study. *Criminal Behaviour and Mental Health, 14,* 39–54.

Vuilleumier, P. (2005). Hysterical conversion and brain function. *Progress in Brain Research, 150,* 309–329.

Wagner, A. W., & Linehan, M. M. (1999). Facial expression recognition ability among women with borderline personality disorder: Implications for emotion regulation? *Journal of Personality Disorders, 13,* 329–344.

Waldinger, R. J., & Gunderson, J. G. (1984). Completed psychotherapies with borderline patients. *American Journal of Psychotherapy, 38,* 190–201.

Wampold, B. E. (2001). *The great psychotherapy debate: Models, methods, and findings.* Mahwah, NJ: Erlbaum.

Waraich, P., Goldner, E. M., Somers, J. M., & Hsu, L. (2004). Prevalence and incidence studies of mood disorders: A systematic review of the literature. *Canadian Journal of Psychiatry, 49,* 124–138.

Weinberg, I., Gunderson, J. G., Hennen, J., & Cutter, C. J., Jr. (2006). Manual assisted cognitive treatment for deliberate self-harm in borderline personality disorder patients. *Journal of Personality Disorders, 20,* 482–492.

Weiss, M., Zelkowitz, P., Feldman, R., Vogel, J., Heyman, M., & Paris, J. (1996). Psychopathology in offspring of mothers with borderline personality disorder. *Canadian Journal of Psychiatry, 41,* 285–290.

Weissman, M. M., & Klerman, G. L. (1985). Gender and depression. *Trends in Neuroscience, 8,* 416–420.

Werner, E. E., & Smith, R. S. (1992). *Overcoming the odds: High risk children from birth to adulthood.* New York: Cornell University Press.

Westen, D., & Morrison, K. (2001). A multidimensional meta-analysis of treatments for depression, panic, and generalized anxiety disorder: An empirical examination of the status of empirically supported therapies. *Journal of Consulting and Clinical Psychology, 69,* 875–899.

Westen, D., Shedler, J., & Bradley, R. (2006). A prototype approach to personality disorder diagnosis. *American Journal of Psychiatry, 163,* 846–856.

White, C. N., Gunderson, J. G., Zanarini, M. C., & Hudson, J. I. (2003). Family studies of borderline personality disorder: A review. *Harvard Review of Psychiatry, 12,* 118–119.

Whiteside, S. P., & Lyman, D. R. (2001). The five factor model and impulsivity. *Personality and Individual Differences, 30,* 669–689.

Widom, C. (1999). Childhood victimization and the development of personality disorder: Unanswered questions remain. *Archives of General Psychiatry, 56,* 607–608.

Widom, C. S., DuMont, K., & Czaja, S. J. (2007). A prospective investigation of major depressive disorder and comorbidity in abused and neglected children grown up. *Archives of General Psychiatry, 64,* 49–56.

Widom, C. S., & Kuhns, J. B. (1996). Childhood victimization and subsequent risk for promiscuity, prostitution, and teenage pregnancy: A prospective study. *American Journal of Public Health, 86,* 1607–1612.

Wilkinson-Ryan, T., & Westen, D. (2000). Identity disturbance in borderline personality disorder: An empirical investigation. *American Journal of Psychiatry, 157,* 528–541.

Williams, L. (1998). A "classic" case of borderline personality disorder. *Psychiatric Services, 49,* 173–174.

Wilson, S. T., Fertuck, E. A., Kwitel, A., Stanley, M. C., & Stanley, B. (2006). Impulsivity, suicidality and alcohol use disorders in adolescents and young adults with borderline personality disorder. *International Journal of Adolescent Medicine and Health, 18,* 189–196.

Winchel, R. M., & Stanley, M. (1991). Self-injurious behavior: A review of the behavior and biology of self-mutilation. *American Journal of Psychiatry, 148,* 306–317.

Wixom, J., Ludolph, P., & Westen, D. (1993). The quality of depression in adolescents with borderline personality disorder. *Journal of the American Academy of Child and Adolescent Psychiatry, 32,* 1172–1177.

World Health Organization. (1993). *International classification of diseases* (10th ed.). Geneva, Switzerland: Author.

Wozniak, J. (2005). Recognizing and managing bipolar disorder in children. *Journal of Clinical Psychiatry, 66*(Suppl. 1), 18–23.

Yalom, I., & Leszcz, M. (2005). *The theory and practice of group psychotherapy* (5th ed.). New York: Basic Books.

Yee, L., Korner, J., McSwiggan, S., Meares, R. A., & Stevenson, J. (2005). Persistent hallucinosis in borderline personality disorders. *Comprehensive Psychiatry, 46,* 147–154.

Yehuda, R., & McFarlane, A. C. (1995). Conflict between current knowledge about posttraumatic stress disorder and its original conceptual basis. *American Journal of Psychiatry, 152,* 1705–1713.

Yen, S., Pagano, M. E., Shea, M., Grilo, C. M., Gunderson, J. G., Skodol, A. E., et al. (2005). Recent life events preceding suicide attempts in a personality disorder sample: Findings from the collaborative longitudinal personality disorders study. *Journal of Consulting and Clinical Psychology, 73,* 99–105.

Yen, S., Shea, M. T., Sanislow, C. A., Grilo, C. M., Skodol, A. E., Gunderson, J. G., et al. (2004). Borderline personality disorder criteria associated with prospectively observed suicidal behavior. *American Journal of Psychiatry, 161,* 1296–1298.

Yeomans, F., Clarkin, J., & Kernberg, O. (2002). *A primer for transference-focused psychotherapy for borderline personality disorder.* Northvale, NJ: Jason Arónson.

Young, J. E. (1999). *Cognitive therapy for personality disorders: A schema focused approach* (3rd ed.). Sarasota, FL: Professional Resource Press.

Zanarini, M. C. (1993). Borderline personality as an impulse spectrum disorder. In J. Paris (Ed.), *Borderline personality disorder: Etiology and treatment* (pp. 67–86). Washington, DC: American Psychiatric Press.

Zanarini, M. C. (2000). Childhood experiences associated with the development of borderline personality disorder. *Psychiatric Clinics of North America, 23,* 89–101.

Zanarini, M. C. (2005). *Textbook of borderline personality disorder.* Philadelphia: Taylor & Francis.

Zanarini, M. C., & Frankenburg, F. R. (1994). Emotional hypochondriasis, hyperbole, and the borderline patient. *Journal of Psychotherapy Practice and Research, 3,* 25–36.

Zanarini, M. C., & Frankenburg, F. R. (2001). Olanzapine treatment of female borderline personality disorder patients: A double-blind, placebo-controlled pilot study. *Journal of Clinical Psychiatry, 62,* 849–854.

Zanarini, M. C., & Frankenburg, F. R. (2003). Omega-3 fatty acid treatment of women with borderline personality disorder: A double-blind, placebo-controlled pilot study. *American Journal of Psychiatry, 160,* 167–169.

Zanarini, M. C., Frankenburg, F. R., Dubo, E. D., Sickel, A. E., Trikha, A., Levin, A., et al. (1998a). Axis I comorbidity of borderline personality disorder. *American Journal of Psychiatry, 155,* 1733–1739.

Zanarini, M. C., Frankenburg, F. R., Dubo, E. D., Sickel, A. E., Trikha, A., Levin, A., et al. (1998b). Axis II comorbidity of borderline personality disorder. *Comprehensive Psychiatry, 39,* 296–302.

Zanarini, M. C., Frankenburg, F. R., Hennen, J., Reich, D. B., & Silk, K. R. (2005). The McLean Study of Adult Development (MSAD): Overview and implications of the first six years of prospective follow-up. *Journal of Personality Disorders, 19,* 505–523.

Zanarini, M. C., Frankenburg, F. R., Hennen, J., Reich, D. B., & Silk, K. R. (2006). Prediction of the 10-year course of borderline personality disorder. *American Journal of Psychiatry, 163,* 827–832.

Zanarini, M. C., Frankenburg, F. R., Hennen, J., & Silk, K. R. (2003). The longitudinal course of borderline psychopathology: 6-year prospective follow-up of the phenomenology of borderline personality disorder. *American Journal of Psychiatry, 160,* 274–283.

Zanarini, M. C., Frankenburg, F. R., Khera, G. S., & Bleichmar, J. (2001). Treatment histories of borderline inpatients. *Comprehensive Psychiatry, 42,* 144–150.

Zanarini, M. C., Frankenburg, F. R., & Parachini, E. A. (2004). *A preliminary, randomized trial of fluoxetine, olanzapine, and the olanzapine-fluoxetine combination in women with borderline personality disorder. Journal of Clinical Psychiatry, 65,* 903–907.

Zanarini, M. C., Frankenburg, F. R., Reich, B. D., Silk, K. R., Hudson, J. I., & McSweeney, L. (2007). The subsyndromal psychopathology of borderline personality disorder. *American Journal of Psychiatry, 164,* 1–7.

Zanarini, M. C., Frankenburg, F. R., Ridolfi, M. E., Jager-Hyman, S., Hennen, J., & Gunderson, J. G. (2006). Reported childhood onset of self-mutilation among borderline patients. *Journal of Personality Disorders, 20*, 9–15.

Zanarini, M. C., Frankenburg, F. R., Yong, L., Raviola, G., Bradford Reich, D., Hennen, J., et al. (2004). Borderline psychopathology in the first-degree relatives of borderline and axis II comparison probands. *Journal of Personality Disorders, 18*, 439–447.

Zanarini, M. C., Gunderson, J. G., & Frankenburg, F. R. (1989). The revised diagnostic interview for borderlines: Discriminating BPD from other axis II disorders. *Journal of Personality Disorders, 3*, 10–18.

Zanarini, M. C., Gunderson, J. G., & Frankenburg, F. R. (1990). Cognitive features of borderline personality disorder. *American Journal of Psychiatry, 147*, 57–63.

Zelkowitz, P., Guzder, J., & Paris, J. (2001). Diatheses and stressors in borderline pathology of childhood: The role of neuropsychological risk and trauma, *Journal of the American Academy of Child and Adolescent Psychiatry, 40*, 100–105.

Zelkowitz, P., Guzder, J., Paris, J., Feldman, R., & Roy, C. (2007). Follow-up of children with and without borderline pathology. *Journal of Personality Disorders, 21*, 664–674.

Zetzsche, T., Preuss, U. W., Frodl, T., Schmitt, G., Seifert, D., Munchhausen, E., et al. (2007). Hippocampal volume reduction and history of aggressive behaviour in patients with borderline personality disorder. *Psychiatry Research, 154*, 157–170.

Zhong, J., & Leung, F. (2007). Should borderline personality disorder be included in the fourth edition of the Chinese classification of mental disorders? *Chinese Medical Journal, 120*, 77–82.

Zimmerman, M., & Mattia, J. L. (1999). Differences between clinical and research practices in diagnosing borderline personality disorder. *American Journal of Psychiatry, 156*, 1570–1574.

Zimmerman, M., Rothschild, L., & Chelminski, I. (2005). The prevalence of DSM-IV personality disorders in psychiatric outpatients. *American Journal of Psychiatry, 162*, 1911–1918.

Zoccolillo, M., Pickles, A., Quinton, D., & Rutter, M. (1992). The outcome of childhood conduct disorder: Implications for defining adult personality disorder and conduct disorder. *Psychological Medicine, 22*, 971–986.

Zuckerman, M. (2005). *Psychobiology of personality* (2nd ed.). New York: Cambridge University Press.

Zweig-Frank, H., & Paris, J. (1991). Parents' emotional neglect and overprotection according to the recollections of patients with borderline personality disorder. *American Journal of Psychiatry, 148*, 648–651.

Zweig-Frank, H., & Paris, J. (1995). The five factor model of personality in borderline personality disorder. *Canadian Journal of Psychiatry, 40*, 523–526.

Zweig-Frank, H., & Paris, J. (2002). Predictors of outcomes in a 27-year follow-up of patients with borderline personality disorder. *Comprehensive Psychiatry, 43*, 103–107.

Zweig-Frank, H., Paris, J., & Guzder, J. (1994a). Dissociation in male patients with borderline and non-borderline personality disorders. *Journal of Personality Disorders, 8*, 210–218.

Zweig-Frank, H., Paris, J., & Guzder, J. (1994b). Psychological risk factors for dissociation in female patients with borderline and non-borderline personality disorders. *Journal of Personality Disorders, 8,* 203–209.

Zweig-Frank, H., Paris, J., & Guzder, J. (1994c). Psychological risk factors for dissociation and self-mutilation in female patients with personality disorders. *Canadian Journal of Psychiatry, 39,* 259–265.

Zweig-Frank, H., Paris, J., & Guzder, J. (1994d). Psychological risk factors for self-mutilation in male patients with personality disorders. *Canadian Journal of Psychiatry, 39,* 266–268.

Index